£18-99

Social Work Ethics

Also by Chris L. Clark

Theory and Practice in Voluntary Social Action
Social Work and Social Philosophy (with S. Asquith)
Planning and Costing Community Care (edited with I. Lapsley)

Social Work Ethics

Politics, Principles and Practice

Chris L. Clark

palgrave

First published 2000 by
PALGRAVE
Houndmills, Basingstoke, Hampshire RG21 6XS and
175 Fifth Avenue, New York, N.Y. 10010
Companies and representatives throughout the world

PALGRAVE is the new global academic imprint of
St. Martin's Press LLC Scholarly and Reference Division and
Palgrave Publishers Ltd (formerly Macmillan Press Ltd).

ISBN-13: 978-0-333-71934-3
ISBN-10: 0-333-71934-4

This book is printed on paper suitable for recycling and
made from fully managed and sustained forest sources.

A catalogue record for this book is available
from the British Library.

Editing and origination by
Aardvark Editorial, Suffolk

Typeset by T & A Typesetting Services, Rochdale

Printed and bound in Great Britain by Biddles Ltd., King's Lynn, Norfolk

Contents

Acknowledgements

I am extremely grateful to several colleagues who read some or all of this book in draft and offered invaluable advice and criticism: to Duncan Forrester for getting straight down to business; to Kath Melia for support and interest; to Fritz-Rüdiger Volz for his generosity, erudition and patience; to Lorraine Waterhouse for constant readiness, in this and all other challenges, to go the second mile. Catherine Gray of the publishers gave thoughtful and cogent advice at all stages and the publisher's reviewer made important and helpful observations. Without all their efforts the product would have been much the poorer.

Permission to reproduce the following is acknowledged with thanks: *The Code of Ethics for Social Work* of the British Association of Social Workers; Box 9.1 from *Issues in Social Work Education* **16** (2). Parts of Chapters 8 and 10 are abridged from my paper *Paternalism and Citizenship in Community Care* (1996).

1

Introduction

Social work is the most contentious of all the human service professions. Building on centuries-old traditions of social responsibility for the disadvantaged in society, and established in a recognisably modern form by the third decade of the twentieth century, social work nonetheless has almost daily to defend its very right to existence. It is not merely that, like all professions from time to time, it has to accept responsibility and criticism for work done poorly or not at all. The controversies that resound through professional practice go right to the heart of the question of what social work is really for. It is the foundations of purpose as well as the superstructure of methods and practice that are perennially insecure.

The signs of this unstable condition are well known. In the public mind there is a broad consensus and understanding about the methods and goals of the health professions; about the education system and the role of teachers of all sorts; about the legitimacy of law enforcement agencies and the lawyers and others who work within them; and about the status and standing of religious leaders. For social work, which shares something of the aspirations of all these groups, there is no comparable understanding. Social workers are not health professionals, but they seek to promote individuals' well-being; they are not formal teachers, but they must try to teach people new ways of thinking about the issues in their lives; they are not lawyers, but they have the practical responsibility of applying some particularly sensitive aspects of the law; and they are not ministers of religion, but they use their influence to promote or suppress certain ways of human living. As in all the professions, controversies come and go about how best to pursue the objectives of the day, and some will have a radical impact. In social work the impact of controversy is magnified because the basic groundwork is insecure.

Society feels ambivalent about the need for social workers. Politicians can be sure that a promise of increased education or health service provision will attract practically universal popular support, but it is difficult to imagine a comparable response to a promise of more social workers. Public support is, at best, reluctant. Social work is the agency charged with dealing with problems most people would prefer to avoid thinking about: poverty, deprivation, family breakdown, drug abuse, living with disability or mental health problems. Since few people choose to dwell on bad news, the reluctance is understandable.

The difficult position of social work is not only due to the perhaps depressing character of the problems it deals with. Crucially, social work sits directly on top of the fault lines of controversy of social values. Family life and the values it represents are undergoing rapid and painful change. Feminism has transformed thinking about family roles and relationships; attitudes and beliefs about sexuality now cover such a wide range that agreement across different parts of the spectrum is impossible; more and more people live alone, whether from choice or necessity. It often falls to social work to mediate compromises across the fault lines of social values. As well as being an uncomfortable position for its practitioners, this is not a role that is ever likely to win full-hearted popular support. Those who become involved in social work interventions will usually only be partly satisfied, at best.

Social ambivalence towards social work is reflected in its institutions. Despite their many-faceted duties and complex responsibilities, and despite repetitive official findings of inadequate training, government policy in Britain restricts social workers to two years' initial training. This period, shorter than any comparable profession, implies the valuation placed upon their work. The status of social workers is reflected, too, in the long-term lack of a formal register of members of the profession, a deficit that is only now being put right. It is almost as if society were reluctant to admit their existence, even though they are needed to implement an ever-increasing body of legislation.

This book is about the ethical and political issues that lie at the heart of social work and give it its special character. It argues that although the controversies of social value that social work practice must address can never be definitively resolved, it is both possible and necessary to identify cogent and useful principles. It is necessary in social work to pursue particular ethical and political goals in the double sense: first, in that neutrality is not possible, since any intervention necessarily represents some values; second, that without a positive grasp of the broader ethical and political purposes of the profession, practitioners will be adrift and ineffectual in the turbulent waters that it is precisely their job to navigate. Establishing a credible and serviceable political ethics is a steep challenge in the present age of dislocation of the old intellectual landmarks of the Enlightenment. The philosophy of the approach recommended here will be that a provisional, imperfect, working and evolving version of the aims of civil society is better than no model at all.

The scope of this book

Social work addresses an especially broad spectrum of human concerns and social issues. Any text about its fundamentals has to take an equally broad view, ranging across several fields of empirical social science, philosophical ethics and normative political theory, applied science and professional craft, policy and politics. Choosing this wide-angle lens means that the exposition of particular subjects will often be quite restricted; indeed, sometimes whole fields of scholarship and research will be abridged in a paragraph or two. The aim throughout this book is to define the essential landmarks while keeping the principal focus on the normative or 'ought' questions at the heart of social work. The selection of topics follows, of course, the author's perception of their salience, just as the treatment of them is bent to the task in hand. The themes of this book represent an individual choice but not, it is hoped, an idiosyncratic one.

This book originates from social work as developed within British society and social policy. However, it is not concerned particularly with British welfare or professional experience. Its focus is the general moral and political issues embedded in the professional practice of social work in all the advanced liberal democracies that are its characteristic habitat. Readers from different countries should find the key issues equally applicable to their situation, even when the history and structure of the profession there differ from the British example.

Who are social workers?

There is some ambiguity about what professional social work comprises and about the identity of its members. This book will be concerned with a range of occupational groups whose members are employed both to assist individuals with problems of social living and to gain their conformance with certain standards of social behaviour. According to this understanding social work is *essentially* legitimated by constitutional and political processes and bases its authority, at least implicitly and often explicitly, on public policy. Social work is not, on this view, a business of private transactions between individuals or between individuals and private organisations. This by no means requires that all social work is carried out by public or statutory agencies. What it means is that all social work, to count as such, is authorised or legitimated as a result of public and political processes. It will be maintained that this remains true even in those regimes where much or most of the delivery of social work services is delegated to non-state organisations.

This definition naturally includes social workers who hold occupational qualifications and job specifications explicitly designating them as such. It also applies to others with similar or associated roles who may not be formally designated as social workers. They include practitioners with a specialised brief within the broad field of social work, including care or case managers, child care workers with children or families who have special needs, workers in child protection services, social workers in the health services, staff who provide residential and day care to disabled adults, probation officers, social education and community workers, and others. Also included are the less formally qualified workers sometimes identified as assistants or auxiliaries who work alongside social workers to provide the same services; non-professionals recruited to help provide social work services, such as foster parents; students and trainees. All of these occupational groups may be found working in state-run public services and in third-sector organisations that receive their income from state subventions, state-supported fees for service and private charitable donations.

Practitioners who work purely on their own account serving a private clientele in independent, fee-charging practice, such as some counsellors and therapists, are excluded from the definition of social work adopted here. Not included are care services bought from independent practitioners and private businesses by private consumers who pay with their own funds, such as much child care and some home help and home care services. Social work does, however, include services of these types provided by the private sector where they are serving individuals at the behest of public welfare services, or where public welfare policy provides the financial means. It is true, of course, that several of these occupations, and others, have points of similarity with social work. Counsellors, for example, often use similar techniques to social workers and work by not dissimilar ethical and professional principles. The point of the distinction is that social work, in the view adopted in this book, is inherently and essentially part of the business of the state, and as such its boundaries should be drawn so as to exclude private market transactions with which public welfare policy is not concerned. Thus for example, if someone employs a cleaner to help them with the housework, that is not to be regarded as social work; but if someone is deemed to need help with the housework because of social needs that are addressed within public welfare policy, then that becomes part of any social work intervention.

Social work is part of the *public* pursuit of welfare through policy and legislation. In the chapters that follow there will be frequent references to human welfare or well-being as one of the defining aims of ethics and politics. However, 'welfare' has also acquired the secondary sense of a specific area of public policy, especially concerned with the relief of poverty and its consequences. Welfare rights are a creation of twentieth-century social policy; welfare spending is the public money that goes on social assistance, social work and the like; to be on welfare is to be in receipt of such assistance. This text makes reference to welfare in both the broad and the specific senses, and should be understood as the context requires.

In social work (as in other helping professions) the traditional focus of technical knowledge and professional ethics is the individual helping relationship. This may be thought of as a private, face-to-face encounter in which the touchstone of good practice is the professional's skilful striving to support the client while avoiding injury or exploitation through ineptitude or ill intent. It is maintained in this book that such a view of social work relationships is dangerously limited. Because social work is an aspect of public policy, the ethics of practice must take fully into account the political issues and choices built in to professional principles and agency structures. Therefore the ethics of social work are *political* ethics. The root questions are the classic problems of ethics and politics: how, and for what, are we to live? How should we treat our fellow human beings? What principles should we adopt to reconcile conflicts in society?

Outline of the book

The aims of this book are pursued in four stages. The first is to acquaint the reader with the traditional and customary ethical teachings of social work. Chapter 2 approaches the subject through a number of *practice examples*. In Chapter 3 the spotlight is on *'values' in social work*. The core aims of social work are often expressed in terms of values and the task here is to appraise what is meant by this popular, but ultimately unsatisfactory, conception. Chapter 4 distils *eight rules of social work ethics* from the established body of literature and practice wisdom. It summarises the development of the field so far and serves as a primer on ethically sound practice.

The second stage introduces ethical theory and offers a critique of social work ethics. Chapter 5 includes *brief introductions to selected ethical and political theories* and goes on to raise some *basic questions about professional ethics*. Chapter 6 looks at the implications of social work being mostly practised within terms increasingly *defined by statute law* and goes on to discuss the bases of *political obligation* and *professional legitimacy*.

In the third stage the task is to rethink the nature of social work to provide a better foundation for its professional ethics. Chapter 7 examines the rationale for *public policies for the promotion of welfare*. It argues that liberal-individualist political theory neglects the dimensions of community that are essential to meaningful lives. Social work only has practical meaning in the context of concrete life projects situated in particular communities and ways of life. In Chapter 8 it is argued that *the purpose of social work is to promote the realisation of ordinary life*. This is linked to the idea of *welfare citizenship*, with its entailments of both rights and responsibilities for welfare.

The final stage of the book proposes that the traditional, narrowly conceived professional ethics or values should be sewn into a much broader canvas of social ethics and normative political theory.

Chapter 9 draws out four basic principles or *stocks of social work ethics*, arguing that professional theory and practice must be ruled by observance of *respect, justice, citizenship and discipline*. In the final chapter, these ideas are applied to a number of representative *topics in professional practice*.

A text of this sort unfortunately cannot avoid the contemporary muddle in the English language over the usage of personal pronouns. In this book the feminine and masculine forms are alternated more or less haphazardly, with occasional recourse to the useful if inelegant singular 'they'. No significance attaches to the choice of masculine or feminine forms, unless the context specifically requires it.

Social workers are rightly sensitive to the hidden implications of different ways of addressing or referring to people of different categories. In this text terms such as 'client' and 'user' are employed with neutral connotation; accepting that newer terms have not displaced the still serviceable 'client' from everyday use in social agencies; and accepting too that the mere use of an old-fashioned or new-fangled term is no reliable indicator of the principles and values embraced by its users. Similarly, the terms 'worker', 'professional' and their synonyms are not intended to convey any particular valuation, but are merely varied to avoid monotony.

Travelling hopefully

It is a commonplace to speak of social work, whether at the level of the local agency or in the broader scene of the whole enterprise, as being in a state of crisis, but it is hardly ever an exaggeration. If social workers sometimes dream of a breathing space of relative normality where they could quietly get on with the satisfying job of delivering quality services to appreciative clients, and attend to steadily improving research, knowledge and skill, they must very often be disappointed.

There are two typical responses to the perception of perpetual crisis. The first is a sense of powerlessness and hopelessness. Problems seem insuperable, vision is lost, cynicism, anger or despair may set in. The only attractive prospect is escape; for workers in the public services this means leaving for a new job or retirement. Only the very practical need to earn a living detains them.

The second typical response to crisis is radicalism, which may be of any specific character, conservative or revolutionary. Radicalism claims that the whole system – of concepts, of theories, of policies, of practice – is profoundly defective. Its demise, already inevitable, should be hastened by the introduction of new aims, new ideologies, new programmes, new attitudes and practices.

This book recommends no radicalism but refuses to accept pessimism. The reader will find values drawn from the main strengths of the liberal tradition in philosophy and social democracy in politics. They are offered in the acute awareness that this tradition is replete with unresolved problems and disputes. Pinker, an academic in social policy, reflects on rediscovering the 'middle way' in social welfare – a concept he borrows from the former Conservative Prime Minister Harold Macmillan, writing in 1938 (Pinker, 1991). Pinker argues that while the specific interpretation of the middle way varies hugely according to the historical context, belief in the viability of a middle way rests upon accepting political pluralism. George and Wilding (1994) demonstrate the crucial historical importance of the middle way in welfare policy. Ironically, the very similar notion of a 'third way' is lately enjoying a renaissance under a Labour government (Novak, 1998). This book shares the assumption that no system of providing welfare should be ruled out merely because it may have originated from political quarters towards which one does not feel entirely sympathetic.

Professionals in every field devoted to human improvement have to learn the difficult art of combining two contrasting modes of action. On the one hand, lest they be deceived about the merit of their efforts, they need the scepticism of science. The scientific attitude avoids assumptions that cannot be well evidenced and projects that cannot be well validated. On the other hand, professionals achieve little of true value unless their efforts are imbued with a moral sense and a positive human spirit. They must meet human problems with a constructive, forward-looking response, and not be rendered ineffectual by ignorance and misery; ready, despite the acknowledged limitations of their craft, to face challenging problems without facile denial, yet not falsely promising what cannot be assured. It is readiness to offer a kind of moral leadership based on understanding the limits of one's knowledge and power.

This book aims to emulate and to model such a philosophy of professionalism. It maintains that although definitive solutions can never be proved, useful advances are nonetheless possible. The theories offered in the following pages make no claim to completeness or finality. They are offered as provisional waymarks for the professional in human services, who needs to make the best of the journey today even though its end is never finally settled.

2

Ethical Issues in Practice

The concerns of social work include every aspect of ordinary life, the commonplace but vital interests of every human being: to get shelter and sustenance, care and comfort, support and opportunity for growth. The breadth of social work sometimes leads critics to say that it is absurdly pretentious, for what authority or expertise do social workers have to lay down standards that are truly the business of every citizen? The very ordinariness of the needs with which social workers are concerned appears to threaten the validity of a distinctive and important professional role. Social workers nonetheless believe that the holistic approach to the individual's problems is essential. For them it is a basic principle that a person's various needs and the interests of the wider community must all be considered in relation to each other. In a world of specialists social workers hold the broad view, balancing different practical and emotional needs and interests with the aim of overall improvement when everything is taken into consideration.

Social work is about the business of ordinary social living, and thus social workers potentially have to deal with almost all the morally vexing questions that affect human society. In actuality, through policy and economy, tradition and practice, certain kinds of problems feature more than others. As a fair first approximation, the prime responsibilities of social workers are as follows: to mitigate poverty and deprivation; to regulate the care and development of children when the family is seen to be deficient; to support the care of dependent or disabled adults; to contribute to the social control of offenders; and to promote social education and contribute to social reform. In the course of these responsibilities, social workers frequently intervene in the relations of individuals to other public agencies including those involved with health care, income maintenance, housing, education and criminal justice.

10

In the following sections a number of key issues for social work ethics will be illustrated by case examples drawn from the social work and general press.

Threats to autonomy

Providing care for adults who, through ageing or disability, are unable to live an independent life unaided is a growing concern in all developed countries. Advances in medicine have prolonged life and increased the survival chances of individuals, who, in earlier times, would have died sooner. Changes in family life and structure mean that former assumptions about who should provide care are increasingly questionable. At the same time, societal expectations about standards of care and quality of life have risen remarkably. It is no longer widely acceptable that those who need fairly constant care and support should routinely be committed to institutions.

The care of adults with disabilities raises difficult issues about their autonomy, which is the right and capacity of persons to exercise choice and live their lives by their own principles. Autonomy or 'self-rule' is widely taken to be the very prime, or at least one of the first, principles of morality (Schneewind, 1993). It also captures the notion that it is not just socially acceptable behaviour that is the object of morality, but the principle that right actions are reasoned and willed.

- A lady in her early eighties who lived alone was admitted to hospital after lighting an open fire in her front room, under the impression that her coal-effect electric fire was broken. The hospital doctor wished an early discharge as there were no acute medical needs, and the patient wished to return home. The house was uninhabitable because of the fire. The social worker found that although the patient appeared to be rational in many respects, the daughter and lodger whom she spoke about as waiting for her at home had died respectively eleven and four years previously. Further investigation revealed several other serious health concerns. The patient was referred for full psycho-geriatric inpatient assessment. (*Community Care*, 2 August 1996, p. 32)

- A pensioner was found dead in his flat after it had been boarded up. Neighbours had reported to the landlord, Scottish Homes, that the flat appeared to have been abandoned. Willie Smith was deaf and said to have a mental age of 12 years. Social workers had been keeping in touch with Mr Smith every two months. He had wanted to live alone and had turned down offers of help. (*The Times*, 2 September 1995, p. 7)

- Mrs P, aged in her seventies, was admitted to hospital for the third time in quick succession. Her daily living skills were assessed at home, where it was found the house was in a poor state and she was unable to use any kitchen equipment. She exhibited disinhibited behaviour and was unable to engage in a meaningful conversation. Mrs P initially agreed to hospital assessment before going home, but family members pressed for rehousing instead. It seemed her relatives were influencing her while her judgement was poor. She was rehoused and support packages were arranged. (*Community Care*, 3 October 1996, p. 32)

A person's autonomy can be impeded by the actions or inactions of others when, for example, there is an identified risk such as accident or assault at home. In other cases a person can adversely affect her own autonomy. Some people, whether from choice or incapacity, look after themselves poorly. This may begin as an autonomous choice, but the resulting poor health and well-being undermine future capacity for autonomy. Some people refuse repeated offers of help, or prefer not to undergo the formal processes of being taken into the care of public service bureaucracies. In extreme, but not rare, cases clients may credibly threaten to do themselves serious harm, including suicide. Where need seems to exist but demand for service does not, autonomy is liable to be eroded whatever course of action is taken.

Many consumers of community care services suffer from dementia, mental illness or learning disability. They are judged to have some limitations of mental competence: in some circumstances it may seem that they cannot make major life decisions with the proper degree of understanding. Their subjective preferences may be difficult to reconcile with practical reality. They may entertain unfeasible options or believe in material facts that are plainly untrue. They may not remember present possibilities and conditions well enough to make an informed choice. Somewhat similar problems may attend the choices of people with learning disabilities. In other cases the capacity for autonomy can be affected by alcohol or drugs, medical and other.

A direct, frequent threat to autonomy is where social workers propose action (or inaction) that is opposed to the client's wishes. There may, of course, be good reasons for doing so, including the rights and wishes of other people involved. Nevertheless, social work is often perceived as a threat to individuals' autonomy, not a safeguard of it.

Social workers may be in positions of very substantial influence over people's lives. A particularly clear example is in residential care. Whether children or young people, or older or disabled people, residents are subject across every area of their lives to the enormous effects of the care they receive from paid workers. It a nice question whether the choices and restraints that are necessarily imposed in residential care are conducive or destructive of autonomy, even where the quality of care is high and the abilities and motivations of staff are beyond reproach. Where standards break down, gross invasions of autonomy can sometimes arise: in punitive control and sexual exploitation, especially with children; in shameful degradation and neglect, especially with the weak and vulnerable.

In keeping with the standard expectations of professionals, social workers are assumed to act in the best interests of the client. Autonomy is threatened when workers approach a problem in a less than fair and open-minded way. Workers may be biased in favour of a specific approach or solution for reasons extraneous to the problem in hand, as for example when there is pressure to use or avoid using a particular resource. They may be susceptible to prejudice, conscious or not, in favour of certain individuals or groups.

Conflicts of interest

Social work enters into sensitive areas of people's emotional and family lives where conflicts of interest are potentially never far away. In any family the motives and rights of one member are liable to be at odds with another's; where a family seeks, or is thought to require, social work intervention, tensions are the rule not the exception.

- A ten year old girl is removed from home because of lack of care. The mother has a history of drug and alcohol related problems, and seems unlikely to improve her standards of child care. The child is placed in foster care, where she is safe but unhappy; if returned home, she would be at risk. The family's wish, and presumed right, to be reunited conflicts with the expectation of adequate parental care. (*Community Care*, 4 July 1996, p. 24)

- An eight year old girl discloses that she has been sexually abused by her father, but tells social workers she does not want her family to be split up or her daddy to be sent away to prison. Allowing the father–child relationship to be maintained, and the principle of consulting with the child over her future, are difficult to reconcile with the need to protect her from continuing harm. (*Community Care*, 13 June 1996, p. 21)

- A couple are divorced after a history of domestic violence. The father exercises his right of continuing contact with the children, which is encouraged both by legislation and expert opinion on the emotional needs of children. Contact is used by the father as an opportunity to harm his former partner, the children, or both (*Community Care*, 18 July 1996, p. 16). In such a case, the mother may feel that the father's contact with the children must be stopped. This could place her in contempt of court, and might also be damaging to the children in a different way. (*Community Care*, 7 March 1996, p. 18)

- Two children, rejected by their parents who had each made new relationships, had a close and loving relationship with their grandparents. The grandparents had reluctantly decided on health grounds that they could not adopt the children, but looked forward to maintaining their contact with them after adoption. Several weeks into temporary foster care, the grandfather was told by the social services that relationships between the birth family and children would be severed upon adoption. The children and grandparents had a happy family holiday while the children were still in foster care. Thereafter contact by visits, writing and presents were strictly regulated. The grandparents were dismayed at the social services' low aspirations for children in care and experienced great distress and sorrow at losing contact with their young relatives. (*Guardian*, 22 February 1995, p. 23)

In child care and protection the right of the child to safety and a good upbringing may cut across the parents' right to bring up their child as they see fit: there is a conflict of interest *between* family members. Similarly, the wish of an infirm or disabled person to be cared for at home may impinge heavily on the opportunities and freedoms of the family members implicated in caring. Such vital interests are not easily given up, neither is it easy to find constructive solutions that enhance everyone's situation.

The needs and rights of individuals are many and varied, and sometimes they cannot all be well satisfied simultaneously: there is a conflict *within* the individual's own range of interests. A need for safety may clash with the desire to continue a risky but valued activity or way of life. Uprooting oneself for the sake of a preferred family arrangement may conflict with maintaining a valued set of involvements and relationships such as a successful school experience, a network of friendships or a rewarding job.

Social work often deals with individuals who pose a threat to the wider community. Individuals or families may choose to behave in ways that their neighbours find offensive, unsafe, threatening or otherwise objectionable. Individuals' choices within, or not clearly outwith, the law may yet be intolerable to those who have to bear with them. In dealing with offenders, social work has a very obvious role of balancing the offenders' interest in rehabilitation, or at least avoiding further entanglement with the law, with the demand of the community for protection from crime. In all these situations there is potential conflict of the client's interests with those of society in general.

Conflicts of interest often show up as problems about confidentiality. To protect the client's interests, the social worker is ideally presumed to reveal nothing of her client's affairs to any individual or organisation except, with permission, to those with a direct legitimate concern. In practice workers have to disclose information without the client's clear understanding or consent in order to pursue the resources that may help to alleviate the problem, or to avert unacceptable risks, or simply as part of the bureaucratic processes in agencies. Under different circumstances, either keeping confidence or breaking it may damage the conflicting interests of various parties.

Lastly, in relation to conflicts of interest, the worker's own interests may conflict with those of the client or the agency. Private and voluntary agencies that depend on payment for services as the basis of their business have an incentive to continue providing the service if it pays them well. They can face the question of whether initiating or continuing service is primarily in the client's interest and only secondarily in their own. Workers also have their own self-regarding interests. In the public or the private sectors they will probably find some kinds of work more personally satisfying, or potentially rewarding in career terms, than others, and this may improperly affect the quality of service that different users receive. Workers sometimes find their clients becoming friends and have then to decide whether acts of friendship, such as giving or receiving gifts, trespass beyond the bounds of working relationships, and whether maintaining those relationships after the end of the working contact is ethical.

Needs, rights and ways of life

Perhaps more than any of the human service occupations, social work undertakes to consider clients' lives as a whole. In developed societies needs and the expertise to meet them are segmented. The doctor does not expect to take on the role of marital counsellor, the lawyer is not a dietician, the housing manager is not an occupational therapist, the financial adviser is not a child psychologist. Yet people who seek or who are required to receive social work commonly do present a complex of interrelated problems covering, say, health, family relationships, housing, legal and financial matters. Social workers are very committed to a holistic perspective on human needs. Although it is much threatened social work would be wrong to relinquish it, since specialisation and fragmentation of professional helping can easily lead to missing the individuality of people's lives in the busy concern to complete specialist tasks.

● A twelve year old boy and his fourteen year old sister look after their mother, who has a disabling disease. Their father has remarried. Because of constantly having to care for their mother, the children have little opportunity to go out with their friends.

They carry much more responsibility than is usual for children of their age. Their schoolwork is suffering. (*Community Care*, 31 August 1995, p. 16)

- Jacob Henry, aged two, was conceived by artificial insemination of his mother, Ruth Henry, with sperm donated by a friend, John Ioannou. John Ioannou is gay and lives with his partner. Ruth Henry is lesbian and lives with her partner. Young Jacob spends Monday to Friday with his mother, and transfers to his father's house for the weekend. Social work agencies are quite satisfied as to Jacob's welfare and propose no intervention in relation to the 'timeshare' child. (*Guardian*, 8 May 1996, p. 10)

- Two young girls from a black family were placed in the foster care of their aunt after their mother, a diagnosed schizophrenic, left them for days by themselves in a room in a bed and breakfast hotel. For five years everyone was happy with the arrangement. A new social worker took over responsibility for the case and began to criticise the foster mother's handling of the children over matters such as the chores they were expected to do, dress and pocket money. The foster mother maintained her standards were normal for black families. The children expressed unhappiness to social workers but this was withheld from the foster mother. When she found out about it she was angry and upset and said the children had to leave. The children's move to other foster parents did not go well and they eventually returned to the care of their aunt. (*Community Care*, 2 November 1995, p. 14)

- The Albert Kennedy Trust arranges supported lodgings for homeless 16- to 19-year-old gays and lesbians, who are placed in the care of adult gay and lesbian couples. The chairperson of the Commons Home Affairs select committee considered it 'thoroughly undesirable' for children with homosexual propensities to be fostered with gay couples. A trustee of the charity took the view that if gay children are fostered in a straight environment they are starved of gay role models (*Community Care*, 21 March 1996, p. 23). Government policy was that gay and lesbian adoptions were considered acceptable only in the most exceptional circumstances. (*Community Care*, 22 August 1996, p. 14)

● A couple fostered a coloured child from the age of four months to eight years. Over 20 years they had fostered more than 70 children, two thirds of them black or Asian. They had previously adopted a mixed-race child. The local authority decided in this case that they could not adopt the child because they were white. After trying to block the adoption the authority required the couple to complete a black cultural awareness course. It was claimed they were reclassified black. (*Sunday Times*, 30 October 1994, p. 1/3)

Social work's broad perspective makes inescapable wider questions of values and ways of life that narrower specialists can afford to, and rightly should, disregard. Among the key disputes of current (and many former) times is the proper form of family life. Lifelong monogamous marriage as the only base for raising children retains a substantial normative power but is far from universally adhered to. In seeking to support workable family relationships social workers deal with family forms that diverge from the traditional norm: for example, single parenthood, under-age parenthood, changed partners, multiple partners, short- or long-term substitute parenting, parenting by lesbian or gay single parents and couples. Social workers thereby place themselves in the middle of unquenchable controversies. Should parents be permitted physically to chastise their children? Is this a matter for personal values and judgement, or should the state intervene to criminalise some forms of chastisement? Should parents be held accountable for the misdeeds of their children? What religious standards, if any, should be required in officially sanctioned substitute care – and are these to be different from the standards expected in ordinary family life? What does it mean to demand that substitute parents have a particular cultural or ethnic identity? Are all practices acceptable simply because they are normative within a particular ethnic or cultural group?

Family responsibilities do not end with those of parents towards their dependent children. This relationship is sometimes reversed, with children taking on the care of their sick, disabled or feckless parents. Such arrangements challenge ideas of normal rights and responsibilities. At the other end of life, adult children apparently have some sort of responsibility to their ageing parents – but understanding of this responsibility varies between individuals, communities and cultures and is not susceptible to standardised quasi-legal definition.

Social work is among the agencies that enforce the social control of offenders and others whose actions are deemed socially unacceptable. Not every class of action that is so controlled is universally regarded as reprehensible: for example, the use of recreational drugs or unconventional forms of sexual expression. By the same token, much behaviour that some people regard as highly objectionable is only weakly, or not at all, condemned by the formal institutions of society, for example adultery or blasphemy.

Social work has tended to favour permissive attitudes to deviance, and has prided itself on its progressive stance in addressing racism, homophobia and other contemporary dragons. In its pursuit of progressive ideals however, social work has almost certainly underestimated the supposed enemy. It is not enough to treat homosexuality as self-evidently on a moral par with heterosexuality in a society where many thoughtful people sincerely believe otherwise and where differences remain in the respective legal statuses and social standing. Social workers have been accused of zealous wrong-headedness in, for example, the requirements relating to the cultural and ethnic identity of substitute parents. Here, too, they have been in danger of assuming they have the definitive answers to questions that, in fact, are not yet settled to the satisfaction of the wider community.

Competing ways of life and incompatible values are typical of the societies that undertake social work. They cannot be filtered out by attempting to transform it into a compendium of technical knowledge and legalistic procedure. Issues about good and bad ways of life come at the heart of social work professional ethics – as they do of ethics in general.

Pressure on public resources

Social work is largely a publicly sponsored activity and is therefore strongly affected by the availability and deployment of public resources. The potential demand for social services is practically infinite but the resources to meet it, sadly, finite. Many categories of demand are ruled out for reasons of priority and cost, but the line between valid need and unaffordable luxury is often arbitrary or accidental. The definitions of need adopted in agencies are inevitably disputable and may be unreasonable; the effect, if not the avowed intention, of agency policy may be clearly inequitable. Workers find they have nothing effective to offer and have to reject genuine cases for help. Clients or their families may have to meet the costs of services that they feel should be free, and this can lead to serious impoverishment or deprivation.

- Under the NHS and Community Care Act 1990, local authorities are increasingly charging elderly and disabled users for home care services. Voluntary organisations that provide services under contract are also obliged to levy charges. Many users feel these charges are unfair and think they should be entitled to free services after a lifetime of tax and National Insurance contributions. Charges apply to people of quite ordinary means, not just the especially wealthy. (*Guardian*, 27 September 1994, p. 2; *Community Care*, 12 October 1995, p. 26)

The area of practice now known in Britain as community care poses tough questions for policy and for professionals in welfare. Continuing care for people who may need attention several times a day, or continuously, is inescapably expensive; and it is often lifelong, since many disabling conditions are not curable and tend to get worse over time. Few individuals can afford such long-term care without state help and even those who can may be thought to have a moral entitlement to special help from public sources. Social workers and others have to make decisions about distributing resources between highly needy individuals in the context of global resources that will always be insufficient to provide optimal care to everyone who needs it. But for politicians and policy-makers, rationing is a nearly unmentionable concept. Where rationing devices, such as prioritisation of requests and waiting lists for services, are adopted in practice to cope with shortage, workers are then faced with problems of equity: what standard should be used for rating some requests higher than others? How can the differing availability of services in different areas be justified?

The characteristic chronic overload of public service agencies perpetually threatens to depress standards. Goodwill will not disguise that the quality and penetration of service frequently fall below what workers and managers aspire to, and politicians claim to implement. Instead of being restricted to isolated incidents, failure can become chronic: the same issue or the same case of professional misconduct resurfaces time after time despite professional and public concern, quasi-judicial investigation and legal action.

It is not only the public who suffer from inadequately resourced services, but staff as well. They may be exploited or badly treated through excessive work expectations, especially, perhaps, at the bottom of the service hierarchy where most frontline contact with clients takes place. Burnout is acknowledged as a serious problem, but action to prevent it is often lacking or ineffectual. Lack of resources or lack of vision can lead to poor training and support, as well as failure to correct unacceptable attitudes and practices such as racism or sexism.

Legitimacy and the failure of expertise

Social workers deploy significant resources to people deemed to be in need of care or control. Their power and influence would be intolerable without the authority of law to ensure legitimacy and a mandate for their interventions. 'Who do they think they are?' is a widespread complaint of an indignant public against official power. Ethical issues arise because the intentions of legislation are neither comprehensively stated nor free from ambiguity. This can apply at the level of both the individual case and the wider issue. Where workers exercise (or refrain from exercising) direct legal compulsion over clients by invoking statute law, there is often room for doubt about the appropriateness of the action in that case. Any exercise of legal restraints over a client is likely to constitute a threat to autonomy, and its legitimacy must therefore be closely examined.

Although certainly necessary, legality by itself is seldom a sufficient safeguard. Some actions may be legal, or not clearly illegal, but still ethically questionable. Legal authority has to be supported by appropriate expertise. Everyone who performs a professional service, whether under public auspices, through private enterprise or as voluntary action, makes at least the implicit promise that his work will be carried out with due skill, care, application and diligence. This is especially important where the consumer is not well placed to estimate the quality of the service, choose another professional or turn down the offer. In the human services the user must largely entrust herself to the designated professional without the benefit of being able to shop around. If the service turns out to be poor the standard of professional ethics will be questionable.

- 'According to claims made by the *Independent* and… Channel 4's *Dispatches*, Lancashire social workers pressured a woman to abort her twins and be sterilised under the threat of putting her child into care. The reason? She was said to have a low IQ and to be prone to aggressive mood swings.' (*The Observer*, 18 December 1994, p. 21)

- A boy of eleven was removed from home to a hostel following allegations of sexual abuse. He was one of 23 children in the Cleveland affair whom the courts ruled should not return home. On his eighteenth birthday, his mother said, he wrote asking her to visit. She was refused access to see him at his hostel. The young man was said to have severe emotional problems. No charge was ever brought against the parents, and the subsequent inquiry cleared them by indicating the boy had been abused by another pupil at his special school. (*Guardian*, 6 April 1994, p. 3)

- An Asian mother of two children turned to alcohol while finding the courage to leave a violent husband. She voluntarily placed her two children, then five and three, in foster care. A year later, she claims, she was not allowed to have the children return. The children were placed for adoption. As the adoption approached, her visits were reduced from monthly to three monthly, then once a year. The mother thought that the decision to have the children adopted without giving her a chance to recover was rash and based on prejudices to do with her race and failure to understand her alcoholism. The local authority took the view that the children could not be left to wait for their mother to get better. (*Community Care*, 7 September 1995, p. 14)

- To protect children in care from potentially dangerous individuals, social work departments routinely screen the police records of potential foster and adoptive parents. To speed the process up, plans were in hand for social work departments to have direct access to the computer-based police criminal records of the general population. (*Sunday Times*, 22 October 1995, p. SC/1/5)

The requisite standard of professional expertise is generally difficult to specify. Doubtless a large part of day-to-day work is everywhere carried out at a level which, if less than excellent, is still acceptable in terms of prevailing norms and standards. Consumers may nevertheless feel that the run of the mill is less than they want or deserve. When the merely average gives way to the distinctly mediocre the question becomes more intense but not necessarily easier to resolve.

Social workers no less than other professionals should expect censure when their work falls below some minimum standard. This immediately raises complex issues. A worker may have clearly failed to observe current norms of good practice but not be wholly culpable; the worker may justly claim that he received insufficient training, or was not given adequate working facilities, support and guidance, or was overworked, or was misdirected by his superiors or colleagues. Another layer of complication is added when workers follow prevailing norms in good faith, only to find that they do not withstand the test of experience. This has been the hard lesson of repeated enquiries into failures of social work. It then becomes an issue whether good faith is a sufficient defence of inadequate or dangerous practice. A sceptical public may feel that even if the workers did not know better, they should have done. Experts may think that they are being asked to produce answers to questions that cannot be answered without substantial research for which resources are not forthcoming.

Standards of ethics in professional practice are not a separate question from standards of technical knowledge and skill, but intimately related. Practice that fails to reach reasonable standards of technical skill is just as much unethical as practice that does not respect general principles of professional morality. The cost to autonomy of invasive intervention in pursuit of statutory requirements is only justified if the intervention is well informed.

Legislation can often be ambiguous, and social workers may disagree with its intentions. For either reason they may wish to influence the political decision-making processes surrounding its implementation. The boundary between professional opinion-giving and improper political lobbying may be very unclear. Because professionals move in inside circles not clearly exposed to public knowledge and debate, they are able to use their influence to gain policy outcomes without proper public knowledge, scrutiny or understanding.

Conclusion

This chapter illustrates a number of common, important and difficult ethical issues in social work. Social work shares the widespread value of individual autonomy, but interpreting autonomy is controversial and intervention sometimes reduces it more than it enhances. Professional practice becomes embroiled in conflicts of interest where no fully satisfactory outcome is possible. Social work intervenes in ways of life and therefore cannot be neutral about them; yet because there is no reliable social consensus, conventional practice is easily exposed to censure. Along with other areas of welfare, social work perpetually operates in an environment of insufficient resources to tackle many priority problems; it has to make politically problematic choices by disputable criteria. In common with other professional practices, social work must demonstrate the soundness of its expertise to prove its legitimacy; but ordinary life, the general target of social work, resists codification as professional expertise. This chapter has shown that we have serious problems on hand, and it sketches the agenda for what follows.

3

Social Workers and Values

The ubiquity of values

Social work values and ethics

Social workers often refer to values and are sensitive, perhaps even over-sensitive, about allegations touching the correctness of their values. The 'values' of social work are staple fare in basic textbooks; the official, institutional voices of social work are equally dedicated to pronouncing requisite values. The regulation formula that practice rests upon 'knowledge, skills and values' is so well ingrained that its conceptual weaknesses are apt to be neglected. As Timms (1983, p. 17) put it, '"values" are placed at every strategic point in the structure of social work'. Although Timms well demonstrated the confused and unsatisfactory character of 'value-talk' in social work, the quality of the dialogue about values has scarcely improved; and there is little to suggest that 'values' might be abandoned in favour of concepts more amenable to precise interpretation and application. Like love in the song, values are everywhere. The continued circulation of 'values' in the common coin of social work signals something important that merits exploration.

Values should be distinguished from ethics; the portmanteau 'values-and-ethics' contains no useful equipment. The several meanings of 'ethics' unfortunately complicate the picture.

1. Ethics is the philosophical study of moral and political virtue and obligation.
2. Ethics may denote a specific prescriptive scheme of obligations, more especially when labelled 'professional'; this is the intention of written codes of ethics. A course of action may be defined as ethical or unethical by comparison to such codes.

3. To speak of ethics may simply refer to customary rules and
    accepted practices in a given milieu, without intending any
    particular moral evaluation of them. Here 'ethics' is close to its
    root meaning of 'ethos' or character. In this third sense,
    therefore, all practice (professional and other) is ethical in that it
    necessarily entails an ethic; but such practice could be held to be
    unethical in the second sense, when evaluated against a
    prescriptive scheme.

In social work it is common to promote lists of 'values' and to treat
them interchangeably with 'ethics'. This is unsatisfactory because it
fails to distinguish between the desired ultimate ends and useful or
recommended approaches to achieving them. To promote a
multiplicity of core values leads to nowhere but confusion. Professional ethics, in the second (prescriptive) sense, must embody the
requisite core values; ideally, professional ethics are derived from
values, but are not identical with them. Values, it will be argued here,
must be few. Professional ethics, however, may helpfully be laid out
in different formulations to suit a range of different practical
problems and situations. The next chapter will set out the main
expectations of professional ethics in social work. In this chapter we
will first tackle the problem of 'values'.

What is meant by 'values'?

The ideas of value and values resist satisfactory definition. Beside
their use as basic building blocks of ordinary language, the concepts
are used in various ways in different fields of discourse. The
commonsense idea of the value of natural assets, goods or services is
appreciated by everyone of normal social competence; economists
rely on 'value' so heavily that their discipline would be unintelligible
without it. The economic notion of value does not transplant
directly into other discourses, but it certainly influences the
commonsense appreciation of 'value' in other contexts. Value in the
economic sense is an intuitive analogy, and perhaps the archetype,
for values in the wider senses.

Philosophers analyse what values might mean in different
contexts. Some philosophers and religious leaders offer theories
about the true values, or standards of goodness, that everyone ought

to try and live by. Others philosophers conclude that the idea of values simply represents the notion of ultimate good or worth and cannot be reduced to anything else; for some of these, values are in the end purely subjective. Prescribing values would be doubly futile if no conclusive proof is possible that certain values are better than others, and if values are no more than subjective and therefore non-disputable preferences or inclinations.

Sociologists carry out surveys of social values and use them to try to account for the character of institutions and societies. The difficulty here is that social values, as properties of individuals and social groups, are not things that can be directly and unambiguously observed. They are constructs attributed by observers that have to be inferred by asking people questions about their attitudes and beliefs, and observing their utterances and behaviour in relation to areas of life where value issues are thought to be significant. Explanations of social action in terms of values constantly risk circularity. For example, if racial equality is estimated to be held in low value on the basis of observed unfavourable conditions for black people, it is unclear how attributing this state of affairs to a *value* of racist white dominance really enlarges understanding of the phenomenon.

Psychologists study the individual's acquisition of moral and other values as a process of development and socialisation. Rokeach offers the following definition:

A *value* is an enduring belief that a specific mode of conduct or end-state of existence is personally or socially preferable to an opposite or converse mode of conduct or end-state of existence. A *value system* is an enduring organization of beliefs concerning preferable modes of conduct or end-states of existence along a continuum of relative importance. (Rokeach, 1973, p. 5; emphasis original)

As with sociology, some psychologists posit the content of individuals' values as a key explanation for human action; and here, too, the same problem of circularity exists.

In social policy values are often adopted as key descriptors of the ideas of reformers, of the social attitudes they reflect, and the policies they recommend and implement. Thus for example, the individualism of the libertarian right that was influential in the 1980s is seen as representing contrasting values to the socialist ideas of the postwar welfare reforms.

The conclusion to be drawn from all this multiplicity and complexity of usage is this: there can be no final definition of the concept of value; the meaning of 'value' cannot be definitively translated into other concepts that are safely beyond the reach of misunderstanding or controversy. The actual substance or content of values is equally impossible to define adequately in abstract terms. Abstract definitions of value eventually collapse into the circularity which affects its counterpart, the idea of the good: roughly, 'good things are valuable because they're good'. 'Value' and 'values' however, are apparently indispensable as well as irreducible, and the disciplines mentioned earlier and others have to aim for working definitions that are adequately serviceable in the context rather than infallibly and universally applicable. Social work, of course, has every reason to borrow the concepts of values used in philosophy, sociology, psychology, social policy and other fields. Since rather different ideas are represented in the respective discourses their application to social work becomes especially complicated.

This, therefore, is the modest principle to be adopted in tackling social work values: we should aim for an interpretation that will illuminate the significance of values in social work, acknowledging that the spheres of values extend far beyond social work's particular range of interests. We shall have to be satisfied with a working characterisation of social work values that must inevitably fall short of rigorous definition or exhaustive explanation. We cannot expect to find unanimity of purpose or even consistency of understanding. We shall hope nonetheless to touch the heart of the matter, however tentatively.

Values concern fundamental goals and issues: we need to talk about values, even though the available conceptual tools may be clumsy and we cannot be sure we know exactly what we mean. Indeed it is in part precisely because the concepts are difficult that we need to talk about them. The point of identifying and debating values is to give expression to intuitions and beliefs about the essential ends of human life and social living. Basic values embrace the grand aspirations or big ideas of morality and politics, such as freedom, justice, autonomy and community. Basic values also comprise ideals about the morally good character and the nature of the life worth living, for example compassion, courage, truthfulness or industriousness. These and other cardinal principles will be debated at many points in this book. It is argued in this chapter that since, to be intellectually appealing or theoretically persuasive, essentials must be few, it is more enlightening to restrict 'values' to those judged supremely important. The following critique therefore aims to suggest what should count as the truly fundamental values in social work.

The scope of values

Discussions of values in social work are sometimes framed so as apparently to include everything about practice. For example, Coulshed (1988, p. 36) suggests that 'If you look again at your in-tray referrals, you will see that... the decisions you reach are based mainly on value judgements.' Similarly, in a discussion of 'values in social care', Braye and Preston-Shoot (1995, Chapter 2) list six 'traditional' values ranging from respect for persons to anti-discriminatory practice, and counterpose six 'radical' values including participation and empowerment. One item of the former list is 'normalization and social role valorization', which in turn covers three components and five accomplishments. This approach is telling, since in leaving no conceivable aspect of social work outwith the purview of 'values' it reflects the all-pervasiveness of values in practice and in the perceptions of observers. As a mode of analysis, however, it is defective since it does not discriminate sufficiently between values and what would be better defined as models or theories, methods or skills. Not everything is usefully categorised as a value, and since the concept is already more than enough inflated, a more parsimonious conception is preferable.

To speak of values is to allude especially to two aspects of belief. First, value-beliefs are beliefs about *morally* good (or bad) ways of living with and treating others in the world. Values, in the senses connoted by value-talk in social work, are not matters of practical usefulness, technical judgement or expediency; indeed values are often said to contradict expediency. For example, a belief in the value of truthfulness might forbid taking an action in a social work case that the client had not been consulted about even if doing so was in some ways beneficial, because failing to communicate relevant information is a form of untruthfulness. The second aspect of value-beliefs is a corollary of the first. Values concern overridingly important, weighty aspects of life. Value-beliefs are held or felt to have a primary, fundamental or intrinsic character rather than a secondary or instrumental character. For example, a belief in the sanctity of life is a belief that life is to be given primary respect and protection for its inherent status and qualities; the sanctity of life (on this view) is not justified merely because respecting life might make people happier or society richer. When we commend or condemn a course of action by reference to values, we implicitly or explicitly appeal to superior, overriding reasons that claim precedence over mundane, practical considerations.

The idea of value relates to the worth of something, and thus connotes what is esteemed good or bad. Much moral discourse is devoted precisely to establishing what the important good things are. Familiar ideas in this vein would include respect, fairness, decency, propriety, and so on. The difficulty for theory is that these concepts are just as resistant to definition as the more general notion of values. A related difficulty is that the scope of values is not easily limited. In speaking of values we also address myriad familiar preferences, customary practices and traditional beliefs that give life its order, texture and meaning. Preferences for ways of living are conspicuously variable between different communities, societies and historical periods; each may be said to be based on different values, and conflicts between ways of living are readily described as conflicts of values. This points to a basic question for moral theory: are there fundamental and universal values that all right-thinking people should embrace, and which simply have to be clearly explained and demonstrated? Or is it rather that values are, inescapably, relative to the actor's view; plural and inherently contradictory; contingent on time, community and situation?

Are workers guided by ethics and values?

Some authors seem to conceive of ethics or values as if they were a kind of external force that operated upon the worker, whether more or less effectively. For example, Levy (1993, p. 1) says that 'ethics regulate and control the behavior of participants in human relationships and transactions'. Kugelman (1992, p. 59) carried out a research study on the 'role that social work ethics plays in informing social work behavior'. A few researchers have attempted to measure individuals' possession of social work values (cf. Pike, 1996). Such approaches are open to serious misunderstanding. On the one hand, since (aside from infants) practically all humans hold values and ethical beliefs, and since it is constitutive of values and beliefs that they affect and are manifest in conduct, to say that workers are regulated by values and beliefs adds little to our understanding. To construe values and beliefs in this sense as having regulatory force is tautologous, for how could they be otherwise? On the other hand, the question of whether values and ethics regulate action can be given a different interpretation if we take it that values and ethics refer to an external creation with authoritative force that workers are expected to adhere to. Whether they do so is then an empirical, scientific question, which will be addressed later.

The analytical and pragmatic assumption (usually implicit and unquestioned) that values comprise some species of free-standing entities, with an independent being of their own, is at best misleading. For example, CCETSW (1996, p. 17) expects students to show evidence of the 'integration of values' in their practice. As Timms (1983, p. 115) puts it, '"Values" are spoken of as if they were part of the actual furniture of the real world, as personal possessions or as part of the organic fabric of a society or of a personality.' But really it is accomplished human actors who hold values; it is only whole persons who are minded to cherish or spurn ideals, beliefs, projects, persons, ways of life, and so on. Values are aspects or properties of the totality of human action, both individually and collectively; they cannot be detached from it except as mental abstractions. To speak of values is thus a shorthand reference for beliefs and dispositions about what is morally or otherwise good: beliefs that will to some extent be shared between different people within communities. It is an error to reify values – that is, to treat as inert objects what should always be understood as the ongoing accomplishments of skilled and knowledgeable persons imbued with a moral sense. Even if not intentionally, reification paves the way for imagining that values are commodities that can be acquired or discarded as easily as changes of clothing. The values listed by CCETSW and other bodies as requirements for professional qualification cannot merely be donned at will, and to represent them as if they could be distorts understanding of the nature of values. The possession of values is not analogous to the possession of objects, nor to the possession of natural attributes. Values cannot be cut out of the profile of the whole person, except conceptually and even then only with great caution. Equally, persons cannot be excluded from the understanding of the cultures, contexts and traditions that they constitute.

Social work values and social workers' values

Lastly, in this process of conceptual clarification, a distinction is needed between social work values and social workers' values, or as it may be alternatively stated, between institutional values and individual values. Bearing in mind the foregoing caution about reification, the values of social work as a social institution – a body of social practice supported by, and expressed through, a range of formal and informal organisations – may be studied by reference to its practical activities, its literature, and the utterances, attitudes and opinions of its leaders and practitioners. We could anticipate some sort of collective profile, as it were, that typifies the occupation, while not necessarily expecting anything approaching perfect unanimity. Whether there exists in reality a global set of social work values, or whether it would be more accurate to conceive of a plurality of different social works, is an empirical as well as a theoretical question.

All this is a different matter to the values of social workers, which refers to the opinions and attitudes of individual members of the profession. We should avoid assumptions about whether social workers actually profess or adhere to the institutional values of the profession, since this too is an empirical question. In the following sections, evidence on both institutional and individual values will be reviewed.

The content of social work values: institutional norms

The 'values of social work' are, it would seem, not far from view. Lists of core values are regularly offered in the literature and just as regularly rewritten, recycled or rarely, rejected by other authors (see for example: Bamford, 1990; Banks, 1995; Bartlett, 1970; Biestek, 1961; Braye and Preston-Shoot, 1995; Butrym, 1976; CCETSW, 1976; Clark with Asquith, 1985; Downie and Telfer, 1980; Horne, 1987; Hugman and Smith, 1995; Jordan, 1990; May and Vass,

1996; National Association of Social Workers, 1996; Reamer, 1995; Rees, 1991; Rhodes, 1986; Shardlow, 1989; Statham, 1978; Timms, 1983; Wilmot, 1997). In its latest stipulations for qualification, CCETSW (1996, p. 18) again puts forward a set of 'values requirements' that candidates must meet. The main points of this are to respect uniqueness and diversity; promote rights to choice, privacy, confidentiality and protection; assist control of behaviour; counter discrimination; and avoid stigmatisation. The attachment to values is remarkable, since as Timms (1983) in particular has demonstrated, the whole system of concepts and propositions within which the dialogue on social work values is conducted is unsound. It shows not merely that social work will not give up its substantive values (whatever they may be), it is also that social work will not abandon the elusive idea of having such important things as values at its core.

Social work is sometimes said to be a 'value-based' profession, at least by implication different from professions not so labelled. In the absence of sufficient groundwork it is not at all clear what the claim means, but it seems to suggest that ideally at least, social work should not allow expediency to take precedence over basic moral purpose. Such a high-minded stance may be commendable but risks being mistaken for sanctimonious moralising. It is not for nothing that the appellation 'do-gooder' is usually pejorative. The claim to be value based also seems to comprise a veiled disparagement of occupations not so dignified, which is certainly provocative and probably unmerited. It is difficult to think of any legitimate occupation whose purposes could not be defined in terms of the promotion of important values. Are social workers more value based than the police (security), teachers (education), farmers (food) or public health inspectors?

The abundant references in the literature notwithstanding, there are, then, major difficulties in capturing social work values. In the search for values it is as if the hunt began with the traps and snares necessary for bringing home the game of the forest, only to find that the object of the quest was not, after all, a wild animal but instead a creature of allegory, imagination and myth that could never be caught by mere mechanical means. The supposed values of social work may resemble real practice as little as the creatures of a medieval bestiary resemble those of the modern science of zoology. The quest is not entirely hopeless for all that. Dimly, as in the mist, the values of social work can be glimpsed, if not fully apprehended.

The literature of social work, and the history of the occupation, unmistakably identify the roots of social work values in the moral thought of western Christianity blended with the intellectual tradition of Enlightenment liberalism. There is nothing fundamental in social work values that is not to be found in the mainstream of western societal values. While this is undoubtedly a rich, varied, complex and in parts contradictory inheritance, it is not one that requires any special elaboration or modification to take account of social work as different in principle from all the other occupations and institutions of modern liberal society. Social work has adopted the inheritance and itself constitutes one mode of its expression. If social work has different values, it is only in a secondary or derivative mode. The literature on social work values serves mainly to restate and reaffirm principles that are familiar as general leading themes of moral and political belief. The debates about social work values scarcely question these familiar principles, but turn rather on the specific interpretations to be given to them.

The western tradition is host to great divergences and profound ongoing controversies. With the many movements of peoples and ideas in the twentieth century, pluralism and value conflict are, ever increasingly, facts of political life. Recognising this diversity poses an important theoretical question: within the wide spectrum of prevailing attitudes and beliefs could there be multiple, competing value-sets for social work corresponding with different foundational moral and political beliefs? Or is it, on the contrary, that there can be only one basic set of values, which is necessary to social work and constitutive of it? The question can be illustrated with the example of religiously based social work. Should a church-based social work organisation be bound by traditional religious teachings about marriage and childbearing, sexual behaviour, abortion and divorce, and so adopt different intervention policies than a secular agency following contrasting contemporary social attitudes? Or should all social work agencies be expected to follow like policies, because they all adhere to similar social work values?

The empirical question remains whether as a matter of fact the institutions of social work cleave to any distinctive point (or points) in the wide modern spectrum of moral values and political priorities. Is social work actually different in its value orientation from other occupations? Do its agencies have distinctively social work approaches and priorities that mark out their values from other agencies? There is only scanty evidence with which to address these matters, but it is reasonable to make the following observations.

Within the broad spectrum of western values, there probably do exist several different conceptions of social work, marked by different priorities or value positions. For example, one of the recurrent themes in the values literature is about the distinctions between traditional (or conservative) and radical versions of social work. Self-styled radicals seek to overcome the perceived conceptual, moral and political inadequacies of conventional theory and practice. There is, however, no constant single radicalism or single traditionalism; these are relative concepts, representing practices that are continually being redefined and reformed. Another example is the claim that there are special and distinctive values in the voluntary sector. The Commission on the Future of the Voluntary Sector (1996), supporting pluralism, thought that independence from government and the other institutions of society was a core value of the sector. This would imply that social work based in the voluntary sector could be committed to different values than statutory social work.

Given the existence of apparently different tendencies within social work and the absence of convincing evidence for a unified set of social work values, we shall work on the safer assumption that there is no single reading of social work values. Rather there must be presumed to exist within social work various tendencies, schools or bodies of opinion about values. This cautious conclusion has surprisingly significant implications. If there is no single definitive set of ruling values, the expectations promulgated by official bodies such as CCETSW and professional associations such as the British Association of Social Workers and the National Association of Social Workers lack the substance and authority that are routinely claimed for them.

Social workers' values and ethics: empirical evidence

There are several kinds of evidence on social workers' values. The most direct is social research specifically addressed to social workers' attitudes, opinions and values, especially in relation to the precepts formulated in codes of ethics and other authoritative texts and prescriptive literature. A second is descriptive and evaluative research about service practice that may, incidentally, produce a profile of some prevalent values. To this may be added case histories, anecdotes and personal accounts from and about social workers, which can be suggestive of the values they hold. Judicial or quasi-judicial enquiries into failures of service may also incidentally reveal something of workers' values. Finally, and most problematically, it is worth considering popular stereotypes about the values that social workers supposedly hold.

Direct research on social workers' ethics and values

Research directly addressed to social workers' ethics and values is very scanty. The few published studies are mostly small in scale and disparate in aims and methods. Researchers have used broadly three approaches to studying social workers' values. The first approach is to apply a standardised, scorable test to individual workers. For example, Dobrin (1989) applied Rest's Defining Issues Test of moral reasoning to a postal sample of social workers and found (in a 21 per cent response) differences between males and females, and between workers in public authorities and private practice. Pike (1996) takes the approach further by developing a standard test specifically designed for social work, namely the Social Work Values Inventory. Since this line of research has not yet encompassed any substantive sampling of populations of social workers or students, the actual distributions of values remain unknown.

Standardised tests offer the potential to carry out consistent measurement in a regular way over large populations. When rooted in the main body of psychological and sociological research, standard tests may offer a means of clarifying the still rather nebulous idea of social work values by comparison with wider knowledge about moral reasoning. Theoretical, methodological and political objections aside, this type of test could conceivably be used to measure if social work students or professionals held the values required by a competent authority. A test of moral values can, however, be of little practical use as a test of fitness to practice unless supported by very clear and entirely authoritative stipulation of what are to count as required and prohibited values. Further, to be practically useful a test must have good discriminating power between acceptable and unacceptable values. Nothing in the research so far supports optimism about either of these questions.

A second, markedly contrasting approach to tracing social workers' values is to observe and ask them about their attitudes and practices in the real-life service situation. Such research is more accurately defined as focusing on social workers' *ethics* – their regular practices supported by conceptions of normatively required action – rather than their *values*, if values denote abstract and general notions of what is good and bad. Qualitative research methods are generally favoured. Holland and Kilpatrick (1991) carried out exploratory interviews with a sample of social workers, from which they discerned three dimensions of variation of workers' views. Workers would be orientated towards agency procedures or basic professional objectives (described by the authors as means or ends); towards client autonomy or protection (described as mutuality); and towards compliance with external norms or internalised views. Proctor *et al.* (1993) studied planning for discharge in hospital social work with elderly people and found four classes of ethical dilemmas. Workers experienced *conflicts between competing principles*, especially self-determination and protection of the client's interests; there were *disagreements* over *discharge destination* and over *medical care*; and there were *conflicts between the parties in cases* involving some or all of patients, doctors, social workers and family members. Clark (1998) interviewed workers in community care and found strong support for traditional ideas of self-determination, coupled with a realistic appreciation that paternalism was sometimes not only necessary, but desirable. Researchers adopting quantitative approaches include Conrad (1988), who carried out a postal survey of 58 social worker respondents designed to elicit information about the prevalence of ethical dilemmas and conflicts in practice. Particular areas of conflict were identified over informing third parties of dangerous or destructive behaviour. Mayberry (1996) carried out a survey of the attitudes of doctors, solicitors, nurses and social workers towards compulsory removal of an individual from home to institution on health grounds, finding (on a low response rate) that the social workers were relatively reluctant to authorise such removals.

Research designed to illuminate how practitioners conceive the ethical requirements of their practice, conduct the practical reasoning and negotiate the obstructions to ethically best practice would have much to teach both about the normative content of professional ethics and about how well practitioners attain stipulated standards. It could also reveal more clearly the dilemmas practi-

tioners face when obliged to try and reconcile conflicting imperatives, and pave the way for better theory. A recurrent theme in the
very limited research on social work ethics is the conflict between
principles of client self-determination and protection, care and
control; this is clearly an important and still unresolved issue. As yet
however, research on practitioners' ethics has hardly progressed
beyond the embryonic stage.

The third approach, midway between the first two, relies upon
testing social workers' responses to fictional but realistic case
situations. Walden *et al.* (1990) used a questionnaire focused on
twelve case vignettes (brief, epigraphic case histories) to explore the
attitudes of a total of 379 respondents comprising workers, supervisors and students towards implementing decisions likely to be
required by the agency. They found, contrary to hypothesis, little
tendency for decisions to vary with the status of the respondent as
worker, supervisor or student. Workers tended to go for a middle
position between the client's and the agency's choice. Kugelman
(1992) used interviews to explore the response of 20 social workers
to a single vignette and found no evidence of perceived ethical
dilemmas arising from commitment to the organisation conflicting
with other professional principles.

Vignettes are a useful and relatively economical way of surveying
attitudes on a well-defined issue. The validity of such research is,
however, crucially dependent on the representativeness of the
vignettes and the accurate focus of the questions posed; an
inadequately designed study based on vignettes risks missing the
target by a mile.

Evidence from studies of practice

Ethics are intrinsic to the fabric of practice and values are not
separable from the totality of action except conceptually. It follows
that almost any description or research on social work has the
potential to suggest something about workers' ethics and the characteristic norms of the milieu. However, it is not the aim of most
research to focus primarily on ethics, and specific findings in this
area are therefore few. The picture even more sketchy because there is
no established framework in which to theorise about, and report
upon, workers' values and ethics. Different researchers have concep-

tualised their objectives differently and consequently it is difficult to synthesise their findings.

Stevenson and Parsloe (DHSS, 1978, Chapter IX) found that social workers felt a strong sense of personal responsibility for the welfare of the clients on their caseload. But they found, too, that many workers favoured tight controls over the granting of cash or help in kind to clients, and preferred to see financial support to poor clients as something that should be kept separate from social work proper. The ethic of meeting clients' needs was thus qualified by an attitude (or value) about the place of social work in meeting financial need. In a wide-ranging review of the research literature, Rees and Wallace (1982) found a spectrum of worker views on the provision of material help from seeing it as of little help, to seeing it as helpful with qualifications, to seeing it as integral to social work.

Sainsbury *et al.* (1982) asked social workers to compare their relationships with clients with those of a 'typical' colleague in the same agency on the dimensions of warmth, empathy, client's dependence, authority, openness/frankness, and purposefulness. Workers tended to see themselves as broadly similar to their colleagues in most respects, but as below typical in the exercise of authority and purposefulness. The authors point out that it was in the latter two areas that clients were most likely to complain about their social worker. These findings suggest workers put a high valuation on warmth, empathy and openness. The workers considered that they showed some or much care towards clients in the vast majority of cases. In their review of the research, Rees and Wallace (1982, p. 101) conclude that 'most workers feel it is important that clients feel they are truly concerned and interested in them and their problems'.

Popular stereotypes

It is widely supposed that social workers tend to hold certain distinctive attitudes and beliefs. Stereotypes are easily recognised in the representations of social work in the general news media, in the words of politicians and other leaders of public opinion and in popular drama and fiction. According to such popular conceptions, social workers may be seen as permissive, left-of-centre liberals, ever ready to condone wickedness that ought to be condemned. Social workers are imagined to be too much preoccupied with irrelevant ideology and over-impressed by the latest fad at the expense of common sense and unpretentious practical service. They may be characterised as self-absorbed, holier-than-thou figures with defective notions of accountability.

Clearly such popular representations cannot in themselves be trustworthy sources of evidence about workers' values. Even insofar as they may reflect important tendencies in the profession, they do not describe the range of social workers' values or the extent of adherence to them. It would no more be true to characterise social workers in this way than it would be, say, to describe all lawyers as avaricious and conservative or all nurses as selfless and dedicated. Nevertheless the content of such stereotypes is well worth exploring. If these are the images of social workers, are they fair or inaccurate? Do they represent the values of social work that it is wished to affirm, or the denial of them? If popular stereotypes are significantly discrepant from reality, should not social workers better attend to their accountability to society in general?

Social workers' values in summary

The evidence about the values actually held by social workers is extremely tenuous. This is due, in part, to the lack of research on the subject, which permits no more than very tentative exploration and speculation. More fundamentally, it reflects the problems of theory. The subject of values occupies a large and diffuse region spread, at least, between the domains of psychology, sociology, philosophy of mind, religion, ethics and politics. Neither the general conceptions of values developed in these disciplines, nor the particular interpretations of values current within social work, provide a satisfactory theoretical framework for advancing the empirical enquiry about social workers' values. So far there are no strong grounds for supposing that useful distinctions can be made between the values that social workers should hold and the values held by non-social workers. There is equally no persuasive evidence that social workers' values are really different from the values of any comparable section of society.

True values?

The review of social work values and social workers' values gives an insight as to why the discourse on values in social work often seems vague and unsatisfactory. The point of value-talk is to address two kinds of problem. First, it is definitional. To talk about values is to signal that the point of interest is questions of the nature and purpose of human living that ought to be recognised as of pre-eminent importance. Claims about values are claims about foundation principles or ultimate aims: or if they are not, they merely degrade the currency of 'values'. Second, value-talk is substantive. It needs to identify and justify basic values if it is to be either persuasive or useful. In social work however, value-talk is neither premissed on adequately clear definitions nor sufficiently cogent about the fundamental values that ought to be pursued.

Whether or not there actually exists a distinctive set, or distinctive sets, of social work values, a further question is still to be debated. This is the *normative* question of whether social work *ought* to represent a distinctive set of values. It is easy to see that social work is a collective response to a fairly specific range of social problems – problems of family relationships and daily living, care for the vulnerable and social control. A useful probe for social work values may be: are these problems that require a specific set of moral principles, attitudes or values for their proper treatment?

Social work often deals with people who at the time are relatively vulnerable in both practical and emotional respects. It should be especially conscious of their disadvantaged status and especially sensitive to the psychological pressures they might be expected to experience. For example, in dealing with children who have been maltreated by their parents, social work values might be thought to require particularly high regard for children's rights coupled with empathy with problems of family life. Or, in dealing with an elderly person who is facing giving up their home and independent life because of disability, it might be said that social work values require special sensitivity to the emotional costs involved as well as a grasp of the practical issues that need to be addressed. It is plausible to suggest, then, that key values will be those that underlie proper care. Care is a multi-dimensional concept that includes within it an attitude of sympathy and compassion as well as the discharge of specific duties (Clark and Lapsley, 1995; Wilmot, 1997).

As well as dealing with people who are vulnerable, social work equally deals with people who are seen to pose a threat to social order; many cases fall into both categories simultaneously. For example, in dealing with offenders social work has a role as part of the formal apparatus of the criminal justice system, while preferring to pursue humane policies that address the welfare of the offender as well as the rights of the injured. In dealing with people with mental health problems, social workers exercise control by formal and informal means, and do so with the interests of the unwell person in mind as well as the possible risks to the community. So it is plausible to suggest that the values that underlie proper control should be set alongside those that underlie proper care.

Basic social work values appear, then, to include those essential to proper care and control. This reformulates, but does not solve, the problem about the normative values that social work ought to represent. Nonetheless, the reformulation perhaps has some heuristic value. What should we look for in proper care and control? Four principles are outlined here in order to orientate one's reflection and focus debate. They will be extensively revisited in later chapters.

The worth and uniqueness of every person

The caring attitude requires full understanding and appreciation that every person has intrinsic worth, whatever their particular attributes such as age, gender, ethnicity, physical or intellectual ability, wealth or contribution to society. Ideally, everyone is to be valued for their uniqueness and treated with the utmost care and respect. In reality, there are innumerable obstacles to the realisation of this attitude.

The entitlement to justice

Control is intolerable unless practised with an attitude of care and a striving for justice. Every person and social group is entitled to treatment on agreed principles of justice. Justice is complex and multi-faceted. It requires the protection of essential rights and liberties, such as the right to life and protection from avoidable harm. Justice is given specific content by theories of human nature and human need, requiring for example the provision of health care and education. Justice attends to the problem of fair distribution, and remedying unfairness. Justice rewards people according to what they deserve – whether honour or reward for effort, or discredit and punishment for wrongdoing. Justice must be supported by demonstrably effective means for its implementation.

The aspiration to freedom

Care seeks the self-realisation and freedom of the cared-for. The idea of freedom complements and interlocks with the idea of justice. Every person and every social group is entitled to their own beliefs, pursuits and projects without interference, but must accept the restraints necessary for others to have similar freedoms. This includes freedom of speech, religion and assembly and freedom to pursue a particular way of life. Although freedom and justice are both highly valued, they can only be defined in relation to each other. Many political questions boil down to the specific interpretation and relative valuation of freedom and justice in particular contexts.

The essentiality of community

Care and control are necessarily practised in communities. The truly valued, fully human life can only be realised by persons living and acting interdependently in well-functioning communities. This applies at every level, whether family, neighbourhood, workplace, community of interest or nation. Community is essential to life, but communities are often divided internally about their aims and purposes, and are often in conflict with each other.

Conclusion: the mirage of values

The mirage of values

The quest for social work values is a frustrating affair. Although paraded at every turn, social work values turn out to be conceptually vague as well as substantively questionable. In social work the notion of values is used in such an elastic fashion that it has little analytic power. It is unclear what sort of thing the general concepts of 'value' or 'values' might denote; and it is equally unclear what, if anything, substantively distinguishes 'social work values' from others. Nevertheless, values are widely presumed to be important, indeed supremely so. This is an axiom rather than a conclusion: values are *of their nature* important.

Because of weakness of theory and the related lack of empirical research on the question, it is very difficult to know whether there is substantial concordance or conflict within and between social work values, social workers' values, and the values and expectations of society at large. The very real possibilities that social work values might be contradictory or morally questionable are obscured by wrapping them all in the same envelope. Overstuffed with both concepts and content, the term 'values' seemingly slackly covers anything of potentially significant moral character: notions of morally good intention; aspirations to treat people in morally significant ways; nostrums and precepts of good practice; approved or disapproved political goals. The lack of clarity is regrettable because it confuses and misleads.

We are left with the question of whether social work values can be made intelligible – or should be jettisoned as irremediably defective. It is tempting to conclude that there are no such things as social work values, or at least, that there is no practical use in talking about them. This radical solution has its attractions but would be a misrepresentation: 'values' remains a powerful rallying cry. There is, then, something called social work values, but it is not what is seems. Social work values are far from comprising the bedrock of sound practice, as convention would have it.

The best likeness of social work values is to a mirage: a deceptive apparition on the horizon caused by peculiar atmospheric conditions. We can perceive something there, but it is a distorted and misleading representation of reality and a poor guide to practical action (spotting objectives and finding one's way). The appearance of the mirage changes as we try to move towards it, and we can never actually reach it. Moreover, differently placed observers will tend to see different things; on the ground there is no one epistemologically privileged, objective view. To make sense of social work values, we shall have to seek a higher viewpoint above the ground where mirages form. To that end, the following principles for interpreting values will aid in reducing error.

Values are limited to fundamentals

The perennial appeal to values shows that social work regards itself as inherently charged with moral purpose. It is said that forms of intervention that might, in some sense, be technically efficient, are not justified if they do not conform to required moral values. Since almost any form of intervention or non-intervention can be held to represent specific distinguishable values, to avoid trivialisation of the term it is preferable to restrict the invocation of values to those occasions where something truly fundamental appears to be at stake.

The fundamentals are questions of moral and political purpose. Not every issue is fundamentally a value issue, although it may with little effort be (mis)construed as such. Disputes about 'values' are best restricted to a small handful of central values about interpersonal action and social life; talk about the values of social work should avoid becoming enmeshed in talk about the whole of social work. In sum, the concept of 'values' is useful only when used parsimoniously.

The short list of values given earlier is suggested as a plausible outline of fundamentals. The list in this bare form does not, of course, adequately explain the meaning or spell out the implications of the suggested principles, which are all highly contested. What the principles do is point to the territory that needs to be mapped.

Only a few core values are compossible

As Timms (1983) showed, a satisfactory scheme of social work values is not to be created by the unreflective compilation of lists drawn from assorted sources. The broad aims of social work underwrite the quest for the widest range of social goods and the mitigation of innumerable harms. It may be tempting to list everything under the 'values' of social work, as it were to enumerate the perils against which insurance is needed; but the pick-and-mix method of specifying values is unlikely to succeed because the good espoused in any one moral value may well conflict with the good in another, and in the real world they cannot all be pursued equally. Values are weighty, but must be few if they are not to be impossibly burdensome.

4

The Rules of Social Work Ethics

The place of social work ethics

Professional ethics as prescription

We have seen in the previous chapter that social work attaches great importance to its values, while often confusing 'values' and 'ethics'. Investigating values proves inconclusive: social work values are impossible to define with any great exactitude, and difficult to distinguish from the common precepts of morality and the ordinary norms of social living. Nevertheless social workers fervently believe that there are morally more and less preferable ways of going about their business. It is also abundantly clear from the nature of the tasks and issues confronted in practice and illustrated in Chapter 2 that they are right to be concerned about the moral implications of their practice. This concern is expressed in professional ethics in the second sense identified at the beginning of Chapter 3: a prescriptive scheme of obligations applicable to professional practice.

In any field of professional ethics there are two main aims, the prescriptive and the critical. Ethics as prescription aims to instruct how professionals ought to deal with morally problematic situations, while the critical aspect examines the premises and arguments on which prescriptions are based. Take, for example, the precept of confidentiality. The prescriptive arm of professional ethics says that information that the social worker acquires about her client ought not to be indiscriminately revealed to other persons. The critical analysis of confidentiality considers the reasons and justifications for this axiom of non-disclosure on the basis of general moral theory.

This chapter explains the standard prescriptions of social work ethics. It is based on the literature about ethics in social work, on formal codes drawn up by professional associations and official bodies, and on wider aspects of the unwritten culture, tradition and informal regular practices of social workers. In addition, legal or quasi-legal expectations in the form of statute law and official regulation often have considerable ethical force. As a statement of social work ethics it both transmits the conventional prescriptions and reflects aspects of the wider character or ethos of the profession. The critical analysis of conventional social work ethics will begin to emerge as its rules are formulated, to be pursued more fully in later chapters.

Statements of the content of professional ethics are useful for a number of audiences. Students are entitled to a clear exposition of the ethical expectations of the profession they are preparing themselves for. Professionals need an authoritative formulation of their ethics in order to ensure that practice adheres to agreed principles, and to help decide difficult cases. Service users are entitled to know what sort of treatment to expect at the hands of professionals, and to have guidelines about when good practice may have been infringed. The community at large should require the professionals who act in their name to be accountable for the moral content of practice.

Setting out statements of professional ethics also has its hazards. Declarations of professional ethics are apt to be received with scepticism or even cynicism. Critics often suggest that a defined set of professional ethics serves merely as one of the accoutrements necessary for an occupational group to grasp the covetable independence and power of professional status. Although the role of professional ethics is purportedly to guarantee service in accordance with defined moral principles, it is sometimes held that their real function is simply to legitimate the control that powerful professionals can exert over relatively powerless consumers (Hugman, 1991). A second criticism of professional ethics is that, for all their fine words, they are not practically achievable in the real world of shortage, imperfection and compromise. There is considerable force in these, and other, criticisms. For the moment they will be set aside in order first to bring the matter of social work ethics more clearly into view.

Sources

Professional ethics are more or less explicitly formulated in the codes of professional associations; in the guidance and procedures devised by public service and official regulatory agencies; and in the goals and methods of voluntary organisations. They are also examined, of course, in the academic and professional literature.

Many advanced countries with established associations of social workers have a code of social work ethics developed by the association. Codes of ethics embody the profession's attempts at identifying the core principles and values that should govern social work. Banks surveyed the codes of 15 national associations of social workers and found substantial agreement over four broad principles of respect, self-determination, social justice and professional integrity (Banks, 1995). There is however much scope for differing interpretation of these principles, particularly since there are large differences in the focus and amount of detail elaborated in different codes. For example, the code of the British Association of Social Workers (1996) runs to some six pages, while the codes of the (American) National Association of Social Workers (1996) and the Canadian Association of Social Workers (1994) run to 30 and 24 pages respectively.

In this context it is worth noting also that codes of ethics are produced by professional associations akin to but not identical with social work, for example counsellors and clinical psychologists. Since their codes may well be relevant in some social work practice settings, social workers so placed should make a point of consulting them. Furthermore, social workers who work in agencies primarily dedicated to other services – health is the leading example – would clearly do well to familiarise themselves with the ethical codes of their colleagues, such as nurses and doctors (see for example Mason and McCall Smith, 1994; Thomson *et al.*, 1993).

Social work is predominantly a public function that is largely sponsored, if not always directly provided, by government at national and local levels. Social workers and their agencies are therefore typically subject to the administration by rule-book that is found in all public service bureaucracies. In Britain copious central government circulars exhort and regulate the local authorities as they implement the wide range of social policies relevant to social work.

Alongside central government guidance must be set the standards and procedures created by local government. To cope with the welter of direction from the centre and to keep their own house in order, local government agencies in turn produce manuals of procedure that can run to many volumes. Occasionally they publish guidelines defining principles of service provision, but these are likely to represent no more than the tip of the iceberg.

The third main class of ethical codes comprises the aims and principles of service practice published by voluntary (or non-profit) organisations in social welfare. It is highly characteristic of voluntary organisations that they pride themselves on a self-chosen, idealistic sense of mission or vocation, in contrast to official bodies, which are governed by statute law and public policy. Perhaps because the service or reform mission is often understood as a voluntary organisation's defining reason for existence, such organisations often give a high priority to spelling out their principles of service, with all their ethical entailments.

For the sake of simplicity, clarity and economy, the strategy adopted in the following exposition is to distil a set of key principles from a broad range of sources. Much of the relevant academic literature has already been cited in this chapter and in the discussion of values in the last chapter. Other sources include the following: Fairbairn and Fairbairn, 1988; Gambrill and Pruger, 1997; Koehn, 1994; Loewenberg and Dolgoff, 1982; McDermott, 1975; Reamer, 1990; Timms and Watson, 1976; Timms and Watson, 1978; Watson, 1985. This summary hearing inevitably gives short shrift to a wide and often disparate range of argument and opinion on a range of complex issues. It cannot to do full justice to every argument, position and nuance in a wide literature. Nevertheless, it is reasonable to conclude that there is a broad consensus about what the professional role requires and prohibits, which is not however to say that there will always be unanimity in the interpretation of general principles and their application to particular cases.

Eight rules for good practice

Social workers are expected to adhere to the following rules of ethical practice. A 'rule' in this context is a widely accepted, generally binding prescription based on experience and customary practice; but rules are not absolute or infallible, and exceptions have to be allowed occasionally where good reason can be shown. There is no particular priority in the order of presentation here; it will quickly become apparent that what is required for good practice under one heading is often required under others too. These expectations overlap and mesh together; they are not independent requirements, but interdependent, each requiring and supporting the others.

Respectful

Ethical practice is respectful, one might even say reverential, of the identity, individuality and rights of every person. Every individual is inherently a being of unique worth, whose special features are to be recognised and valued however they may compare with one's own characteristics, beliefs or attitudes. It follows that respect is equally due to all persons without regard to such contingencies as race or ethnicity, age, gender, sexuality, physical or intellectual ability or cultural background.

Since it is a practically universal human characteristic to be more attuned to the uniqueness and value of some individuals while remaining relatively insensitive to others, practitioners and their organisations should take positive steps to address shortcomings of respectfulness whether deliberate or inadvertent. They should recognise and understand the universal tendency to treat more sympathetically those who are, or whom we perceive to be, similar to ourselves while neglecting the similar claims of those who are or seem different. Thus, for example, practitioners should ensure that members of ethnic minorities and speakers of minority languages are not treated in a disadvantageous or demeaning manner as a result of lack of mutual understanding or lack of sympathy with a way of life. Similarly, they should be careful that the way of life of someone with learning disabilities is not undervalued because of its differences with prevailing norms in the wider society.

Practitioners should be constantly aware that their interventions are probably intrusive as well as potentially helpful. They must maintain a nice balance between reaching out to provide apposite help and refraining from intervening in order not to trespass upon the autonomy of the individual. Practitioners and managers should ensure that the individuality and privacy of service users is not contradicted by the operation of impersonal service systems. For example, they should guard against routinisation to the point where individuals are fitted to the service and not the other way about, and they should ensure that information about individuals' personal circumstances and affairs is communicated only to those with a valid reason to hear or read it.

Honest and truthful

Social work services should be offered and given in a manner that is honest, open, truthful and transparent to users. This means more than merely avoiding intentional or accidental misrepresentations or falsehoods. It requires positively striving to ensure that the user is well informed about, and has an appropriate understanding of, aspects of the service process that he may not have considered or appreciated. The word of social workers must be trustworthy; undertakings made must be kept unless there are genuinely supervening reasons. Similarly, any taint of fraud whereby a client is deceived about the basis on which service is given, or its content, must be definitively avoided. For example, a client should not be led to believe that the worker has knowledge, qualifications, experience or authority that she does not possess.

Within many professions individual practitioners have traditionally been banned from advertising their services in such a way as to imply their superiority or even promote their visibility over other practitioners. On the other hand, generic advertising to attract the public to use, for example, lawyers in general without identifying particular law firms, is more often permitted. There are strong reasons for supporting generic advertising in social work to ensure that users know that services exist and what to expect from them. Where social work is a public agency function, advertising seems positively necessary for potential users to know what public policy has determined to provide. Where it is voluntary or not-for-profit agencies that provide a service, advertising seems well justified for similar reasons and considering that state subventions and individual donations often support such services.

Professional services are offered on the basis that the professional will give paramount consideration to her client's interests. It must nonetheless be openly recognised that the professional is also motivated by some elements of self-interest. The professional has to ensure that her interest in the process does not displace the client's good. The problem is especially obvious where a service is provided in return for a fee. Even in the context of salaried officials working for public services, there is the possibility that the worker will have self-interested motives. She may, for example, find a piece of work particularly attractive or burdensome, and thus be induced to pursue a course of action less than optimal for the client's best interest.

The service contract in social work is much more often implicit than explicit. The nature of the service is far less obvious and familiar than the exchanges people routinely enter into when they go shopping, visit the doctor or send their child to school. Many social work users have no idea what to expect when they present themselves to the agency. Research has shown that users are often under significant misapprehensions about social work, and that social workers themselves have been less than clear about it. Furthermore, social work is not surrounded by a body of common and statute law comparable to that which defines ordinary exchanges in the market. Users are on the whole relatively poorly placed to ensure they receive fair dealing, and to complain effectively if they do not. Unlike, say, medical practice, suing for bad professional service is very rare in social work.

The creation of the often implicit, unspoken contract between social worker and client therefore calls for particular care to satisfy the principles of honesty and truthfulness. The obligation is upon the professional and the agency to ensure that the service user knows as soon as practicable what he is entitled to expect, and what may be offered on a discretionary basis. Agencies should therefore provide their clientele with ample information in appropriate forms at every stage of the process, including before any enquiry or request is made. The user should also be informed about what obligations or restrictions may fall upon him as a result of entering a service process. He will be expected to cooperate by giving information about himself and may have to reveal, say, his financial affairs, or disclose aspects of his intimate relationships.

In professional services the professional carries out some series of operations with, on behalf of, or actually upon, the client, patient or service user. Outside the professional relationship, such operations would often constitute an assault or an invasion of rights, dignity, or privacy. To ensure that no such invasion occurs, the professional is bound to seek the consent of the client. The clearest example of this is the consent form that a patient signs before undergoing an operation. It is much more usual however for the client's consent to be implicit. Merely by placing himself, literally or figuratively, in the hands of the practitioner, the client is presumed to have consented to the series of operations that is expected to follow. Consent is implied by seeking the service and accepting what is offered, just as a contract is implicitly created by seating oneself in the hairdresser's chair. However, many social work interventions are carried out not with the willing consent of the user, but under duress. Where consent is not possible, it is nevertheless a duty to be honest about the terms of the engagement. For all these reasons, there is much to commend the use of explicit contracts or working agreements with clients. It must still be remembered that clients usually remain in a relatively powerless position, so contracts should not be used to excuse manipulation or deception.

An important aspect of openness in service provision concerns the use and status of client records. Social workers used to follow the conventional professional rule and treat their case notes and records as private to themselves and their professional colleagues. More recently this practice has been overturned in favour of the principle of open records in which not only does the client have a right to see his records, but where ideally the client is positively encouraged to participate in the creation of the record and its use to further the work. Openness in records accords with the principles of honesty and truthfulness, but it must equally be explicitly recognised that some records cannot be open. Accuracy in records is obviously necessary for truthfulness. Truthfulness may be abridged by incompleteness, which raises the issue of how full a record is necessary.

Finally, the principle of honesty in the contract extends to the termination of service. It should be clear what will bring about the end of the contact and whose terms will determine this. It is also helpful to be clear about the relationship that will exist between worker and client after the end of the service, when the special licence that sanctions professional intervention has lapsed.

Knowledgeable and skilful

Many clients choose to use services because professionals enable them to tackle problems that are beyond their capabilities. In the traditional professions of the religious ministry, law and medicine, practitioners are recognised to hold special knowledge, experience and authority not otherwise available to the lay person. This now applies equally to a wide range of other professions and occupations including social work. The client may lack the requisite knowledge, for example of an area of the law, or of the requirements surrounding adoption of a child. The client may lack the authority: many operations and processes, from supplying a social enquiry report to a court to installing gas appliances, are licensed exclusively to authorised individuals or corporate bodies. The client may lack the ability, for example to carry out a physically strenuous task or simply to cope unaided with the ordinary activities of daily living. The client may lack the desire, as when people turn over their financial affairs to be handled by a tax consultant. The client may lack the means, as those in poverty lack the money for essentials. Some recipients of professional services, perhaps especially social work, are obliged to receive a service that they have not chosen that is expected to remedy a social problem. Whether clients seek the service or have it imposed upon them, expertise is crucial; without it, there cannot be confidence that the professional's intervention will be appropriate, beneficial and non-harmful.

Professionals are, therefore, expected to be knowledgeable on a range of subjects defined by the scope of their work; ethical social work must be properly informed and expertly practised. In social work prime areas of knowledge include psychology and human development, social problems, and so forth, as well as knowledge of models and methods of intervention. The command of this knowledge is not sufficient by itself; professionals are also expected to be competent or skilful. Their practice should embody that effective application of knowledge that is recognised as skill.

The professional's knowledge is never perfect. Service practice with people who face challenging difficulties in the means of maintaining or changing their daily lives, in their personal relationships, or in their relations with the institutions of society requires that the professional should recognise her limitations and regularly seek advice and consultation from colleagues with relevant expertise. The professional needs to ensure that she is suitably educated for the roles she undertakes and trained for the tasks she assumes. Professionals in positions of formal authority have a duty to ensure that their students and colleagues are offered appropriate education and training.

The knowledge of the profession is never perfected. Much, perhaps most, social work practice is of uncertain effectiveness and open to significant improvements. Progress in furthering knowledge of the problems that social work tackles and in improving practice depends on research. Every social worker should learn the inquisitive, curious, critical, and sceptical attitude to knowledge that drives research. Social workers should set the support of research high in their professional priorities.

Careful and diligent

Between professional and client there is a fiduciary relationship, that is one in which the client rests his trust in the expertise, integrity and good faith of the professional. The professional has care and stewardship of the potentially vulnerable client's best interests. Ideally the relationship is built on a sense of trusting and mutual fidelity. Sometimes the client will be in conflict with the professional and disinclined to trust her. The professional nonetheless retains the fiduciary obligations of the relationship, even if the client does not feel reciprocally bound by a sense of trust.

Social workers are entrusted with individuals' delicate affairs in the expectation that they will be safe and well looked after. Clients are often especially vulnerable, disadvantaged or threatening to the general welfare. Social workers have to discharge the responsibilities undertaken in the implicit or explicit contract; they must be careful to carry out their duties well, and dare not be careless in their performance. The contract, whether formal or informal, depends on trust between the parties; trust will rapidly be destroyed if the client believes or feels that the worker is failing to take care of his interests.

Since the client's interests are usually best advanced by full attention and effort to his problems, workers undertake to pursue matters with due diligence and without neglect. They should perform their duties in a timely and reliable manner. Qualities of conscientiousness, determination on the client's behalf and commitment to the client's interests are hallmarks of good professional practice. Willingness to go the second mile is highly valued; minimalist, barely adequate service attracts disaffection and complaint.

Effective and helpful

Clients turn to professionals, or are required to turn to them, in the expectation that their problems will be alleviated. Expertise is essential to meet this expectation, but it is not sufficient. The experience of all the professions sadly proves that the knowledgeable and competent provision of a service is no guarantee that the client will actually be helped by it. In medicine, for example, the pre-modern uses of leeches and purges, although done according to the best knowledge of the day, were often irrelevant or unhelpful to the patient's underlying condition. In litigation it is quite possible for the lawyer to give the client technically correct legal advice while neglecting the client's best interest overall. A well-known example from social work concerns the use of approaches to counselling or 'casework' modelled after psychoanalysis. For perhaps 30 years, this was the ruling orthodoxy in social work theory. Eventually research began to emerge that implied that even in the hands of experienced and skilful practitioners such interventions were often of very doubtful effectiveness. Social work has since moved away from relying on psychodynamically inspired counselling as its principal model of intervention. One should not therefore conclude that social work has learned the general lesson of the importance of research. Macdonald and Macdonald (1995) argue, with more than a mite of justified pessimism, that ethical practice in social work is still being defeated by unwillingness to address effectiveness questions seriously.

Professionals must seek to ensure that their interventions are not only carried out with due competence and in good faith, but are effective in the sense that they lead to the desired outcomes. Good intentions on the practitioner's or the agency's part are not enough. Interventions may fail under two general sets of circumstances. A method may be generally effective, but inappropriately chosen or badly applied in a particular case. Alternatively it may be that the method is never dependable and should simply be discarded, just as obsolete medical treatments are discarded. Professionals should use the methods and findings of social research to study the effects of their work, and be ready to seek alternatives or desist if it is shown that their interventions are on balance unhelpful to the overall interests and welfare of the client.

Not every type of intervention that is effective, in the sense that it reliably leads to an intended outcome, can be judged helpful, in the sense that it is, on balance, valuable to the client. For example, residential child care often seems to assume that the young person who leaves care at 18 should no longer be a responsibility for public welfare. In achieving the aim of deleting the case from the agency workload, policy and practice neglect that young people leaving care are no less likely than other young people leaving the parental home to need several more years of moral and financial support before attaining a healthy independence.

A highly valued end in social work is to empower the client or service user. Empowerment means, among other things, to place in the service user's hands a meaningful choice of courses of action for the present, and to create valuable options for the future. A helpful intervention will often be one that tends to empower the user. Some necessary interventions, nevertheless, are inevitably disempowering, as for example when parental rights are abridged to protect a child.

Legitimate and authorised

Like other professional activities, social work routinely entails actions which, were they not carried out under the special conditions of professional service, would be regarded as improper or illegal under ordinary social mores. Intervening as a stranger in people's personal relationships, life plans and daily affairs is acceptable only if it is legitimate; it must be sanctioned by law. Social work interventions are, in effect, carried out under licence whereby specific permission is granted for that which is otherwise generally prohibited, just as driving is permitted only under licence.

At minimum, legitimacy requires refraining from the positively illegal. For example, social workers should not as a rule provide or condone a child care service that does not meet relevant regulations about standards of accommodation, staff training, or care methods. Often a stronger basis of legitimation is expected and necessary, whereby action is not merely permissible but positively required under specific enactments that social work agencies have a duty to implement. For example, social workers are legitimately entitled and expected to take action if it suspected that a child is being maltreated in the family.

Social workers must have authority to carry out the work they intend to do, in the shape of instruction or permission from the agency that employs them and underwrites their work. Not every conceivable piece of social work is on balance desirable or feasible, and workers must ensure that the work they take on has the backing of the agency on whose behalf they undertake it. For example, workers are usually expected to practise within a specified local district or a section of an agency, and to carry out work that they have been specifically allocated; they are expected to refrain from work outwith the agreed programme of action. It is also essential to workers' authority that they be appropriately qualified for the work they carry out. Correspondingly, agencies must ensure that workers are authorised and trained to carry out the expected duties. For example, agencies have to delegate to their workers the powers to make appropriate decisions about the treatment of cases, the running of service units or the spending of funds.

The sources of legitimacy and authority lie, then, partly in the law that creates social work agencies and determines their duties. Some of this legislation is mandatory and requires specific action under defined circumstances, as for example in the treatment of offenders on probation. Much more is broadly enabling or permissive, serving to give public authorities a wide range of powers to support various types of work without precise specifications about how it should be implemented. For example, s.12 of the Social Work (Scotland) Act 1968 stipulates that

> It shall be the duty of every local authority to promote social welfare by making available advice, guidance and assistance on such a scale as may be appropriate for their area.

Legitimacy is not, however, founded exclusively on statute law expressly created to define social work services. It depends in part also on the political processes that give varying attention to different social problems at different times, and the framework of social policy which thus emerges. The spread and balance of activities in social work agencies changes considerably as different issues rise or fall on the political agenda. For example, the Local Authority Social Services Act 1970 enables local authority social services department in England to undertake community work alongside more mainstream social work activities. During the 1970s policy in many local authorities found space for local community work; by the early 1980s the emphasis changed and community work largely disappeared from English local authorities without any specifically relevant legislative initiative (Thomas, 1983).

Some forms of social work owe their legitimacy to a general presumption permitting social action as an aspect of the core political freedoms of free speech and assembly. Especially in the voluntary sector, individuals and groups have freedom to initiate and carry on forms of social service not envisaged or required in legislation. In many countries voluntary associations have to be legally registered; it is not required in Britain. Organisations have to submit to special requirements if they wish to claim the advantages of non-taxable, not-for-profit operation.

Underneath policy and law, legitimacy rests ultimately on a broad social mandate and the sanction of the community. Social services have to be seen to be broadly in line with priorities and values prevailing in the wider community. When social work departs from such communal, implicitly expected standards and its legitimacy is cast into doubt despite the stipulations of statute, the political results can be spectacular.

Collaborative and accountable

All professionals have to work together with their colleagues in order best to serve their clients' interests. In social work the primary responsibility for the service usually lies not with a single practitioner, but with the agency that employs the worker; workers must collaborate effectively if the agency's responsibility is to be well carried, since the work must pass from hand to hand at different stages of the process. The sharing of responsibility should benefit the service user who thus gains, directly or indirectly, from a range of contributions, expertise and opinions. For similar reasons collaboration must extend beyond immediate office colleagues to members of other disciplines and other agencies.

Put in this way, the principle of collaborative working may seem uncontentious, but in social work it has been a notorious point of failure. An understandable sentiment to shelter the interests of the client behind a screen of privacy has probably interfered with a clear sense of the boundaries of proper collaboration. Between social work and other occupations, barriers of status, organisation, method and professional ethos frequently interfere with satisfactory collaboration and result in inferior service. Professionals need to be mindful that both they and their colleagues are likely to have much invested in the progress and control of cases. They may be tempted, perhaps unconsciously, to protect their power and influence over work that brings them satisfaction or reward, or which they regard as their territory. Equally, they may be inclined to neglect work that they feel is someone else's responsibility, and fail to communicate what seems peripheral to their own concerns. Thus the apparently innocent requirement of collaboration is easily neglected in the daily processes of maintaining influence and control.

Effective collaboration is fostered by clear rules of communication, often taking the form of a professional etiquette in which conventions of language implicitly define mutual expectations and responsibilities. Professional ethics thus includes understanding and using the accepted norms of communication in matters such as forms of address, communicating information about clients or requests for assistance. For example, social workers who write reports to assist judges in sentencing offenders often couch their recommendations according to a formula intended to convey information and advice but not presumption. These formulae may vary considerably from court to court. However, professionals need to be mindful that conventional formulae can also be used as a cover for poor communication, inadequate action and dissimulation. Professional etiquette should be used with understanding, but not uncritically. Where professional communications seem saturated with standard formulaic statements, the authenticity of the collaboration is questionable.

Accountability is an intrinsic part of collaboration. It refers first to the requirement upon a professional to perform her duties, in collaboration with colleagues, to the expected standard. Second it requires the professional to demonstrate the performance to the appropriate individuals, colleagues and authorities. Social workers typically are accountable to their team-mates, supervisors and managers. Like other professionals, they are also in some senses accountable to their clients. Accountability in social work is complex, and will be considered again in Chapter 5.

In the course of their work, professionals are given certain power and discretion to use the agency's resources properly and wisely.

Service agencies are labour intensive and the key resource is most often the professional's time. It is clearly part of professionals' accountability to use agency resources, including their own time, according to the legitimate purposes and with due regard for economy and effectiveness.

Since professional services are normally best provided on the basis of collaboration between workers and agencies, accountability between colleagues usually expects that they will complement and reinforce each other's efforts and not detract from each other's standing. This expectation becomes problematic if a professional considers, or has cause to believe, that a colleague's actions are harmful to a client or to the agency. The expectation of support between colleagues may have to be reversed in exposing malpractice. In social work as in other professions, the importance and the difficulties of whistleblowing are gaining increased recognition (Hunt, 1998).

Reputable and creditable

The last of our eight interconnected expectations of professional ethics is that the professional and the agency she works for be creditable. The agency should command public and professional confidence in the quality of the service it offers, and the professionals should merit respect for their probity, integrity and dependability. All these are necessary to ensure that the public are not deterred from using the service because of a poor reputation, or stigmatised when they are obliged to become service users. Furthermore, a discredited service is unlikely to survive in the longer term, and so the interests of users may be damaged in this way also.

Public confidence is formed in response to the public face, and inevitably the public face is judged according to prevailing social conventions. Professionals are expected to dress and behave in such a way that the attitudes implicitly conveyed, and expectations implicitly generated, are consonant with the nature and terms of the service being offered. Just as customers in a car salesroom expect to be attentively assisted by smartly and conventionally attired sales staff, users of professional services expect conventionally appropriate modes of dress, speech and behaviour accurately symbolic of the nature of the relationship being offered. Although such superficial appearances might be considered essentially irrelevant, nonetheless they impact upon essential aspects of professional service. An example of these issues arose when a candidate for a professional social work course presented himself for interview smartly dressed in conventional female attire. Course staff felt that while individuals should have the right to express themselves in the dress of their choosing, professionals have to give precedence to the sensibilities of clients – a view that the candidate accepted.

Professionals in other services, and the public at large, will also judge a social work service by other tokens than the personal appearance of its staff. The treatment users receive on the telephone and in reception areas; the quality, clarity and courtesy of written communications; the comfort, cleanliness, and amenity of agency buildings; the attitudes and dispositions of staff, are all matters that strongly affect public sentiment towards the service. No casual visitor to a range of social work offices will need much convincing that agencies frequently discredit themselves in these ways.

More troublesome issues of creditability arise if a professional is known or suspected to have engaged in actions, or to pursue personal preferences, that might be thought disreputable or disgraceful. Extreme cases, for example a conviction for gross fraud or sexual assault, probably occasion little doubt over whether the individual is suitable to work as a professional. Far more disputable are those actions or preferences over which public opinion is divided. For example, if a social worker is known to use prohibited drugs privately for recreational purposes, and yet is invariably drug free at work, should her conduct be permissible? Or to take another example, if a social worker lives privately in a homosexual partnership within a community that esteems such a life choice immoral, how should the agency address the negative impact upon its reputation?

The maintenance of professional credibility and standing in the community will tend towards keeping to conservative standards in order to avoid disgrace and disrepute. But some such standards are not intrinsically relevant, and others may be thought ripe for refutation. Professionals and agencies must therefore actively create and maintain their public standing, and take responsibility for contributing to changes of public opinion.

The achievement of professional ethics

The rules of social work ethics show that the profession is highly conscious of its obligations and has devoted significant effort to specifying its ethical principles. There is a recognisable core to social work ethics, one not dissimilar indeed to the ethics of all human service professions. Although practice ethics as framed in the codes of the professional associations, in official guidance and in the mission statements of independent organisations offer useful points of orientation they are afflicted by several fundamental difficulties. General principles are often difficult to interpret precisely in particular situations; accepting the principle often provides no infallible solution. Allied to this is the problem of conflicting principles, where trying to fulfil one rule may prevent fulfilment of another. Codes and rule-books are rarely clear about how to resolve such conflicts.

An outstanding feature of the ethical codes of the professional associations is their voluntary character. The codes are devised by voluntary associations that have no constitutional authority over the professional conduct of social workers. Social workers are under no formal obligation to follow the code unless they choose to join the relevant professional association. If they do so, compliance with the code becomes largely a matter of honour, for at least two reasons: first, because abstract principles are controversial in content and difficult to interpret in practice; and second, because mechanisms for enforcing compliance hardly exist in most places.

An effective system of professional ethics must address the *interpretation* of ethical principles and the *enforcement* of ethical standards. As with any system of general rules, there has to be interpretation and application to specific cases. In social work the systems for interpreting ethical principles and adjudicating cases are generally weak. The weaknesses are both theoretical and institutional. In the theoretical dimension, the codes and procedures asserted by the professional bodies and the service agencies do not show convincingly how to resolve conflicts of rules. In the institutional dimension, social work largely lacks bodies with intellectual and institutional authority to determine difficult cases and apply sanctions when ethical standards are neglected. Unlike, say, medicine, there is often no requirement for social workers to be registered with a body that has powers to withdraw the licence to practise on grounds of ethical malpractice. In a few places ethics committees have begun to consider cases and sanctions, but their influence is still small. The weaknesses in the theoretical and institutional dimensions amplify each other, since the lack of a forum with formal powers of adjudication stunts the development of practice ethics; and the weakness of theory deprives the case for the creation of formal powers of political credibility.

5

Founding Social Work Ethics: The Critique of Theory

A note on method

In the preceding chapters we have visited the land of social work values and described the rules of practice ethics where they lie, as it were, discovered on the ground. Thus, describing social work ethics deals with one class of questions but directly raises at least two more. First, what is the substance and content of basic theories of right living and right action, upon which rules of practice could reasonably be founded? How can the principles and values professed and practised in social work be related to the main belief systems and philosophical orientations that inform the moral understanding of the wider community? The second class of questions (known in the philosophical literature as meta-ethics) is about how to justify beliefs and evaluate the merit of conclusions. What are the theoretical presuppositions and methodological tools that will enable us to judge one approach or argument as superior to another? Before going on to the main business of the content of ethical theories, a word about the meta-ethical questions is appropriate.

Pluralism

The analysis that follows is based on an assumption of *pluralism*. Pluralism is the presumption that there will often be genuine, independent merit in more than one of the available schemes of explanation, prediction and precept for practical action. This applies to all kinds of questions, scientific, moral and practical. Pluralism accommodates the uncontroversial observation that available theories often fail to provide categorical answers to practical questions; their results are *underdetermined* in that they leave multiple possibilities open. For example, if we are trying to understand the causes of crime we find ourselves contemplating a whole range of theories as diverse as genetic predisposition, faulty socialisation, poor opportunity, defective social structures, and so on. All of these may appear to have some merit but none seems to provide a complete explanation, exclusive of all others.

Pluralism therefore rejects the notion that any single theoretical and metaphysical approach can be relied upon to lead to the ultimate, right answers. It approaches different explanations with an open mind in which as little as possible is ruled out on first principles. Pluralism believes that when addressing complex, real-life problems, where the simplifying assumptions of the theoretician do not accurately apply, the most advantageous approaches may not necessarily be the least complex. Take for example town and country planning for the control of development in housing, industry and transport. Advanced societies in densely populated parts of the world cannot function acceptably with a single simple principle, say that a landowner should be allowed to do as he wishes with and on his land. What is needed in practice is a highly complex system of laws and consents, permissions and controls, checks and balances, so that the many legitimate interests in land use can best be satisfied.

The obvious problem for pluralism is that without a foundational scheme for arbitrating between different theories and prescriptions there is no definitive way of resolving contradictions. Often we may arrive at similar practical conclusions by way of different premises and methods, in which case the issue raised by adopting incompatible theories may only matter to philosophers and theoretical purists. Moreover, people with ordinary practical concerns may well be positively reassured if different theories lead to the same outcome, whatever the disagreements of the theorists. Sometimes, however, rival theories in science, or rival approaches of morality and politics, point to opposite conclusions. This is characteristic of the important controversies of any given time. So for example in the treatment of animals, the belief that animals are merely one of the many resources of the natural world to be wisely exploited for food and other human uses collides with the belief that animals have rights analogous to human rights and should therefore not be eaten. An over-elastic pluralism may simply leave us unable to come up with a usable answer.

Pluralism is unable to offer any simple answer to this problem. But, by the same token, it has the advantage of being free to evaluate the merits of a wide range of approaches. The pluralist seeks the most plausible solution *on balance*, being prepared to give credence to a range of approaches and theories while recognising that the theoretical disputes that divide them are not capable of being finally resolved for the time being. We have to decide how to treat animals today, but there is no answer yet to the dispute about whether it makes sense to talk about animals having rights. For the time being we need to give this position a serious hearing, even if in the end we decide it is cancelled by other, more persuasive arguments.

It will be maintained that several key concepts of ethical and political theory, and of disciplined practical action, have what might be termed the character of *indispensability*. Although not theoretically unchallenged or unchallengeable, these concepts seem to capture principles that are intuitively so important that no credible theory can do without them. They mark the limits of the pluralist's elasticity, the best points of reference available to us today. For illustration, consider the important example of respecting persons. Although the idea is theoretically problematic in several ways, it seems quite unsafe to reject it and build a theory of professional ethics that makes no place for respecting persons. The idea of indispensability requires that we should retain the concept, even if problematic, and find some way of accommodating it with other principles of like magnitude and significance. The relativism to which pluralism is committed means that no absolute defence of the indispensable principles is possible, and the process of balancing principles must be admitted as a fallible guide. The status of indispensable principles is to be understood as dominant until proved otherwise, as necessary until shown to be wrong or redundant.

It is assumed here that no single theory is comprehensive and persuasive enough to earn the comprehensive defeat of all its rivals. Practical action on problems of social living and politics positively requires the undoctrinaire, pragmatic and often cautious approach commended by pluralism. There are no prima facie grounds for believing that theoretically singular approaches to practical problems are inherently preferable; indeed, experience shows that theoretically plural approaches often seem to work better. Pluralism also embraces differences of social value not only as a matter of empirical fact but also as something to be positively welcomed. The pluralist argument is that because none of us ought ever to feel sure that we have the final answer to the goals of social life, we should (for theoretical and practical reasons) accommodate challenges and we should (for ethical reasons) be ready to re-evaluate rival values.

Much of mainstream moral and political philosophy tries to erect theories founded on single first principles, or small groups of closely related first principles. Contrariwise, much recent work in applied ethics, and especially in professional ethics, soon concludes that theoretical purism leads to unconvincing or unworkable solutions. Dworkin addresses the passionate and bitter controversy over abortion, finding in individuals' moralities and in public sentiment two incompatible basic objections to it, neither of which can, however, be dismissed (Dworkin, 1993). In their leading textbook of medical ethics, Beauchamp and Childress decide that both the main, theoretically incompatible, approaches of western philosophical ethics have to be admitted (Beauchamp and Childress, 1989). Their mixed framework of principles, descended from the intuitionism of W.D. Ross, marks the terrain upon which the issues have to be settled. Writing about community care, Wilmot bases his book on four key concepts: care and community [sic], justice, autonomy and responsibility. These concepts are 'balanced against each other in tension' (Wilmot, 1997, p. 26).

Finally, it might be argued that pluralism is a more serviceable response – perhaps the only possible response – at a time when faith in the Enlightenment project of a rational basis for social and political order has to a large extent disintegrated. Gray commends an 'agonistic liberalism' dedicated not to the defence of traditional liberal rights and freedoms, but marked by constant '*agon* – the rivalrous encounter of ideas and values in a context of peaceful coexistence' (Gray, 1995, p. 132). It is in this spirit that pluralism faces the perplexing issues of professional ethics.

Towards a critical practice ethics

Staking out the rules of good practice is useful for the purposes of practical application and education but does not mark the end of professional ethics. We are left with as many questions as answers. In this chapter we shall investigate the roots of social work ethics and values in three main traditions of social thought. These traditions offer useful purchase on the timeless slippery questions of right action, but leave several acutely important issues inadequately answered. We shall consider in particular the problem of establishing universal foundations for morality in societies divided by differing religious beliefs, ethical standards and cultural practices; the complex accountability to different persons and authorities as a special feature of social work; and the ambiguous character of social work expertise.

The longer trajectory of professional ethics moves from description and prescription towards analysis and thence a critical praxis. To avoid paralysis pluralism needs a framework that will capitalise on the strengths of the established traditions, and a method that will enable the practitioner to devise credible responses under conditions of uncertainty and conflict. The mature ethics is a *critical* ethics that goes beyond received rules and challenges the strengths and weaknesses of conventional ethics. It is based on the knowledgeable and understanding adoption of key principles and equips the practitioner to meet the challenging of rules.

In this book the chosen path to a critical ethics is inductive and dialectical. It has moved through description and prescription; proceeds now to question the sources of ethics; and goes on in the following chapters to propose a framework of concepts that affirms, replaces and transcends what has gone before.

Three strands of ethical theory

The values and ethics of social work originate in, and express, three main traditions of moral thought and social action. Within most versions of social work ethics – although not across the wider field of social and political thought – the first is predominant and tends to shade out the other two.

Individualism and the ethic of personal service

The ethic of personal service places the unique human being at the centre of attention. The prime aim is to promote the welfare and best interests of the individual who presents herself for professional help. The professional concentrates his effort through the personal relationship, which is the medium of helping and is informed by an ethic of respect and service. Within this individualistic perspective, the rest of the world fades into the background.

The concept of the counsellor who focuses on the value of, and the needs of, the unique individual is perfectly at home with the individualism of liberal theory. The modern counsellor we find in the social work and related literature is descended from the figure of the pastor as confidant and adviser. Biestek, a Jesuit priest and probably the best known moralist in social work, formulated what are still widely regarded as key principles in the 'casework' relationship: central regard for the value and uniqueness of the person, whatever good or bad they may have done; the promise of acceptance and understanding; the authenticity of the individual's projects, within the bounds of the moral law; the assurance of confidentiality (Biestek, 1961). Modern counsellors in social work and kindred occupations have assumed the mantle of the pastor (presumptuously, some would say), and grafted on knowledge from psychology and elsewhere (Halmos, 1978a).

The ethic of personal service is founded upon the deep appreciation of the value and uniqueness of every person. It holds that every individual has intrinsic worth, irrespective of any contingent attributes such as age, gender, talents, wealth, or contribution to society. Moreover, the individual continues to be uniquely valuable even if he or she sometimes acts in a morally unacceptable way. The value of the individual is echoed in the ethical precepts of respect and honesty that were identified in Chapter 4. These familiar ideas are strongly expressed in the Christian tradition; philosophically, they are best developed in the ethics of Immanuel Kant (1724–1804) and numerous followers.

The Kantian theory has the advantage of providing a base for our moral intuitions about the value of persons without relying on a theology that no longer speaks to many people's view of the world. Of course it also presents difficulties. Kant's deontology insists on fulfilling one's moral duty according to universal rules for all times and situations. This doctrine of duty seems sometimes too narrow and severe, neglecting other equally important aims of human life, and leading to implausible or counter-intuitive consequences. The theory is unsatisfactory on how we should act towards human beings with temporarily or permanently impaired rationality, who happen to comprise a significant proportion of social work clients.

BOX 5.1
Kantian ethics: deontology or theory of duty

Kant's moral philosophy regards persons as creatures endowed with reason who are thus capable of making moral, and other, choices. The capacity to apprehend what is morally good and bad is independent of the effects upon our selves of the material world; morality consists in faithfulness to the universal law of reason.

Our obligations are to the community of moral agents, that is to other beings with a capacity like our own for morally meaningful choices. The capacity for moral agency is a property of the individual will and is independent of contingencies such as wealth, status or personal desires. Reason requires that all bearers of moral agency should be treated universally and impartially. Kant expresses this as the *categorical imperative*: 'Act only on that maxim through which you can at the same time will that it should become a universal law.'

There are moral imperatives that we must obey not merely because they may be expedient, but because failing to do so would be a contradiction and betrayal of our own rationality and moral sense. Kant's ethical theory is an ethics of duty, or *deontological* theory (from the Greek word for duty). Kant develops this in a number of applications, insisting for example that one must always tell the truth, or always keep promises, even if the consequence seems likely to be a bad outcome. The deontological perspective sets adherence to moral duty as the yardstick of conduct.

The principle of respecting persons flows directly from Kant's conception of persons as beings capable of autonomous moral choices, and the principle of universalisability. We must respect the other's autonomy because if we fail to do so we negate our own rationality. Kant presents the principle of respect as an alternative formulation of the categorical imperative: 'Act in such a way that you always treat humanity, whether in your own person or the person of any other, never simply as a means, but always at the same time as an end.'

Further reading

Short, accessible introductions to Kant's ethics are offered by O'Neill (1993) in Singer's *Companion to Ethics*; Chapter 10 of Rachels' (1993) *The Elements of Moral Philosophy*; Chapter 6 of Raphael's (1981) *Moral Philosophy*. A more extended debate is contained in Baron, Pettit and Slote's (1997) *Three Methods of Ethics*. Singer's (1994) anthology *Ethics* contains several relevant articles. Paton's (1991) *The Moral Law* is a translation of

Kant's key text accompanied by an indispensable summary. Acton's (1970) textbook *Kant's Moral Philosophy* is an exegesis of Kant's work, and Chapter 6 of Norman's (1983) *The Moral Philosophers: An Introduction to Ethics* develops the Kantian theme of respect for persons.

A modern Kantian approach to the ethics of the caring professions is Downie and Telfer's *Caring and Curing* (1980). Reamer's (1990) text on *Ethical Dilemmas in Social Service* adopts the neo-Kantian moral theory of Gewirth's (1978) *Reason and Morality* (see also Gewirth, 1986).

The most important challenge to Kantian theory comes from various forms of consequentialist or utilitarian philosophy.

BOX 5.2

Consequentialism and utilitarianism

Consequentialist moral theories focus on the outcomes or *consequences* of actions. For the consequentialist, an action is morally good or bad insofar as it produces good or bad consequences. In order to decide which outcome from a range of possibilities is preferable, one needs a common standard of value. In classical utilitarianism, the consequentialist theory advocated by Bentham and Mill, the value to be maximised is pleasure, or happiness, and the absence of pain. Whereas deontological theories specify what is morally good in itself, consequentialism functions by aiming to maximise a non-moral good (such as happiness). For this reason consequentialism is sometimes called a second-order moral theory. Within utilitarianism, the principle of universalisability is established by providing that every individual's experience is to count for the same as every other's. But within utilitarianism, there is no conclusive way of choosing between the greatest total sum or *aggregation* of happiness and the best possible *distribution* of happiness.

Pleasure and the absence of pain can be experienced not only by rational adult persons but by all (presumably) sentient creatures. Utilitarianism therefore extends moral rights to at least the higher animals. Depending on the overall balance of pleasure and pain, the claims of animals may sometimes override the claims of humans.

Deciding what to place as the central value to be promoted is a perennial problem in utilitarianism. Pure pleasant sensation seems to disregard the intuition that some forms of achievement are inherently nobler or more valuable than others. Modern forms of utilitarianism have substituted other concepts for pleasure or the absence of pain as the basis for calculating morally preferable outcomes, adopting preference satisfaction, interests or welfare instead.

Utilitarianism aims to demonstrate that it automatically takes care of common intuitions about what is morally right. Respecting persons follows from counting every one on the same basis. Distributing resources in such a way that utility is maximised automatically takes care of fairness.

Further reading

Utilitarianism is introduced in the chapters by Pettit (1993) and Goodin (1993) in Singer's *Companion to Ethics*; Chapter 7 of Rachels' (1993) *The Elements of Moral Philosophy*; Chapter 4 of Raphael's (1981) *Moral Philosophy*. As with deontology, a more extended debate is contained in Baron, Pettit and Slote's (1997) *Three Methods of Ethics*; and Singer's (1994) anthology *Ethics* also contains a number of articles on consequentialism. Bentham's and Mill's classic works are available in Warnock's (1962) and numerous other editions. Chapter 4 of Plant's (1991) *Modern Political Thought* and Chapter 2 of Kymlicka's (1990) *Contemporary Political Philosophy*, as well as elaborating on utilitarianism, demonstrate its power as a foundation for political as well as moral philosophy.

Utilitarianism generally offers a more convincing rationale for the humane and therapeutic treatment of persons whose conduct is morally problematic, such as offenders or those who otherwise fail in their social obligations. Mill's theory remains not only philosophically powerful, but is a strong part of the whole tradition of social engineering that gave rise to social work and other modern welfare professions. However, utilitarianism is weak on protecting the rights of individuals against the claims of advantage for society as a whole.

The liberal-individualist mainstream of English-speaking moral philosophy is still largely occupied by the debate between Kantian and utilitarian theory. Both have survived numerous pronouncements of their demise. Deontological and consequentialist theories often lead to basically similar practical conclusions, but they are based on incompatible first principles; to support both families of theory seems to involve a high price in philosophical inconsistency.

However, it is highly significant for practical ethics that the result of the contest is no better than a draw. In the context of contemporary real-life ethical problems such as abortion, euthanasia, health service rationing or punishment, thoughtful decision-makers are usually willing to abandon neither the moral insights of deontology nor the real-world arguments of utilitarianism. In their textbook of medical ethics Beauchamp and Childress come to the interesting if controversial conclusion that 'it is doubtful that a utilitarian theory that follows Mill and a deontological theory in the Kantian tradition require significantly different courses of action' (Beauchamp and Childress, 1989, p. 72). Where practical decisions must rest on public consent, we apparently cannot escape what Frankena (1963) terms 'mixed' theories of morality.

Whatever their theoretical differences, the Christian, Kantian and utilitarian traditions concur in their attitude of respectful service to individuals who present themselves for professional help. The central idea of the value of the person and the respect that is due to persons counts as indispensable to professional ethics, even from the rival perspectives described in the following.

Social reformism and the ethic of justice

Whereas the ethic of personal service focuses on helping the troubled or troublesome individual, the primary aim of social reformism is amelioration of the social conditions that are seen as the root cause of many individuals' needs for help. The social reform perspective supposes that welfare problems such as poverty, family and relationship dysfunction, poor educational levels, unemployment, crime and so forth are to a very large extent the product of bad social arrangements and policies and are not attributable to personal deficiencies of the individuals who have the misfortune to be affected by them. Writing for social work, Braye and Preston-Shoot (1995, p. 3) '[take] it as axiomatic that inequality and oppression in the form of racism, sexism, ageism, disablism, mentalism and heterosexism exist at individual and structural levels... and are expressed through organizational policy and practice and through society's institutions'.

Reformism challenges the injustice of enormous manifest inequalities of wealth, status and power in a civilised society. This is the hallmark of Fabianism and other forms of democratic socialism (see, for example, George and Wilding, 1994). The concern with structural inequality and powerlessness has a mixed parentage. One influence is the tradition of social thought which stretches from Hegel and Marx, to later figures of critical theory such as Marcuse, Habermas and Freire, and through to some branches of feminism. But in Britain at least social workers rarely read in this tradition, and in the age of the eclipse of socialism it is more difficult to sustain the arguments. There is also a strong concern with justice within liberalism, however, sharing the same roots as deontology and utilitarianism.

Throughout the history of social welfare the individualistic perspective and the social reform perspective have turned around each other in slow perpetual motion, now one, now the other, dominant from time to time and place to place. The early pioneers of welfare who prepared the way for the modern profession of social work were arguably at least as concerned to change general social conditions as they were to save individuals from their plight. The following examples illustrate the social reform perspective in action.

In *community work* welfare professionals including community workers, social workers, health education workers, youth workers, community education workers and others engage with people in local communities through local groups and committees. Their aim is to work together with local people to remedy problems that affect the local area generally, such as unemployment, housing and planning issues, poor public services, or other lack of amenity. It is a fundamental tenet that the problems which local people face are the result of defective social policies and service systems and not the consequence of individual pathology or fecklessness. Community workers often perceive the contrast in conditions between the areas in which they work and more favoured places as issues of social injustice; they believe that poverty in deprived areas is the inevitable counterpart of wealth for more fortunately placed members of society; they judge that ultimately solutions to welfare problems have to be cast in terms of the redistribution of wealth and power.

The *radical social work* in Britain of the 1970s was informed by broadly socialist and sometimes Marxist ideas (Clark with Asquith, 1985). Socialism aimed to bring about increased equality and major redistribution of wealth and power by direct government control over industry, education, health, housing and many other spheres. Common provision for all members of society under control of elected representatives was favoured; privilege and elitism based on inherited status, rather than merit earned, were detested. Radical social work saw socialist goals as indispensable to social work itself; it examined, with much angst, the fact that social work was usually not performed by organisations with socialist aims. Radical social work remained more a cry of protest than a coherent programme, and went into decline with socialism generally from the late 1970s. Even with the collapse of socialism in the 1980s and 90s however, most social workers probably retain at least a partial awareness that their clients are very often the casualties of wider social systems which operate in systematically unfair ways.

The concept of *empowerment* is a contemporary expression of the concern for justice in social welfare. Rees proposes that:

> The process of empowerment addresses two related objectives: the achievement of the more equitable distribution of resources and non-exploitative relationships between people and the enabling of people to achieve a creative sense of power through enhanced self-respect, confidence, knowledge and skills. (Rees, 1991, p. 66)

From this perspective structural disadvantage and powerlessness are seen as the leading causes of people needing help from social workers and other professionals. In similar vein, the principle of *normalisation*, an approach to care for people with learning disabilities and other conditions which emphasises their entitlement to the opportunities and benefits of ordinary life, outside of institutions, shares much of the ethic of empowerment (Ramon, 1991).

Social reformism, therefore, represents a more overtly political position than the ethic of personal service. It focuses on the social collectivity and sees relationships between individuals as conditioned by the social and political milieu. It embraces the insight that powerlessness is as much about self-perception and (false) consciousness as it is about objective inequality. Reformism, plainly, takes for granted that structural inequalities exist as an empirical fact, although these are not necessarily beyond dispute; for example, the Central Council for Education and Training in Social Work has been heavily criticised for its assumption that racism is endemic in British society.

Despite a long history in social work and related interventions, the ideal of social justice is very much less well expressed and developed in social work ethics than is the idea of respect for the person and its cognates. In a parable about the imagined denunciation of the social services, Jordan puts these words into the mouth of the radical activist who confronts the director of social services:

> Let me tell you what we don't seem to see from your department or the probation service. First, we don't see clear statements or actions on injustice. I know you have taken positions on specific issues – racism in the criminal justice system, child sexual abuse, the rights of carers, and so on – but there isn't an *overall* position on injustice. (Jordan, 1990, p. x; emphasis original)

The eight rules of professional ethics extracted in the previous chapter reveal little more than an implied connection with justice. To fail to respect people's rights, or to treat them dishonestly, or to fail to provide an appropriate service of adequate quality, might each be construed as injustice; but the matter is not developed in any way comparable to the ideals of respect and individual service within the personal helping relationship. This reflects an important asymmetry or bias in social work. In principle, its global concern to remedy defects of resources and social relations in the sphere of everyday life would lead to a broad agenda of social reform. In practice, the tradition of individual service has usually predominated over socio-political issues, that some might argue are more fundamental.

The ideal of justice thus remains comparatively indistinct in the ethics of social work. This may reflect a preponderance of 'personalists' (Halmos, 1978b) over political activists in the profession; it seems very likely that social work predominantly attracts people who enjoy face-to-face contact with the client as their main mode of work. 'Social workers are people people', proclaims the National Association of Social Workers on its Internet home page (www.naswdc.org, July 1998). Such a bias may equally be reflected in the socialisation of its workers; Mills (1970, p. 100) claimed many years ago of social workers and others that 'their professional work tends to train them for an occupational incapacity to rise above a series of "cases"'. However, we cannot properly understand the goals of social work without recourse to some ideal of justice. The concept is indispensable to explaining the broader ethical and political aspirations of the profession, and the theory will be further examined in Chapter 9.

The ethic of public accountability

The third strand of social work ethics derives from its character as a *publicly* sponsored and funded activity and the fact that it requires some special skill and knowledge to do properly.

It was suggested in Chapter 1 that in comparison with many professional groups, social work is especially closely bound to the public realm. Although all the professions routinely claim to be dedicated to the public good, in general they do so on the basis that their institutional independence from the state is essential to guarantee the rights and welfare of the client and the ultimate benefit to the community. Thus for example many lawyers are private practitioners who offer their services in a market; and medical practitioners tend to think of themselves as independent professionals who may choose voluntarily to enter into a contract with the state for the provision of medical care to patients. Reviewing the sociological research, Macdonald (1995) pictures the professions as relatively powerful and autonomous groups that contrive a bargain with the state for monopoly, or at least dominance, of their professional activity. Professions strive to pursue their self-chosen project by getting the state to grant them power and control in their respective domain. In social work, in contrast, the concept of private practice, independent of state sponsorship, has no comparable application, because it is constitutive of social work that it is performed at the instigation of the state and on behalf of society through its public institutions of politics, legislature, government and law. This does not of course preclude private, profit-making and voluntary, non-profit agencies from being brought in to deliver the services instigated or sanctioned by the state.

Since social work is necessarily publicly sponsored, it is quite properly expected to demonstrate that it is responsive to the wider political community as well as the people it directly serves as clients. From this perspective the professional's moral values or political principles, as they might be derived from the theories sketched earlier, are of peripheral relevance. Of greater moment are the manager's and politician's desire or perceived need to ensure that social work is accountable to its political masters, seen to be effective in the tasks it is supposed to address, and kept to tolerable costs. Social work has significant legal powers and duties which reflect public policy. These powers and duties must be properly regulated, especially the power to dispense public funds; the power to restrict liberty; and the duty to protect the vulnerable. The concern for public accountability overshadows regard for professional conduct based on supposedly universal principles of morality.

The requirement of public accountability raises questions about what structures and institutions would best serve it. Social work might, for example, be organised as a self-regulating college of independent practitioners in the manner idealised in the medical and legal professions and in some (non-episcopalian) churches. It might be a monopoly state service run by salaried civil servants, who would be directly accountable in the same way as public servants in other sectors of government. It might be carried out by private companies on contract to the state, or by non-profit making philanthropic agencies. Whatever may be the merits of these and other models, in fact the dominant ethic of accountability in social work is bureaucratic. Social workers for the most part are officials who work in bureaucracies, whether those of public bodies or those of voluntary philanthropic agencies. They are bound by hierarchical command structures and abstract but detailed formal rules of procedure. Their special knowledge derives from their position as functionaries within the organisation rather than the independent esoteric knowledge of the professional. They are expected to place loyalty to the organisation over other principles of action, including claims of moral or professional principle. In a word, their ethic of accountability is based on the values of bureaucracy.

Bureaucracies are valued for their capacity to perform complex technical tasks in a reliable and efficient way; to do so they must employ technically competent personnel. The ethic of accountability therefore raises to prominence the expertise of the professional. When an agency fails in its duty, the public expects heads to roll; high moral principles and sound political intentions do not excuse practice below a level which an ordinarily capable practitioner should be expected to perform. We shall see that the definition of expertise is a serious problem in the profession of social work.

Key issues for social work ethics

Professional ethics are based on the moral and political values and theories of the host society; several important such theories have been briefly described in the earlier review. Whatever the merits of these theories in the sphere of ordinary morality, a number of especially important issues for social work require further exploration. This section will consider the problem of moral and cultural pluralism; multiple accountability as a defining attribute of social work; and the ambiguous nature of social work knowledge and theory.

Pluralism and moral theory

The aim of theories of morality and politics is to define right action. The substance of social work is helping people to achieve the commonplace necessities and ordinary attainments of human living, under the aegis of political institutions that partly define and regulate what those necessities and attainments should comprise. Social work therefore entails some or other vision of the good society. This has immediate, strong implications for practice. It is possible in some professions to practise with considerable technical detachment from the basic purposes that the work serves. For example, the engineer who develops aircraft engines will probably work in much the same way irrespective of whether the engines are destined for jetliners or warplanes. In social work (and other socially orientated professions) the technical skill is intimately coupled to the basic aim; as one changes, so often must the other.

The aims of social work would be far easier to particularise and reach agreement about in a society where basic values were universally shared and where consensus existed over the ordinary expectations and obligations of social life. No such state of affairs exists in many of the developed societies that support social work. On the contrary, the disintegration of traditional communities and ways of life has led to increasing pluralism as an empirical fact of society. It may even be thought that the appearance of social work is itself a symptom of the social disintegration it is supposed to address; a popular myth has it that in traditional communities social work was unnecessary because social needs were taken care of in the ordinary intercourse of daily life, without the need for paid officials. However, it is very easy to exaggerate and romanticise the community support and consensus that is supposed to have existed in times past (Abrams *et al.*, 1989; Bulmer, 1987). Western societies have for centuries been internally divided by religion, culture and economic interest. At different times and place such conflicts obtrude particularly painfully: in Northern Ireland; for the Jews of Europe; in the Balkans. There is nothing new about conflicts of basic values; what is somewhat new is the invention of social work as a means of coping with some of the conflicts.

Liberal political theory as developed in the west can be understood precisely as the endeavour to provide a rationale for social life in the modern world where religion and tradition no longer provide a sufficient common core of aims and beliefs. The central preoccupation of liberalism is to devise a basis for politics that will allow individuals to choose their own way of life, while allowing equivalent rights and freedoms to those who make different choices. In the more recent mood of post-modernism, the liberal ideal of affirming every individual's right to pursue his or her projects, within a mosaic of different communities of culture and interest, has been called into question. On a pessimistic note, some theoreticians question whether there can be any rational and credible basis for consensus over the goals of political and social life. The world views of people with different religious, cultural and ideological affiliations may simply be irreconcilable. The liberal project of toleration is under attack for alleged theoretical incoherence. This position constitutes a radical challenge to the legitimacy of many social institutions, including social work.

We have seen therefore in the discussion of values, in the setting out of conventional rules of professional ethics and in the tracing of three currents of ethical theory that there are abundant sources of guidance as to how professionals should act in carrying out their duties. The inevitable consequence of this richness is contradiction: in trying to act correctly by one set of standards, workers risk contravening another of at least superficially equivalent authority. For example, in child protection the principle of honesty may arguably have to be somewhat abridged for the sake of effectiveness; or in dealing with a dangerous offender, the principle of respect for his privacy may have to be modified by concern for the rights of others.

Conflicts of principle are so common that workers sometimes describe all the moral issues of practice as dilemmas. Although that is an oversimplification, it doubtless true that determining to follow established principles of good practice may seem more like the beginning of one's moral problems than the end of them. Conflicts of principle may centre on interpretation or may reveal deeper theoretical divisions.

Issues of interpretation are raised in cases where it is considered that despite superficially contradictory indications of how a matter should be resolved, a fuller and deeper exploration will reveal that the conflict is more apparent than real. The matter hinges therefore on the interpretation to be given to key principles. For example, it is often suggested that it is incorrect to interpret the principle of self-determination as a license for anyone to do as he wishes, irrespective of the effect on himself or others. A true view of self-determination, on this argument, would recognise that its real essence is not enhanced but corroded by condoning self-destructive acts such as threatened suicide, or acts injurious to others such as robbery. The general argument that the key principles of professional ethics are sound but merely in need of authoritative interpretation and explication paves the way for official or unofficial professional ethicists to specify the proper resolution of dilemmas in practice; their endeavour is to show the correct path on the basis of general principles propounded as sound and universal.

A second type of conflicts of principle occurs when despite being agreed over how to deal with a situation in practical terms, different participants nonetheless invoke different foundation premises and theories to justify their moral decision. To take a well-known example, many professionals and ordinary members of the community alike agree that it is wrong to allow a woman to terminate her pregnancy for supposedly frivolous reasons such as wanting to go on holiday or not being pleased with the baby's sex. Despite their consensus, the grounds for such a conclusion can be quite different. Dworkin (1993) proposes that there are two fundamentally different kinds of objection to abortion: one based on the view that the foetus holds rights similar to any other person's, and the other based on the view that the foetus – although not a person – is a thing of value that should not be wantonly destroyed. It may be a relief that there is practical agreement, and those with a pragmatic bent may conclude that the philosophical differences do not then really matter in the real world. However, a consensus based on the coincidence of conclusions rather than agreement over principles is always fragile and liable to collapse, as the continuing argument over abortion clearly illustrates. Eventually, the underlying conflicts have to be tackled.

Complex accountability

It is a particularly important feature of social work that in their cases workers have multiple accountability to different individuals and authorities for a range of different, and sometimes conflicting, responsibilities. This will be termed *complex accountability*, and it goes with social work being intrinsically a public function. The classic conception of the professional role envisages the professional exclusively committed to act for the client's interest and welfare. Other parties in the case are expected to have their own adviser and advocate, where relevant. If social work were a private professional practice it would be straightforward to claim, in line with the standard model of the professions, that the worker's allegiance lay first to the client and second to the honour and institutions of the profession. In social work this is much more the exception than the rule. Complex accountability arises in two common sorts of situation.

First, the social worker often has to act within families and other social groups where there are conflicts of opinion and of interest: for example where a parent fails adequately to care for a child; or where a disabled person relies on other family members who may be reluctant to provide all the requisite support. In such cases the social worker's position can be dangerously ambiguous: whose side is she on? An analogous dilemma can equally afflict the community worker: if members of a community hold opposed views about official plans or community-generated projects, how can the worker support legitimate local aspirations without being fatally compromised?

Second, the social worker often, indeed characteristically, has to mediate between the individual and the institutions of society: for example in dealing with offenders, the worker often experiences conflicts between the demands of the law and the criminal justice system, the best interest of the offender and his family, and the interests of other people in society such as victims or potential victims. Social workers have to respond on behalf of society to the demands of people whose way of life is deviant or disapproved, such as drug users, or those who are merely minorities such as refugees or ethnic minorities. Equally the social worker, as a public servant, often has to deal with the effects of poverty and unemployment in the context of a social policy which could be said to have created, or failed to remove, the problem in the first place.

It might be objected at this point that the special relationship of social work to the public realm has been exaggerated. Whatever the myths of professionalism, is it not true that, for example, health care is, to varying but large extents, organised and paid for by the state? Are not doctors equally bound in practice to public policy? Davies (1983) has argued that the dichotomy between professionalism and bureaucracy has been overstated, based on too narrow a sociological perspective; one should rather aim to understand conflict in organisations and institutions within a wider socio-economic and political context. Now it is undeniable that modern states do not leave essential services, such as health, purely to the fate of private contracts between individual consumers and independent practitioners. The difference is that while private contracts between consumers and professionals for the delivery and receipt of, say, health care or legal services, are still perfectly intelligible in principle and indeed widely found in practice, privately sponsored services superficially similar to what social workers provide would no longer be social work. Social work is necessarily always an instrument of public policy, which may of course utilise private and voluntary organisations for its implementation. In this respect social work is more analogous to schoolteaching. Teachers, whether in public, private or denominational schools, work within a legal and policy framework that defines the content, manner and intended outcomes of schooling. The state has entirely taken over the authority to prescribe compulsory schooling, and education professionals cannot legitimately operate outside it. The police and the armed services are also analogous. A enforcement agency is only a police force if it is specifically authorised by legislation and public policy to ensure the rule of law, otherwise it is a private bodyguard or security company; an armed force is only an instrument of the state if it is under duly authorised political control, otherwise it is a rebellion. Intervention in social welfare is only social work if it is carried out within a framework of public policy that legitimates its objectives, otherwise it is either private beneficence or a commercial service.

Complex accountability within the public function of social work has significant consequences for its professional ethics. It means that the ideal of individualised personal service based on an ethic of respect, important though it is, cannot by itself cover the range of issues that social workers must address. It shows too that the ethic of justice is not one which can be simply defined by reference to the narrow interests of one group, such as clients, but must be addressed in relation to the complex and competing interests of the many parties who have a legitimate interest in the processes and outcomes of social work. Public accountability embraced in the third ethic identified earlier will indeed be complex accountability. The avowed professional principles and codes of social work ethics do not offer satisfactory ways of dealing with complex accountability.

The ambiguity of social work expertise

There are many varieties of opinion about what professionals are and what they should do, but on one point at least everyone is agreed: professionals are distinguished by their special knowledge and expertise. Moreover, their expertise is not merely an art to be pursued for art's sake, but is held to be instrumentally useful for meeting the important, socially valued needs of individuals who from time to time may use the professional's services (Koehn, 1994). Ordinary members of society do not hold professional expertise and it is not acquired except by long years of study, training and practice. Professional expertise is often exclusive, in that only trained professionals are likely to have been enabled to acquire it, and only duly licensed practitioners are permitted to practise it. Professions claim that the value of their expertise to society justifies the privileges of professional status. The other side of this coin is the ethic of professional accountability, already discussed. Accountability is the proper price for professionals' relative freedom to define and practise their expertise. Accountability requires valid professional knowledge and the effective deployment of expertise; if the service is incompetent, accountability is seriously compromised.

Every feature of this generally uncontroversial model of professional expertise is problematic in social work. This has major implications for its professional ethics and therefore merits explication.

The subject of most professional occupations is more or less esoteric, involving specialised activities that are beyond the commonplace experience and knowledge of ordinary members of the community. In social work, however, the principal subject is no less than the everyday preoccupations of ordinary life: achieving

tolerable satisfaction of the common human needs of bodily health
and safety, sound affective relationships, psychological security and
growth, and a fulfilling standing in the community. The primary
knowledge of social workers lies within the realms of everyday know-
how and life experience, which explains the high value often given to
life experiehce as a prerequisite or qualification for social work. The
primary knowledge is quite the opposite of esoteric, since it is part of
the common knowledge and common sense dispersed throughout
the community. This accounts for the frequent scepticism that social
workers have any special expertise; but it is not inaccurate to say that
social workers are experts in the commonplace tasks and goals of
daily life. Social workers prefer to say that their special contribution
is an holistic view of the client which rather than compartmental-
ising needs according to poverty, health, housing or other concerns,
considers the whole person in relation to all the issues in his or her
life as a whole.

While much of the knowledge of social workers is commonplace,
it is not for that reason trivial. Social workers frequently work with
individuals whose knowledge, attainments and expertise in the skills
of daily life are in certain respects defective or inadequate to meet
their changing circumstances. For example, the demanding skills of
parenting may be widely known, but social workers deal particularly
with parents whose command of these skills is so poor as seriously
to threaten the welfare of their children. Social workers counsel
offenders whose ways of dealing with the ordinary demands of
society are self-defeating or pathological, and who need to learn new
social skills. Social workers assist people to deal with changed
personal and family circumstances, such as loss of physical or
mental capacity, or bereavement, where their circumstances and
previous life experience are not sufficiently protective for them to
cope successfully.

Not all the knowledge of social workers is commonplace: social
work also deals in a range of specialised interventions that require
special expertise. These interventions are means to help individuals
achieve the goals of ordinary life. For example, the first aim in
working with children and families is to help achieve satisfactory
family functioning; but if this is impossible within the existing
family, it is social workers who arrange alternatives such as fostering,
adoption or institutional care. The recipes for success in alternatives
to ordinary family care are not matters of common knowledge, and

indeed have been the subject of much research, and less controlled experimentation, throughout the history of social work. Similarly, the first aim in working with adults who have not attained, or cannot sustain, a decent independent life in the community is to help them achieve a productive independence in the life of their choosing; but if a normal amount of adult independence is unfeasible, it is social workers who create innovatory alternatives such as supported accommodation and domiciliary services. Again, the methods for success have been and remain the subject of much development, experimentation and research.

Social workers' expertise lies, then, partly in creating supplements, alternatives or remedies for the family, to benefit people who cannot obtain from their families the nurturance and support that others are fortunate enough so to obtain in good measure. To do this work effectively a number of methods of intervention have been developed. Examples highlighted in the *Companion to Social Work* (Davies, 1997) include person-centred counselling, family therapy, task-centred work and cognitive-behavioural therapy. The expertise of social workers partly lies, or should lie, in the knowledgeable understanding and skilful application of such methods of intervention. The point to stress here is that while what social workers hope to help their clients achieve lies within the ordinary goals of daily life, the process of helping clients to do so requires non-trivial technical knowledge and skill in the methods of helping. It is crucial not to confuse the relative ordinariness of the outcomes that social work intervention may be trying to achieve, with the special knowledge and skill that may be needed to achieve it.

In the context of social work expertise it should not be omitted that practice is largely framed by statute law and constantly regulated by government direction. Social workers must plainly have a sound knowledge of relevant areas of law, and an understanding of the issues reviewed in Chapter 6. Where this is lacking – most notoriously, as revealed in the enquiries into failures of child protection – the consequences for standards of practice are manifestly damaging.

The knowledge and expertise needed for social work is located in large part within the common knowledge of the community, while in some areas it has a more specialised and technical character. Whatever its content, like any other professional body of knowledge it needs to be developed and practised through years of training and experience. Regrettably, the provision for education and the opportunities for experience are often poor in social work. Workers may have to operate in areas of ordinary life where their experience is limited, such as marital relationships, parenthood and bereavement. The professional education of social workers struggles to equip students with even the rudiments of that wide knowledge of life and that range of specialised and technical skills that would truly qualify them as experts in the range of their responsibilities. Therefore, while it is beyond doubt that social workers, like other professionals, require special training, knowledge and skills, it cannot be lightly assumed that they possess it. There are also reasons for thinking that social workers have often been bad at applying the results of research which nourishes and develops the knowledge of the profession; that in place of soundly based knowledge they substitute an idiosyncratic mixture of local practice and personal style, more in defiance than in benefit of the fruits of ongoing research.

Social work expertise, then, is paradoxical in several important respects. Although partly specialised, much of it is rooted in ordinary knowledge. While this ordinary knowledge is widespread and commonplace in the community, acquiring it is no facile accomplishment and much of its content is far from trivial. It is problematic for the profession, but part of its essential character, to be the purveyor of the ordinary. Social work knowledge is also ambiguous in that it can plausibly be viewed either as relatively limited in range and depth – and thus trainable in a year or two – or, alternatively, as encompassing such a broad sweep of the experience and wisdom of mankind that no one could ever master more than a fraction of it. Truly, both views are defective. The ambiguity of social work knowledge is deepened by the fact that many of its practitioners seem to be poorly disciplined in it. Thus a valid case can be made for professional status, but it is undermined by the observation that many social workers seem to get by without actually having a powerful command of the (ambiguously defined) knowledge that they need.

The ambiguity of social work knowledge and expertise weakens the accountability that is one of the key justifications and defences of professionalism. It is, perhaps, an awareness of this questionable accountability that has driven various interest groups to attempt, or insist on, the mechanical codification of social work knowledge. A not insignificant industry has grown up to define, apply and regulate comprehensive sets of competencies which novice professionals are expected to attain. However, this method of attempting to overcome the problems of social work knowledge is fatally flawed. Knowledge on the broad scale required for any profession which has human living as its central subject is not reducible to sets of competencies, and to attempt to do so is futile; detailed expertise cannot be rigorously assessed where no satisfactory instruments have been created (Clark, 1995).

Conclusion

This chapter has argued that the conventional content of social work ethics, which was previously described in Chapter 4, can be traced to three main currents of ideas in the western religious and philosophical tradition: the ethic of pastoral care and its modern expression as individual service and casework to the afflicted; the ethic of social reform inspired by a thirst for justice and a dream of liberation; and the ethic of public accountability developed in the culture and practice of large scale organisations typical of modern societies. The roots of professional ethics are to be found in these ideologies, and conflicts in ethics often reflect the competing priorities embraced by these three traditions.

The review of professional ethics points to a number of fundamental issues for theory. This chapter has discussed the problem of defining what is ethical in societies whose members do not share common histories, culture, beliefs or values; the especially significant problem of complex accountability in social work; and the ambiguity of the prescriptions of theory and method. These will be cardinal issues in the search for theory that now ensues.

6

Law, Legitimacy and Professional Accountability

Social work and the law

Law, policy and administration

Social work is constituted, in large part, by its relationship with the state. This chapter will examine how that relationship is mediated through the institutions of the law, policy and administration, and will consider the influence of these institutions on practice. The position of social work as an instrument of public policy raises significant issues for professional ethics, which will also be considered in this chapter.

It is relevant to keep in mind the respective roles of the different institutions of law and administration (see Atiyah, 1995). The role of making law, at least in its primary form, lies principally with the legislature or parliament, which enacts new laws and modifies or repeals old ones; in Britain such laws are known as statutes. The power to enact legislation may exist at more than one level of the national state, as for example in the USA which has both state and federal legislatures, or in Britain under the newly created Scottish Parliament and Welsh Assembly. In England and some other countries with cognate legal systems there exists additionally a substantial body of unenacted, so-called common law which represents the practices of custom and tradition; with the passage of time more and more of the common law is being replaced by statute. Law is also, in effect, created as judges interpret legislation and the common law in cases where their import is unclear.

The processes of policy-making generally take place within the framework of basic or constitutional law and are carried on by elected politicians and their political advisers; appointed public servants;

representatives of specific interests such as voluntary associations and pressure groups; and more or less independent bodies such as universities and research institutes. When desirable objectives are unachievable within current legislation, efforts to create new legislation may follow. For example, following a policy review, the Griffiths report (Griffiths, 1988), the National Health Service and Community Care Act 1990 addressed the escalating costs of care for elderly people and gave local authorities new powers to determine the support older people might receive. Existing law frequently allocates ministers and civil servants the powers to implement specific requirements or apply directions for the management of public service, and these directions often have the practical force of law. In Britain they typically take the form of circulars to local authorities and published guidance on good practice. Thus the formal legal requirements of the NHS and Community Care Act were underlined and amplified in voluminous publications from the Department of Health (Lewis and Glennerster, 1996; cf. Payne, 1995).

The implementation of legislation falls to various bodies. At national level public administration is the job of ministries and semi-independent, politically appointed agencies (sometimes known as quangos or non-departmental public bodies). At the local level, local departments and service organisations perform a wide range of service functions authorised and paid for by public policy: for example, the maintenance of public roads and spaces and the provision of schools and hospitals. The implementation of legislation may also be delegated to voluntary or private organisations to carry out under government mandate. This forms a highly significant part of social service provision in some areas of policy and in some national service systems. With a few exceptions mainly confined to very small organisations, the mode of organisation of the bodies which implement policy and legislation is bureaucratic: hierarchically structured with well defined vertical accountability, involving a high degree of specialisation of functions, impersonal in the allocation of roles, ruled by an ethic of professional merit and technical competence, bound by comprehensive sets of formal rules and procedures.

When individuals offend against the public law the criminal justice system has the role of apprehending them and dispensing punishment. Disputes between individuals or organisations that do not represent a transgression against the state can be adjudicated

under private law: for example, matters of trade and commerce, or
the resolution of family disputes.

The intimacy of social work's relationship with the law is thus
demonstrated in its potential and necessary involvement in all these
arenas of public life: the debates over social policy; the making of
legislation in relation to areas such as the family, disability, the
treatment of offenders; the implementation of public policy through
the organs of public administration; the dispensing of criminal
justice; and the mediation of private disputes between individuals.
The relationship is so dense that without it social work in its modern
forms would not exist. But it seems that social work has difficulty
comprehending the importance of the relationship with law and its
institutions. In regard to policy, the government's former chief
adviser on social work commented that:

> The greatest barrier to effective communication for many people was
> their difficulty in understanding why and how government operated as
> it did... Even people with extensive experience of the politics and
> processes of local government had difficulty in transferring knowledge
> to the national level. Social workers, with their strong commitment to
> vulnerable groups in the community, had particular problems with an
> ethic which differed markedly from their own in serving the political
> objectives of a national government. (Utting, 1997, p. 281)

Social work's ambivalence about the law is also illustrated by the
long reluctance, now mostly dissipated, of social work educators to
tackle the subject seriously in professional training (Ball, 1997). In
criminal justice social work, probation officers have often been
suspected of more or less covertly harbouring the idea that their role
was not to strengthen justice but to soften the harshness of its
ministration. Such examples could be multiplied but would merely
reinforce the conclusion that social work has a characteristic myopia.
The client, close to, is sharply seen, but vision is progressively
blurred when it comes to understanding social work's wider relationship to the institutions of society, including the law, and the basis of
legitimacy of those institutions.

The broad institution of social work is necessarily a creature of law
and public policy. It is specifically charged with the administration of
important segments of law and public policy, especially in connection with the family and with the treatment and rehabilitation of

offenders. The professional ethics of social work must therefore squarely address its principles and obligations, not only in the narrow remit of professional relationships with clients, but also in the wider sphere of public life and accountability under the law. This chapter will unfold these concerns.

Legislation and social work

In dealing with clients, social workers are likely to encounter almost any of the common situations with legal implications that directly affect people at a personal level: difficulties as consumers of goods and services both from the public and private sectors; being victims of an offence, such as assault or theft; family conflicts, such as divorce; facing unresolved disputes with neighbours or other members of the community; being charged with or found guilty of a criminal offence; and so forth. For this reason, social workers need a working understanding of the main areas of law likely to affect ordinary members of society, and of operation of the legal system. At minimum social workers must be able to recognise correctly a legal problem when they encounter it, and direct the client to appropriate sources of advice.

Social workers are likely to need a particular depth of knowledge in those areas of law and administration that are particularly significant within the type of work that they do. For example, where poverty is a frequent issue, a knowledge of unemployment and of welfare rights is indicated; where housing problems are rife, a knowledge of landlord and tenant obligations, housing management policy, homelessness legislation, and so forth; where marital violence is the focus, a knowledge of housing rights, divorce law and access to children, the law of assault, and the like; in medical settings, the rights of patients and their families. These and other issues will be daily grist to the mill in particular practice settings, but none, with the possible exception of welfare rights, would generally be thought of as a matter in which social workers are the leading specialists. Nonetheless, social workers have a serious responsibility to be sufficiently conversant with those areas of the law likely to affect ordinary people in their private lives, because the legal aspects of common life problems may well be very significant and the clients of social work are usually disadvantaged in access to legal advice and representation.

Beside their general responsibility to be conversant with the law, social workers are responsible for very specific duties exclusive to their agencies or very strongly associated with them. In these areas the implementation of social policy and the associated legal processes cannot, or ordinarily do not, proceed without the specialist opinion and intervention of social workers. The most prominent area is child care and protection, including substitute care when the natural family no longer functions; a popular textbook of law for social workers (Ball, 1996) devotes one-third of its content to children and families. In the criminal justice system, social workers have traditionally advised the courts about the treatment of offenders, and counselled offenders especially those placed on probation. (In England, however, the requirement for this work to be carried out by qualified social workers was recently abolished.) In regard to care for people with disabilities, social workers have traditionally played a distinctive role alongside the health-related professions. Under the NHS and Community Care Act 1990 local authorities are expected to discharge their responsibilities for social care through social work and services departments, traditionally led and staffed by social workers. These are leading examples of areas of law, public administration and service practice in which the special role and expertise of professional social workers is built in, and which particularly demonstrate the position of social workers as agents of public policy.

The objectives of these areas of policy and administration in which social workers have been allocated a central part to play are not obviously in accord with the aims of the profession as social workers commonly express them. Whereas the traditional ethics of social work emphasise care for the person, the individuality of the client and her right to self-determination, the legislation which social workers in particular execute seems to turn mostly around social control. It often involves intervention in which the usual presumptions about the boundaries of private action have been set aside. Thus while the manner of parents' care for their children is ordinarily regarded as no business of officials, the presumption of privacy in family life is overturned in the face of suspicion that certain standards of care are not being met. The private living arrangements that adults contrive for themselves are normally no concern of the state, but if they appear to be extremely unsatisfactory or dangerous then social workers and other officials will be expected to intervene. In a secular society the morals that individuals choose to practise are not chiefly the business of officialdom, but individuals who flagrantly disregard societal norms will find themselves counselled, cajoled and coerced, by social workers and others, to mend their ways.

Social work, therefore, is among the social institutions that circumscribe, as well as enhance, the liberty of the individual. And yet social work plainly shares with the liberal tradition of political thought that is both its progenitor and its inheritance a primary value of individual freedom and self-realisation. The question of why, as free autonomous individuals and bearers of human rights, we should be expected to accede to the power of the state and its institutions is traditionally known as the problem of political obligation. Since social work is heavily implicated in important areas of law, obligation must be a central issue for professional ethics. The following sections examine this problem.

Why should citizens obey the law?

Over the history of civilisation political philosophers and religious leaders have examined a wide range of arguments on whether, and why, one should obey the law. As concerns the individual, it may be said that obeying the law is advisable simply because of the practical consequences of not doing so; the lawbreaker risks loss of advantages, punishment, and ostracism, and his life may be the worse while he flouts the law. As concerns the good health of society in general, maintaining a rule of law is apparently indispensable to social stability and human flourishing. It is easy to agree with the general thesis – although there will be disputes over particular issues – that many evils, for example poverty, exploitation and risk of violence will follow if citizens do not obey the law. It can also plausibly be held that most people obey most of the law most of the time, and this in itself is valuable because it is conducive to stability and prosperity.

The question of political obligation can partly be sidestepped to the extent that in practice the demands of legality and morality coincide. If theft is both morally and legally wrong, it may be said to make little practical difference whether the reason for refraining from theft is to conform with morals or to comply with the law, since the implications for conduct are the same. A moment's reflection shows that this is a weak and unsatisfactory position, because there are many situations where the demands of law and morality do not, in fact, coincide. For example, some people consider promiscuity wrong on moral or religious grounds, but in most places the law is now silent on this particular moral question. There are also situations where the law and morality appear to be in direct conflict, as for example when the state imposes military conscription upon individuals who consider that fighting in the current war is morally wrong. In modern societies both the law and morals are constantly in flux, and here and there inevitably out of step with each other. More robust grounds for obeying the law are needed than simply coincidence, which is both unreliable in practice and unconvincing in theory.

The problem, therefore, is to show that obeying the law, beyond being convenient or useful, is also *morally* required, and this is the object of theories of political obligation. Against the idea of obligation it may be held that, while adherence to the law is generally morally justified, in certain particular situations departing from the law is morally preferable. Or, in a stronger argument, it may be held that there is no overriding general moral argument for obeying the law, while admitting that to do so is often useful. In the following paragraphs some of the most important arguments for and against political obligation will be briefly sketched. Fuller discussions of this subject are given by Horton (1992), Stirk and Weigall (1995) and Bellamy and Ross (1996).

Divine or religious authority

One of the earliest arguments for political obligation was that the law regulating human affairs was directly based on the will of the gods, or God, and religious commandment. The figure of Moses is perhaps the most famous example; numerous other religious traditions share the same features of a prophet who acts as messenger to communicate ways of right living to the people, followed by a priesthood to guard the observances. In traditional societies the function of religious leadership was indistinct from the function of maintaining civil order; priest and king could be closely allied, or the same person. A version of this concept persisted in Britain until the seventeenth century; a ghost of it perhaps still survives in the institution of an established church.

In western liberal democracies the doctrine that obeying the law is grounded on the religious authority of the ruler is now largely obsolete as the basis of the political constitution. This is not so, however, in all places. A notable example is Islamic fundamentalism, which in a number of countries has reasserted that the basis of law and civil society should be the authority of the Koran and traditional religious teaching. Although social work as it is known in the west hardly exists in fundamentalist regimes, collisions of religious authority with the expectations of the law based on liberal political institutions are nevertheless a real problem. The social worker who must deal with a young person forbidden on religious grounds to act in ways that are perfectly permissible in secular law is experiencing the direct conflict of theories of political obligation.

Moral and civic duty

A second traditional line of thought holds that obeying the law is a moral obligation which necessarily falls upon every member of the community and is not even in principle negotiable. This position is often legitimated by reference to the law being based on divine authority. The power of the idea that doing one's duty under the law is utterly inescapable is vividly illustrated in dramatic tragedy, where the hero faces an irreconcilable conflict between personal obligation or love, and duty to the state. The price of defying the law is moral and social extinction by shame and banishment from the community, or actual death.

Western thought since the Reformation has questioned the individual's obligation to obey civic authority and asserted his right to make his own religious, moral and political choices. Liberal individualism has indeed entrenched the rights of the autonomous individual as the dominant ideology. However, individualism is criticised for blindness to the essentially social character of human life, especially by communitarian theorists who place social duty among the core values. They hold that obligations to society cannot be explained away within any expanded version of individualism, but must be treated as foundational. The theme of communal obligations will be taken up again in the next chapter.

The argument from authoritative competence

A third defence of political obligation depends on the idea that laws are created and administered by authorities which best, or alone, understand what will conduce to the good of the community. Since ordinary people do not possess the knowledge or expertise to determine cases or judge the good of the community, they should defer to the designated experts. The citizen's duty of obedience to the law is founded on the benefit to society of social affairs being regulated by those who possess the requisite authority based in knowledge.

There are numerous versions of the expertise or authoritative competence argument. In the *Republic* Plato gives to the Guardians the role of ruling over the common people in society. Where obligation is founded on divine or religious authority, there will invariably be a caste or class that has the role of interpreting it. In many pre-modern societies, authority was closely linked to patriarchy so that only men of certain standing were empowered to interpret and impose the law. In modern times it is sometimes argued that political decision-making should be left to scientific and technical experts who alone understand the issues to be decided. For example, it may be held that the building of roads, the planning of new towns or the redevelopment of old ones should be left to architects, planners and engineers, since ordinary people do not have the necessary expertise; and that in the process citizens should be lawfully bound to accede to properly applied restraints on their freedoms, such as those on the design and location of housing or the compulsory purchase of land.

It is no longer feasible to defend obligation on the basis of deference to expertise, for at least two sorts of reasons. First, the rise and fall of particular authoritative expertise is now such a frequent phenomenon that we have all been taught to be sceptical. Where once traditional teaching and authority survived for generations, now the discrediting of experts is a commonplace, and with it has come the loss of faith in grand systems of theory. Second, even where the authority of experts is accepted, the presumption is now in favour of the opinion of the ordinary citizen, howsoever ignorant, over the art of the expert. The role of experts is to inform and advise, but not to impose solutions over the heads of the community.

The utilitarian argument

The basic principle of utilitarianism (see Chapter 5) is that the rightness of actions or rules is to be assessed according to the outcomes they produce. Given a standard for comparing outcomes – such as happiness or satisfaction – morality is deduced by comparing the consequences of different courses of action. This leads to a comprehensive theory of personal morality. A great theoretical advantage of utilitarianism is that exactly the same approach can be applied to the questions of politics and law. The right policy or law is the one that will lead to the best outcomes, on balance. Thus for example, if the policy objective is to reduce road accidents caused by drunk driving and random breath tests are an efficient way to achieve this, then a policy of random breath tests is desirable whatever the alleged intrusion upon civil rights.

The utilitarian argument for obeying the law is that doing so will produce on balance the best outcomes for the individual and for society as a whole. However, utilitarianism faces the same problems when it comes to justifying political obligation as it does in personal morality. The first is that utilitarians have to determine what is the one good to be set above all others, and prove that the choice is incontrovertible. Like other moral theories, utilitarianism therefore rests in the end on a theory of human nature (Plant, 1991).

The second problem, or rather pair of problems, is to do with calculating the best outcomes. Utilitarians have to show that a meaningful reckoning can be made of the advantages and disadvantages, in terms of the promotion of the basic good, of different actions or rules. Further, they have to decide how to balance the sum total or aggregation of the good achieved with the distribution of this good between different members of society. In reality this calculation is often so complicated as to be practically impossible; we simply cannot know well enough the outcomes of every conceivable course of action to make this the sole basis of choice. How, for example, could we judge whether a policy of prohibiting the inheritance of land would in the end lead to a better or worse use of natural resources for the good of humanity?

The third problem is that utilitarian considerations sometimes seem to fly in the face of ordinary moral intuitions and practices. Utilitarianism seems to justify violation of human rights if the consequences to society as a whole are worth it. For example, political dissent might be suppressed on the grounds that the safety of the state requires it; but suppressing dissent makes it impossible for the wider society to judge the merits of the argument.

Fourth, it has been argued that utilitarianism really fails to address the question of political obligation at all (Horton, 1992). Act-utilitarianism, which holds that the merits of every single act should be judged according to the anticipated outcomes, is essentially irrelevant to supporting or refuting the obligation to respect the law, which of course is a system of rules. On the other hand, rule-utilitarianism – which says that we should abide by general moral rules designed to produce the best outcome overall, although not necessarily in every particular case – could provide a useful framework for assessing the quality of laws and therefore the validity of the obligation to obey them.

The conclusion to be drawn about utilitarian arguments for political obligation is a mixed one. It is plainly desirable that we should comply with laws that promote the good of society, which supports utility as a ground of obligation. By the same token, since it is equally clear that we cannot be sure that every law does in fact promote the good of society, we cannot safely conclude in general that obligation follows from the propensity of the laws to promote social good. Utility is left as a very important consideration in justifying political obligation, but it fails as a single principle.

The social contract and consent

Social contract theory, in essence, envisages that the rights and duties between individuals in society are defined in some kind of founding contract or agreement. Having chosen to become members of the society we are then morally obligated by a promise to obey and uphold its laws, just as in joining a club one undertakes to accept its rules. This does not, of course, preclude trying to change specific laws from time to time, provided one respects the ground law or constitution.

Literal interpretations of the social contract are soon shown to be fatally flawed. First, with rare exceptions there is no reason to suppose that the founding fathers (or mothers) ever actually set about explicitly creating a social contract that defined rights and duties between each other; societies simply develop organically, and by the time the concept of law has any meaning they are already established for longer than history can recall. Second, even if, counterfactually, a social contract had been established by the founding fathers, it is difficult to see why the undertakings of ancestors should be binding upon their descendants. If instead we imagine that the social contract is recreated between every individual and society at a certain point – say, the age of political majority – this falls to the third objection that in practice hardly any one has a choice in the matter. Most people become citizens of a given polity just by being born and growing up in it. They have no choice about its rules, and only seldom have a choice to give up the citizenship of their birth in favour of another one.

Since (with rare exceptions) there is no such thing as a historical social contract, some theorists have instead invoked the idea that a social contract is implicitly created by consent. In this version, my passive consent to the law of the land counts as a promise to obey it. However, this is also subject to the third objection and furthermore, as Horton (1992, p. 82) comments, 'people sometimes consent to arrangements which are irrational, unreasonable or unfair'. Nevertheless, although the consent of the individual is not *sufficient* to justify political obligation, under the ideal of democracy it is certainly *necessary* that the people should consent. It is now impossible to believe that we should be bound by laws that are not supported by will of the majority, or its representatives.

The power of the idea of the social contract does not, then, reside in any description of the actual, empirical world. The point of the social contract is as a thought-experiment and it is the theory of Rawls (1973) that has regenerated interest in it. This proposes that we should accept as just and binding the set of mutual rights and obligations that free and rational agents would create for themselves if, hypothetically, they were in a position to legislate for a yet-to-be-created society. Rawls' theory will be revisited in the context of justice, to be discussed in Chapter 8.

Conclusion: utility, consent and human rights

Which theory, or theories, of obligation carry greatest weight? Like the other perennial questions of moral and political theory, political obligation eludes final solutions. All the ideas sketched here are powerful enough to merit serious attention, and all are morally significant in that many people have conscientiously held to them. None is sufficiently persuasive to absorb or exclude all others definitively, however (Horton, 1992). There is more to this than mere theoretical untidiness, since what divides people and societies is fundamental beliefs and values that cannot be amalgamated by clever philosophising.

The problem for social work, as for other activities that depend on the authority for the state for their legitimacy, is that strong grounds for proving individuals' obligation to obey the law are needful but impossible to demonstrate conclusively to everyone's satisfaction. The problem is very much worse in politically and culturally plural societies. What recourse is open to a conscientious profession?

In Chapter 5 it was suggested that social work and other comparable interventions are underdetermined, that is, available theoretical and empirical knowledge is often not sufficient to show that a particular course of action is clearly correct or unmistakably superior to all others. Practical decision-making should therefore observe the indispensable principles, whereby every theory or piece of information that still merits serious consideration after rigorous challenge should be given an appropriate weight in the adopted solution. The same principles of pluralism and caution apply equally to the use of competing moral and political theories. In regard to political obligation, several theories are persuasive but none is conclusive. There will be very strong grounds for obligation where a class of actions is supported by several persuasive principles. Grounds for obligation will be less robust where a class of actions is only weakly or partly supported by important principles, and will be questionable where they appear to contradict important principles. Practitioners should hesitate to enforce obligations to obey the law that are not well supported by indispensable principles.

In modern liberal democracies there are three indispensable principles for political obligation. The first is utility: obligation is justified when the laws are shown to promote the benefit of society as a whole. The idea that laws should promote social benefit is perhaps so much taken for granted as to require little defence. Political parties canvass support by pointing to the socially beneficial changes they will institute. Utility is nevertheless a source of constant controversy and a difficult principle to realise, since many laws have detrimental effects on some individuals and the test of utility requires that there will be benefit overall. For example, taxation enables a whole range of vital provisions to be put in place, but is detrimental to – or experienced as such by – very large numbers of individuals. Similarly, the punishment of offenders is presumed to be in part at least for the benefit and protection of society in general, yet the evidence that it does so is often ambiguous: consider for example the control of 'recreational' drugs.

The second essential is consent: obligation is justified when the laws command wide support of the people. The necessity of this principle is again illustrated by its taken-for-granted character. Every modern government claims to embrace democracy; every modern liberal constitution embodies the idea that governments derive their authority from having been freely elected by the people who have consented to the proposed policies and the laws that will flow from them. Except under tyranny, laws that do not have the general consent of the people soon become unworkable.

The third indispensable principle is a defence of individuals' moral integrity: obligation is justified when it does not involve an unwarranted infringement of any person's fundamental rights. The defence of the individual's rights is almost universally acknowledged as a necessary check on the pursuit of overall social utility which government policies may represent. The universality of this concern is illustrated by such international commitments as the Universal Declaration of Human Rights, the European Convention on Human Rights and the International Convention on the Rights of the Child. Some government actions upon individuals must be rejected however attractive the claimed or potential overall social benefit. For example, depriving an individual of his freedom without due process of law is universally regarded as an unacceptable infringement of human rights, so citizens should not consider themselves morally bound by laws that implicate them in any such process. With regard to consent, the defence of individuals' moral integrity recognises that policies and governments which have the general consent of the people may nevertheless be repugnant to minorities, and therefore should be exercised with due regard for the rights and interests of minorities.

Obligation, then, is on good grounds when all three conditions of utility, consent and protection of rights are reasonably satisfied. Where the conditions are less well satisfied, obligation is correspondingly weaker. At this point in the argument, these conditions are more formal than substantive. We have stipulated utility, consent and the protection of rights, but we have still to work out precisely what is to be understood by them: there are competing versions of these ideals and competing ideas about how they can be realised. In the remainder of this chapter we shall examine how the grounds of political obligation apply to the profession of social work.

The legitimacy of professional authority

Is the power of professionals legitimate?

Professions function in a social and political context that legitimates their operations and organisations. They have the authority to deliver influential advice and weighty recommendations, and in some circumstances the power to coerce people against their will. The existence of this power poses the important question of legitimacy. What right do professionals have to influence or compel ordinary citizens? What is the content and basis of their rights as professionals?

To claim that professional power is legitimate means to say that it is justified in three respects.

1. The first test is that the professional power is exercised according to law. The law represents the best available approximation of the considered view of society on duties and obligations, right and wrong conduct. Legitimacy plainly necessitates that professionals should work within the law.
2. The second test is that the law itself should satisfy the conditions for political obligation as already discussed: it should have the consent of the people, promote utility and preserve human rights.
3. The third test is that professional power should be truly guided by expertise, since otherwise it will fail to promote utility and protect rights.

Under ideal, and indeed imaginary, conditions, the power exerted by professionals might be perfectly authorised by the political community, and be shown to rest on a secure framework of laws and public institutions supported by society at large. Ideally professionals would exercise impeccable expertise and would not make errors of fact and judgement, which damage the interests of users and undermine the public's confidence. Since these conditions obviously do not obtain in the real world, the question of legitimacy is urgent. Why should clients accede to professional authority given that the powers of professionals often seem to have a dubious basis both in law and in knowledge, and that the actions of professionals sometimes seem to contradict the expectations of ordinary morality? The question has a counterpart for professionals: what privileges and sanctions attach to their professional role that set it apart from the private individual?

The ambiguity of 'helping'

Social workers like to think of themselves as *helping* professionals; but since helping connotes a voluntary relationship that either side may choose not to pursue, the notion implies that the client is at liberty to decline the help. If the client were under no pressure to accept help, then the issue of legitimacy might be less serious. A client who mistrusted the professional could simply choose to ignore her advice or avoid contact. Such is the current status of various so-called 'alternative' mind and bodily health treatments, for example herbal medicine or therapies based on meditation. No one is obliged to take them; they are presumed to constitute no significant danger; no official role is allocated to their practitioners; and whether they should be regarded as beneficial therapy or as quackery is left mostly to the judgement of the individual consumer. Their legitimacy is based on the freedom, in a market society, to offer goods and services without specific permission but subject to any laws designed to protect the consumer or other interests.

The social work self-image of helping profession is rudely challenged whenever the course of intervention leads to a collision with the expressed wishes of the client. Children are taken from home; adults are compulsorily detained in institutions; clients of all kinds are compelled to accept interventions, constraints and restraints much at variance with their own notions of the help they need. The collision is apt to be especially painful to the sensibilities of social workers, as well as their clients, when it involves actual physical force. Teaming up with the police to carry out a dawn raid on a family, although not to be held up as necessary, desirable or frequent practice, is nevertheless the logical culmination of the status of social work professionals. In such forcible interventions social workers end up appearing not only to condone but to sanction the objectionable use of force, since they are carried out legally, and ostensibly in the name of welfare.

It is thus clearly incorrect to typify the social worker as a helper whose intervention the service user may freely choose or decline. While there remains a place for professional relationships established on this voluntary basis, social work as a whole has to be understood in the context of its relationship to the state and the purposes of the state. The myth of the privately contracted helping relationship has nevertheless been highly influential in the history of social work, and especially in the formation of ethical codes. While the motivation of social workers is doubtless to help, the function of their profession in society is also to regulate and control.

The basis of professional–client relationships: a three-cornered compact

The relationship between the state, professionals and citizens (of whom some become clients) is constitutive of the conditions of legitimacy. In the liberal-democratic tradition this relationship can be modelled as a three-cornered compact or partnership embodying a mutually agreed set of expectations and principles for the powers and responsibilities of the parties. In idealised terms, the following features are said to support the legitimacy of a profession. As between citizens and the state, in a democracy the state derives its authority from the support of the people and their consent to be ruled by the government of their choice. The state has no other basis for enforcing its rule than the ultimate agreement of the people that it should do so in the public good. As between the state and professionals, the presumption is that the state charges professionals with certain duties and empowers them with certain authority to support purposes duly adopted by the state within the framework of law. As between professionals and citizens or clients, the presumption is that professionals undertake to act for the client's good and the public good within the range of powers and activities legitimated in the other arms of the partnership relationship.

The principles of partnership and consent informing this idealised three-sided relationship obviously merit support. The widely subscribed professional ideals of disinterested service and intervention by consent could scarcely be realised otherwise. However, the model falls far short of a working description of reality. In reality the relationships often entail poorly defined or contradictory expectations in significant areas. The actual relationship between citizens and state cannot be reduced to the simple model of citizens empowering the state to act on their behalf. Real states deploy a range of powers and interests, acquired over historical time, which often ill reflect the current sentiments of the community. Further, communities are often divided in such a way that a genuine consensus is unobtainable. As between the state and professionals, it cannot be assumed that the former will effectively define the scope of the latter. Powerful professions often bend their efforts to have their interpretation of professional authority dominate over the voice of the community as expressed by the organs of the state. As between professionals and clients, a large literature and much popular opinion question whether professionals truly are motivated to act in their clients' interests.

Professional legitimacy and political obligation

Bringing together the principles of political obligation and the basis of professional legitimacy, we are led then to the issue of whether the power of social workers and other professionals is legitimate. We can begin to investigate this question by asking whether professional authority as defined in the idealised three-cornered compact could plausibly meet the grounds for political obligation sketched earlier.

The first justification of political obligation was utility. It is reasonable to think that the arrangement whereby the state entrusts the responsibility for a range of specialised functions to independent or semi-independent professions is generally conducive to utility. In the western and western-inspired societies that have adopted the model, the arts and sciences fostered by professionals have flourished and despite the many reservations that one would enter, have arguably enhanced standards of living. By contrast, in the communist world where expert practitioners were completely assimilated into the state, the failure was spectacular. Nevertheless, the authority created in the three-cornered compact is clearly no dependable guarantee of utility. Everyone in western societies has direct experience of poor or damaging professional service.

The second justification of political obligation was consent. In this respect the legitimacy based on the three-cornered partnership is frequently rather tenuous. Although professionals and their organisations may function correctly according to law, it must often be doubtful that citizens have fully understood in advance what powers were to be exerted by professionals. For example, one keynote principle of the NHS and Community Care Act 1990 was the promotion of choice for users and potential users of care services. In practice welfare professionals often have the job of imposing the reality of little or no choice.

The third justification of political obligation was the protection of rights. As with utility, the experience of western societies suggests that there is much about the three-cornered compact that is valuable for the protection of rights. Professionals arguably need their distance from the state if they are to be free to defend the interests of citizens, especially when clients might be in conflict with the state. On the other hand, it is not self-evident that the many professionals who work directly for the state – including, for example, many doctors and social workers – are any less effective in protecting the rights of clients than their independent counterparts, who must often charge clients for their service.

The question of why citizens should legitimately be compelled to obey professionals, including social workers, therefore remains pressing. Koehn (1994) offers a defence of professional authority, especially in law, medicine and the religious ministry, by focusing on the relationship between the professional and the client. Koehn observes that trust in professionals is currently being challenged on the grounds that professionals do not have any special commitment to the public interest, but are merely self-serving; that professional ethics cannot be essentially different from ordinary ethics; and that legitimacy should be based on professionals' proven role and effectiveness and not by appeal to a spurious status. Koehn identifies two sorts of possible basis for clients' trust in professionals. The first is professionals' expertise; but as Koehn argues, expertise is unreliable. The second basis is because professionals are service providers who obey the client's will under a contractual obligation to empower the client; but as Koehn shows, much proper and necessary professional action cannot be covered by any precise kind of contract. Koehn proposes instead that reliance on the professional's authority must be based on a general pledge of service by the professional to the community. The pledge of service entails that:

> A professional is an agent who freely makes a public promise to serve persons (for example the sick) who are distinguished by a specific desire for a particular good (for example health) and who have come into the presence of the professional with or on the expectation that the professional will promote that particular good. (Koehn, 1994, p. 59)

Koehn's reformulation of the basis of the professional–client relationships is correct to stress that much of the substance of such relationships cannot be known in advance in specific detail. On the other hand Koehn neglects the role of the state in sanctioning and creating professional–client relationships, leaving them to appear much more like private agreements than they truly are or should be.

Conclusion: under the law?

The legitimacy of social work quite often appears to be in tatters. Legitimacy requires that intervention should be carried out according to law and this is doubtless accepted by most social workers, but inquiries into failures of service show that their knowledge and understanding of the relevant law is not infrequently defective. For example, in the Carlile child abuse case the social worker and apparently all his colleagues were unaware of a statutory provision that could have been used to compel the parents to allow a medical examination of the child (Blom-Cooper, 1987).

Legitimacy requires that the law should be a genuine expression of the will of the community, but in fact the opinion of the community is very often divided about how to deal with the sensitive and contentious issues and problems allocated to social work. There are, for example, wide divisions of opinion over how much protection or independence parents ought to give their children.

Legitimacy requires that intervention should be informed by pertinent expertise, but this is often not realised because of problems at two levels: either the workers concerned are not as knowledgeable about the matters in hand as they reasonably should be, or there is simply too little soundly based knowledge in existence to make practice reliably effective.

The conclusion to be drawn here is that observance of the law will usually be necessary to professional legitimacy but will frequently not be sufficient. Occasionally, following the law may actually undermine professional legitimacy, since the law inevitably embodies conflicts and contradictions and can point to courses of action that must be rejected on wider ethical and expedient considerations.

In the wake of the Beckford and Carlile child abuse enquiries it was argued that social work needed to refocus itself as, in effect, a branch of applied law (Ball *et al.*, 1988). This is too narrow a conception of the aims and value of the profession. It was argued in Chapter 5 that complex accountability is a defining characteristic of social work: it must serve the interests of *all* parties in situations of personal and family difficulty. The partisan view of the legal agent negates the inclusive scope of social work: social workers are rightly devoted to realising a wider conception of welfare. And it is doubtful that they have the temperament and inclination to shape their professional role according to the narrow vision of the law.

Social work is practised under the law, because without legality it can have no legitimacy. The centrality of law for social work has perhaps been realised only rather belatedly, even making allowances for the changing character of professional work and the relatively recent escalation of the legal powers that fall to social workers to implement. It is an error, however, to place social work too much under law, if by that it is meant to limit social work to the exact application of relevant law. There are wider aims and farther boundaries to the legitimacy of social work than those delineated by law. The regulation of social work must be conceived accordingly, and this will be theme of the next chapter.

7

Welfare, Politics and Social Work

Social work is part of welfare; but welfare is a complex idea, subject to controversial theoretical and political interpretations. This chapter examines key arguments for welfare. It argues that, in order to provide a better foundation for social work as part of welfare, liberal theory needs to be reinforced with a stronger account of the communal aspects of social life.

In the next chapter these ideas are applied to support a general concept of social work as the realisation of welfare citizenship.

Welfare, the private and the public

To analyse and build the ethics of social service, we must revisit the question which, perhaps, many practitioners entertain above all in the earliest stages of their professional engagement: why social work? For what reasons should political society provide, at no small public cost, for a system of service organisations and workers whose main role, apparently, is to supplement the entirely ordinary activities of family members? Given that social work only reaches a relatively small fraction of the population, what are the special features that distinguish recipients from non-recipients? Such issues rapidly generate a train of subsidiary questions. To what bodies should services best be entrusted? What outcomes are to be required, and what mechanisms of accountability? How should the balance be held between ever-rising demand and limited societal willingness to meet the costs? Is there any truth in the accusations that social services actually have a detrimental effect on welfare?

The question here turns on the extent of *public* responsibility for welfare: in what respects the welfare of individuals should be regarded as a matter for politics and public policy. It is understood, of course, that individuals make and accept a range of responsibilities and duties for the well-being of others, their kin and their communities, under the law and within their own sphere of choice and moral action. In the liberal political tradition, this is treated as a private matter for the individual to decide upon according to his or her values and priorities. It is not for the public realm, through its political institutions, to dictate or interfere. What is at issue then is the point where individuals' action (or inaction) in respect to the welfare of others becomes a matter for intervention supported and sponsored by public institutions such as the various arms of government, the police or the judiciary.

The public-private distinction is a general one, applicable across the whole field of social relations. For example, custom and culture commonly expect relations between neighbours at least to be peaceable and respectful of conventionally defined rights to property, privacy, and so forth. A framework of law defines these expectations and provides remedies should someone's actions be considered offensive. There is thus a clearly recognised and acknowledged public responsibility for certain minimal standards of neighbourly behaviour. What is much less clear is whether law and public policy should have any particular remit for promoting neighbourly relations beyond the minimal safeguarding of peaceful respect of rights. In fact such larger goals have been sporadically adopted by a whole range of social policies, such as those promoting community development in new housing areas, or methods of social work that have invoked the mutual helpfulness of neighbours. It is entirely plausible to go either for or against the mix of policies currently pursued. On the one hand, it can be argued that whatever the virtues of good neighbourliness and local social action, these are properly matters to be left to the initiative and choice of local residents, which government should leave well alone. On the other hand, it can just as well be argued that some communities are in fact dysfunctional and will never offer residents even minimally adequate standards of welfare in their private lives unless public social policy intervenes.

The ambiguity of the boundary between public and private applies not only to individuals but also to organisations and institutions. In the liberal constitution, bodies as varied as business firms, sports clubs and private charitable foundations all belong to the private sector. The remit of government is limited to ensuring fair play under laws that are neutral with regard to the specific objectives of business, sport or charity. In reality the simple distinction between public and private sector organisations has been extensively modified. Businesses are induced to come into being or locate in particular areas by public subsidies, infrastructure projects, and the like. New kinds of businesses are created and others destroyed by changing public policy, for example controls on the dumping of waste. Policy and law intervene in the affairs of private sports clubs, for example by prohibiting racial discrimination. In the public social services, private organisations in the so-called 'independent' sector are increasingly given the central role for the supply of services under contracts made in a quasi-market.

The boundary between public and private in the areas relevant to social work is especially problematic. The intimacy of family relationships might well be thought the very last area into which the state should be permitted to intrude; the whole drift of modern thought over several centuries recoils at the notion that the private world of home, family and personal relationships should be regulated by officialdom, however benign. Until relatively recently there was little to challenge the assumption of patriarchy in which conventional expectations were often embedded. Nonetheless it has also been long recognised that families do sometimes fail to ensure even the barest standards of care and safety, and publicly sanctioned mechanisms are needed to fill the gaps. Reflecting as it does deeply held, yet constantly fluctuating societal views about the proper minima of family life, the public-private boundary is paradoxically both passionately contested and constantly changing. The political ethics of social work must seek that the boundary be properly understood and respected.

The arguments for public welfare

All modern developed states support 'welfare' services. The welfare state requires at least the standard services of health, basic education and the relief of poverty. Some modern states have aimed for comprehensive coverage of these, and many other, social welfare ends, encompassing almost every member of the population and every conceivable need. Others have proceeded much more cautiously, restricting welfare policies to those seen as minimally necessary

(Esping-Andersen, 1990). The extent to which different countries have committed themselves to policies for welfare has varied not only with their wealth – which is only to be expected – but also with social opinion, political regime, history and culture. Thus for example, the former East European regimes aimed for very high levels of state provision of welfare in the context of only moderate economic wealth, while in the USA high national wealth has accompanied a generally reluctant attitude to public welfare spending.

The idea of welfare is integral to human well-being and flourishing, and is therefore part of the bedrock of social and political theory (Barry, 1990). However, in modern usages 'welfare' usually does not denote the whole aim, scope and end of morals and politics; but 'welfare' has a broader sense and a restricted sense. The broader sense is manifest in the popular concept of the 'welfare state' that proudly provides for the needs of all citizens for essentials of food, shelter, health, education and social care. The narrower sense of 'welfare' connotes dependence on state sponsored services for what individuals are, as a rule, expected to provide for themselves; the implication is clearly that an individual's welfare usage is an irregular condition preferably to be terminated as soon as possible. Being 'on welfare' is, on this view, undesirable (for example Marsland, 1996). In the narrow sense welfare suggests reliance, not on universal services such as education, but on selective services whose usage tends automatically to imply a personal shortcoming on the part of the user. Prominent among these are the direct financial relief of poverty, and social work for those seen to be unable to manage the normal, everyday demands of life. Contributions to the debate on welfare are always coloured by the concept deployed; indeed the debate about welfare is to a large extent about the relative merits of the broad and narrow concepts.

The following paragraphs briefly and perhaps too coarsely outline the leading arguments for state welfare – from the technical and instrumental to the broadly moral, political and philosophical. Since the narrow idea of welfare already contains a partly concealed evaluation, we shall begin with the broad view, which does not presuppose that welfare policies inherently serve undesirable persons or ends. The aim is to show the relevance of different concepts of 'welfare' to social work. More detailed analyses are amply available in the literature (see for example Butcher, 1995; Deakin, 1987; George and Wilding, 1994; Pierson, 1991; Thane, 1996).

Political expediency

State welfare services, it may be held, are useful in the process of making political bargains. In return for the promise of resources or services politicians hope to gain electoral support or escape from political embarrassments. For example, it is widely supposed that the promise of welfare reform following the Second World War was among the factors that led to the postwar victory of the Labour Party. For governments, welfare services are sometimes necessary to placate political opposition and ensure a compliant public.

The argument that welfare measures are justified because they are expedient is dangerously double-edged. Today's expedient measure may, because of shifting political opinion, be inexpedient tomorrow. For example, public sentiment towards welfare claimants can easily shift from regarding them as genuinely unfortunate individuals who merit social assistance to regarding them as malingerers or free-riders who should be made to submit to the same disciplines as other, responsible, citizens. It seems clearly unsatisfactory to evaluate the merits of claims to welfare entirely on the basis of fickle public opinion, which can often be ignorant, punitive and unfair. It would also frequently be unworkable, because public policy and provision is often not able to respond as quickly as public opinion changes without incurring unfairness or inconsistency. For example, when the NHS and Community Care Act 1990 somewhat shifted the responsibility for paying for the care of dependent elderly people away from the public sector towards the elderly themselves, many felt that the solemn promise of the postwar welfare state had been broken.

Economic efficiency

Welfare services, although they cost public money, can be an aid to overall economic efficiency by promoting a healthy and motivated workforce, and thus save more than they cost. For example, by promoting healthy and well-functioning families the economic and social costs of ill health and psychological maladjustment can be reduced. Equally, a well-functioning social insurance system can reduce the costs to society of managing indigence.

This argument is easy to appreciate in principle, but very difficult to evaluate in relation to specific services. The increase in efficiency that social services may promote has to be set against the possible decreases in efficiency caused by higher taxes. Appraising the outcome means tackling the technical problem of measuring the outputs under various conditions, a difficult task given that there is no obvious or agreed global measure of welfare. The benefits foregone by the process of raising taxes are equally difficult to measure, as are any possible indirect benefits – for example, creating employment in depressed areas – brought about by running welfare services. Much of the debate in the last 15 years has been about whether, overall, welfare is a beneficial service or an enormous disutility.

Avoidance of public affront and social instability

Some welfare problems, for example childbearing outside marriage (in a bygone age) and homelessness (in the present time) are perceived as a threat to common standards, decency and public order. Welfare services can reduce the incidence or impact of socially threatening phenomena, thus promoting political stability.

Without doubt one of the functions of welfare is to remove the socially offensive, or at least hide it from public view. The resurgence of street begging offers an interesting contemporary example. Many people find begging disturbing, distasteful, offensive or threatening. Politicians have responded with promises to clean up the streets. They and the public will be satisfied if begging is controlled to small, tolerable levels, whatever may be done (or not done) about the underlying causes.

Public affirmation of shared basic values

On this view, governments need welfare services to demonstrate that they support principles and values widely cherished in the political community. To fail to look after seriously neglected or imperilled children, say, would seem inhumane, repellent and intolerable. In effect governments are forced to respond to public sentiment over certain issues, as for example when it became politically imperative to introduce tighter controls on handguns after the Dunblane school massacre. The support and realisation of shared basic social values is perhaps the closest of the arguments mentioned thus far to social workers' reasons for entering and supporting their profession.

To promote social solidarity

Welfare services may be seen as a way of promoting positive valuing and support by members of the community, one for another. On this view mutual obligations are not fully expressed or discharged either within the narrow confines of the morality of family and interpersonal relationships, or in the abstract rights and duties laid down in law, or the impersonal, instrumental transactions of the market place. Rather, it is a function of formal welfare to repair and build the fabric of social solidarity that enables people to express their altruistic care for each other. This is not merely a benefit to those in need, but an essential opportunity for every fully developed human life.

The classic exposition of this view comes from Titmuss (1970), who argued in *The Gift Relationship* that the free donation of blood for the benefit of an unknown stranger is a morally, as well as practically, preferable system to one based on market exchanges. Versions of the idea that social welfare services should promote social solidarity are found quite widely in social work and related fields such as community work. For example, early postwar community work in new housing estates incorporated the idea that neighbourliness and local organisation were both ends in themselves and means of achieving needed practical improvements in local facilities (Goetschius, 1969). More recently, the Barclay (1982) report advocated community social work as the method of choice for local personal social services. All these visions of welfare entail going beyond the spheres of strict obligation, whether defined in morality or in law. They aim to build social improvement on the need of human beings for mutual support, which also recognises that they benefit themselves by helping each other.

To promote the essential ends of justice

Welfare services address a range of conditions, misfortunes and disadvantages that do not fall randomly in society. For example, poverty and its concomitants such as unemployment, poor health, poor housing and poor family environments are not accidental occurrences in an otherwise well-functioning scheme of things. Many analysts and theoreticians argue that the well-being of those in more fortunate positions is obtained precisely at the expense of those in poverty, and therefore social improvement requires positive efforts at redistribution. Others think that while the uneven distribution of advantages may not necessarily represent any intentional exploitation of one group by another, nevertheless the current state of affairs is unacceptable because the pleasures of the rich cannot justify the pains of the poor. On either view there is an issue of social injustice: the operation of society is seen to entail unfair distributions of advantage and disadvantage; welfare services are one, necessary means of beginning to redress the injustice.

The justice argument for welfare services, like the efficiency argument, is easy to appreciate intuitively but much harder to demonstrate with concrete force in particular applications. Demonstrating injustice requires a clear conception of justice against which to compare an actual state of affairs. It also requires clear empirical evidence. Social justice, the most contested concept in all of social philosophy, will provide a rationale for welfare only if given extended development. The theme of justice is taken up again in Chapter 9.

As part of citizens' rights

The final argument for welfare is based on citizens' rights. This approach, which has enjoyed much renewed interest in the last few years, relies heavily on Marshall's analysis of citizenship (see Box 7.1).

Citizenship is a fruitful, and indeed indispensable, concept in welfare theory and policy. The citizenship argument for welfare has the merit, like the justice argument, of attracting support in principle from nearly all quarters of opinion; it also shares the weakness of the justice argument, that extended development is required before it can do useful work towards resolving the dilemmas of policy and professional ethics. It is discussed further in the next chapter.

BOX 7.1
Marshall on citizenship

In his famous essay *Citizenship and Social Class*, Marshall (1950) introduced the analysis of citizenship that has dominated later thinking on the subject. Marshall held that there were three overlapping categories of citizenship rights. *Civil rights* comprised liberty of the person, freedom of speech, thought and faith, the right to own property and conclude contracts, and the right to justice. *Political rights* comprised the right to participate in the exercise of political power as a member of a body vested with political authority or as an elector. *Social rights* comprised the whole range from the 'right to a modicum of economic welfare and security to the right to share to the full in the social heritage and to live the life of a civilised being according to standards prevailing in the society'. The latter lead to education and social services. Marshall argued that broadly speaking the three categories of rights had emerged as separate entities in, respectively, the eighteenth, nineteenth and twentieth centuries.

The idea of social rights has been extremely influential. Reformers have sought to implement a whole raft of social rights, such as rights to better pay and conditions at work, better health and education services, and more comprehensive and differentiated social welfare provisions. Philosophers argue about whether social rights really belong in the same category with traditional human rights. Ordinary citizens have become accustomed not only to welfare rights explicitly so called – particularly in the field of income maintenance – but also to a range of provisions from legal aid to subsidised medicines to free school meals. Recent critics have argued that the whole idea of social rights has become dangerously over-inflated, generating large and unrealistic expectations while at the same time losing sight of the correlative duties of citizens.

Further reading: Andrews, 1991; Barbalet, 1988; Marshall, 1950; Turner, 1993.

Beyond public and private

Recent debate about welfare has often been cast as a perennial struggle between the opposing forces of the state and the market (for example Loney *et al.*, 1991). The contest operates at several levels. If, along with varied social benefits, markets unfortunately generate diswelfares, in what areas and to what extent should public policy aim to

remediate them? Unemployment is a key example. Is it morally preferable or practically more effective to concentrate on maximising job
opportunities through macro-economic management, and meantime
provide only minimal financial shelter to those affected by unemployment? Or should policy treat unemployment and its consequences as
primarily a social question, since persistent unemployment
permanently corrodes the self-realisation and life chances of individuals affected by it, and undermines and corrupts the way of life of
entire communities? On the latter view, market-orientated intervention aimed merely at reducing global unemployment figures would
seem totally inadequate, even if it were conceded that the best cure for
the ills of unemployment is the chance of a decent job.

The state-versus-market issue arises in another guise where policy
does explicitly aims to correct market-generated diswelfares, but this
time as a question of means. For example, policy aims to ensure that
everyone reaches retirement age with entitlement to an adequate
pension. Different means of achieving this aim place more or less
reliance on market-orientated mechanisms. Postwar National
Insurance was a state-run scheme intended to guarantee adequate
pensions by compulsorily enrolling everyone; there could be no
market in state pensions, which individuals were not at liberty to
refuse to contribute to, buy or sell. Since that time governments have
progressively, and sometimes stealthily, moved towards privatising
pensions; now individuals will increasingly be obliged to make their
own arrangements in the market, albeit a market much regulated so
as to achieve the aims of public policy. Another examples is in the
provision of personal social services, where the turn of policy since
the 1989 White Paper on community care (DoH, 1989) has
emphasised private and voluntary sector provision, purchased in a
quasi-market in which government underwrites much of the direct
cost of services.

The state-versus-market debate is set to run and run. The end of
markets (once anticipated by Marxism) and the disappearance of the
state (envisaged by some communists and anarchists) now hardly
seem credible scenarios; we can be sure that, for the foreseeable
future, welfare will continue to be provided by an increasingly
complex mix of state and market systems. A key underlying assumption does, however, require to be challenged. The market model
assumes that within it individuals pursue their private interests.
Similarly, where the actors in a market are corporate bodies such as

private businesses or public enterprises, those bodies will act to maximise their respective interests. Welfare policy, however, is firmly in the domain of the public; it is presumed to be primarily the business of the state to pursue public welfare policies, even though it may on occasion adopt private sector mechanisms to do so. This dichotomising of the public and the private fails to give adequate recognition to what may be thought of as the third sphere of social life, which will be termed here the *communal*. The communal overlaps both the private and the public. Understanding it is essential to explaining the existence and justifying the purpose of much social welfare work, including in particular the characteristic goals and activities of social work.

The categorisation in liberal political thought between the private and the public is an artificial postulate; it is a presupposition based on a particular view of human nature and moral agency. Liberalism aims to provide a rational defence of individual freedom against the powers of tradition, obscurantism and tyranny; to do so involves thinking of human beings as bearers of independent moral status, capable of autonomous choices. Thus in the liberal view, morally independent persons are seen as freely choosing the constitution and laws within which they agree to frame those public areas of life essential to ensuring security and basic rights. Individuals' tastes, goals and life projects should be left out of the political account except insofar as necessary to prevent infringing the like freedom of others. This view of human nature and politics has, of course, been hugely persuasive and historically significant, and still forms the core of western political constitutions. It has paved the way for modern ideas of political freedom. However, the liberal distinction between private and public realms is an oversimplification. Human beings do not emerge into the world as autonomous moral agents capable, among other thing, of rationally choosing and pursuing their own ways of life within an ensured private sphere. Humans are formed within particular relationships that are conducted in particular environments and lived according to particular values; they learn in their upbringing to value certain places, communities and ways of life above others, and they naturally fear and mistrust strangers and threats of alien ways of life. The particularity of socialisation and social life is absolutely essential, since no one can learn moral agency or the value of life other than in the context of real, compromised choices and real, imperfect lives.

To the abstract liberal concept of autonomous moral agency must be added the particularity of community. No worthwhile human life is possible that does not both embody, and present opportunity for the pursuit of, specific and characteristic expressions of the social character of human living. Human beings and human communities are richly varied; within the world shrunk by modern communications and expanding knowledge of other societies both historical and contemporary, it is no longer tenable – if indeed it ever was – to claim that one particular religion, culture or way of life is necessarily morally preferable to others. Liberalism has taught that enforcing ways of living without the consent of the people is oppressive. Now, paradoxically, the ways of life within which liberalism was engendered are left, as it were, hanging in the air without the intellectual foundations upon which liberalism was built (Gray, 1993).

Because community is indispensable to every fulfilled life and every imaginable society, morals and politics must address community – the world of the communal – along with the sphere of individual rights and duties and the arena of public policies, laws and institutions. The communal is the space of social life that cannot be completely reduced either to the public or the private. This can be illustrated by thinking about the status of the Christian churches in the west. For many centuries, the churches enclosed the key arenas of communal life. They provided the focus for community celebrations such as thanksgiving for the harvest, and the means of collective psychic response to disasters. The churches provided the stage for rites of passage such as weddings and funerals, and were the source of moral teaching on the responsibilities of daily life. Religion defined the language of artistic and intellectual expression, and the churches were the forum of artistic exhibition and performance. Where communities shared a common form of religious expression, these and many other aspects of the communal were enacted relatively unproblematically through the activity of the church. However, where religious conflict erupted, the boundaries and content of the communal were disputed. In modern times these issues have been magnified by the disintegration of traditional religious adherence and practice, and by conflict between different and sometimes hostile traditions. It is no longer agreed what authority the churches should have. For example, some people believe, in the name of religious freedom and equality, that religiously segregated schools should be incorporated within the free state education system; others believe that this is socially divisive and undesirable for the general good of the community.

Defining the communal for modern, complex societies presents several theoretical challenges. What are to be its boundaries with the wholly private and the wholly public? What are the legitimate expectations of individuals upon the communal, and vice versa? How are we to deal with the irreducible plurality of the communal – the fact that no single conception of the communal can ever be incontrovertibly superior to others? One of the issues at the heart of this problem is both analogous and related to the question of how human nature constrains morality, and can be stated as follows. The object of moral and political theory is to promote human flourishing; what this precisely means depends upon one's view of human nature. Similarly, the content of the communal depends on one's view of human nature. Liberal theory has tackled the problem by postulating there can be bare minimum standards that all would accept – described as a 'thin' theory of human good – and building moral and political theory from this starting point (see Box 7.2). Against this communitarians have argued that no 'thin' theory provides an adequate description of, or prescription for, a fully human life, which must entail the particularity of community. The problem for the communitarian approach is to distinguish the good that is embedded in communal ways of life from the reprehensible that may also be represented as intrinsic to valued ways of life. For example, some cultures value forms of human mutilation and sacrifice. It is difficult to believe that these practices can be justified merely because they represent a form of cultural expression. Less extreme examples can be just as contentious: foxhunting and bullfighting are highly cherished in their respective communities, but regarded as barbaric by sections of the wider societies in which they are practised.

Liberalism, welfare and community

The standard arguments for state welfare are rooted in the liberal theory of the state. Although there is much debate about just how far the state should (and could) take on collective responsibilities for individuals' welfare, the core presumption of western welfare systems is that it is not the state's business to control or direct the central projects and values that individuals must choose for their own lives. Libertar-

---

BOX 7.2

Human nature and human good

What is the overarching goal or ultimate good that politics should try to defend and promote? The question is crucial, because the answer provides the benchmark against which different political theories and arrangements are to be assessed. Answering the question depends on our understanding of human nature.

Liberal theory assumes that human nature is very adaptable so there can be innumerable good ways of life; theory, therefore, should invoke only the minimum and universal requirements that would apply to every human being in every society. According to Rawls, there is a small set of primary goods, defined as the things it is rational to want since they are necessary for the framing and successful execution of a rational plan of life. The primary goods are political rights and liberties, opportunities and powers; income and wealth; and self-respect.

Gewirth (1978) argues that rational agency depends on certain primary goods, which can be classified as those guaranteeing political freedom and physical and mental well-being. Doyal and Gough (1991) proceed fairly similarly, arguing that the basic needs are for physical health and autonomy. Their theory of human need is particularly addressed to social policy.

Further reading: Doyal and Gough, 1991; Gewirth, 1978; Plant, 1991; Rawls, 1973.

---

ians take a strong line against state interference, conceding the need only for few and minimal interventions. Socialists go much further in prescribing the contours of social obligation and what should be permitted as a reasonable range of social conditions. Neither tendency (excepting some minority strong socialist ideologies), however, believes it is the job of state welfare to prescribe the wider aims of life as a whole. State welfare in liberal democracies relies on a thin, or fairly thin, theory of the social good, addressing itself primarily to the (partial) relief of severe poverty, the provision of basic education within mainstream assumptions, the repair of ill health and so on.

The liberal concept of freedom to pursue one's own mode of life protected by a thin theory of the good is a defining achievement of Enlightenment thought. For all its problems and shortcomings it is difficult to believe that many people would now choose to relinquish the concepts of human rights, individual dignity and equality before an impartial system of law. Even a sometime sceptic such as Gray, who rejects the intellectual coherence of liberalism, values the outcomes that it has (contingently) produced. By the same token, a thin theory of welfare cannot alone be satisfactory as the basis of a fulfilled life. It does not furnish the meaning, richness and depth that give individual lives their particular character and purpose. By rejecting substantive general prescriptions for the full and meaningful life, liberalism creates a void. It invites the individual to fill this void for him or herself. But the freedom to choose one's way of life is in large part illusory, because fulfilled human lives do not originate in isolation; the fulfilled life is social in character, woven out of the complex web of cooperation, support and affirmed, shared experience.

Liberal individualism requires, therefore, to be complemented by a theory of community. The argument here is pluralist in two senses. It holds that a monistic social theory – a theory that maintains that moral and political questions can ultimately be decided by reference to a single, overarching principle – is bound to be inadequate to answer the complexity of real social questions in real societies. This necessitates pluralism in the second sense: that there is, and must be, an irreducible range of differences in social values and ways of life. It will often be impossible to produce conclusive arguments showing the superiority of some choices over others. However, the pluralism advocated here is not infinitely elastic. It accepts the liberal argument that there are indeed some absolute minima of human welfare, derived from a thin theory of the good and expressed in the classic conceptions of basic rights and freedoms.

The essential features of the British welfare state were established in the context of war and its aftermath. Social solidarity and commitment to the national interest from all sections of society reached a high-water mark that has probably never since been recovered. The idea of national planning for welfare fitted well with the war experience and British political culture. Much has happened since that vitiates the assumptions of that time. Traditional religious practice as an affirmation of shared belief has declined dramatically. Peoples recently originated from other parts of the world now comprise substantial minorities with distinctive religions, cultures and values. The expectations of and about women have been revolutionised.

Minorities such as people with disabilities and people with different sexual orientation have achieved a degree of recognition that was hardly dreamt of even a generation or two ago. These and other changes have enormous implications for all of social welfare and social work in particular. Social work as the creation of welfare policy embodied, perhaps for the most part unconsciously, the assumptions that different sections of society and different communities would by and large follow similar ways of life informed by similar values. There was only relatively weak recognition of the particularities that differentiate communities and which ought, therefore, to distinguish social work practice.

Social welfare as an area of public policy – of which social work is a constituent part – has to be realised within, and by means of, specific, concrete conceptions of community and what is to be valued and pursued for the sake of the good life. But how is community to be pursued in the context of state welfare?

The state with its social welfare institutions is very different in nature and scale from the communities in which individuals' lives are rooted and expressed. The familiar welfare state makes few concessions to the diversity of the communities in which its policies are realised. Thus the law and administration of social insurance and measures for the relief of poverty are almost uniform across the British state; the *National* Health Service aims to provide constant standards of care irrespective of locality (but often fails to meet this objective). Other arms of the welfare state, especially education and the personal social services, are administered by local government which has some limited discretion, but only within the framework of national laws and strong central government regulation. This picture of relative uniformity in state services must be set against the diversity of contexts, traditions, cultures and tastes that distinguish communities. Communities based on shared residence in a given locality typically number no more than a few thousand. Communities based on other affinities may be much smaller, as for kinship, or much larger, as in loyalty to one's city (Willmott, 1989). Yet it is in the fine grain of communities that individuals find the locus of their essential daily routines, their important relationships, their daily work, their valued recreations, and the familiar detail of the home area. Insofar therefore as community depends on state welfare services, it will be badly served by national systems that expect and impose relatively high uniformity between different areas. National standardisation is unsympathetic to the localised variation upon which the fulfilled life actually depends.

The flourishing of real lives takes place in, and only in, communities. As an arm of state sponsored welfare, social work now has to develop in such a way that it reflects and draws from the character of the communities it should aim to serve. This means questioning assumptions that the practices adopted in one community of locality or interest would be appropriate for others. It does not, of course, mean accepting the expressed wishes of communities as the necessarily infallible guide, since communities sometimes express attitudes and values that flout basic rights rooted in liberal thin theory of the good. The consequence of recognising the communal as constitutive of social work would be a wider range of driving interests for the profession, and much more local variation in the specific character of practice. But more can yet be said to limit the scope of social work to sensible proportions; social work always needs to avoid pretending to possess such a broad agenda that it becomes indistinguishable from the whole of morals and politics. This is the theme of the next chapter.

8

The Ordinary Life and Welfare Citizenship

Social work: promoting the ordinary life

Social work aims to promote welfare; it shares this global purpose with the other arms of the liberal welfare state. A strength of the professional culture of social work is that it is highly committed to the indivisibility of welfare; it emphasis that for every individual, well-being in the areas of safety, health, housing, financial security, education, meaningful occupation, beneficial personal relationships and so forth cannot really be split apart. For example, social work with children in families recognises that they need not just some but all of physical care and safety, health care, adequate housing, sound and loving parenting, schooling, and opportunities for constructive challenge and productive social relationships outside the family. Social work recognises that safe, happy and productive lives are not easily made in communities marred by poverty, ill health, crime, deprivation and the other familiar ills that welfare tries to redress. Thus social work sometimes seems to purport to address nothing less than the whole of social life. The official definition of the British regulatory body for training reads: 'the purpose of social work is to enable children, adults, families, groups and communities to function, participate and develop in society' (CCETSW, 1996, p. 16).

This is plainly unsatisfactory. It is unspecific and too vast to be achievable by one service sector or profession alone, and risks making the occupation ridiculous. It does not enable consumers, policy-makers or the general public to choose with understanding when to use social work, nor does it enlighten them about what they might expect to gain by doing so. What is needed is a conception of social work which, while embodying the holistic view of human needs and human living to which social work is justly committed, is also specific enough to designate a reasonable area of operation.

It will be argued here that the core purpose of social work is to promote the realisation of ordinary life. The point of departure for social work intervention is a material discrepancy between normative standards and actual conditions of ordinary life. Workers and agencies seek to respond when the conditions and opportunities in which identified individuals are discovered, or find themselves, are thought to be incompatible with the ordinary standards of normal life as generally understood within a particular community. For example, there is a prima facie case for social work intervention where an infirm elderly person is unable to look after herself at home within commonly held, tolerable standards of safety and comfort; or where a child's wellbeing in the hands of his family is open to serious doubt. These are cases when the reasonable expectations of ordinary life are not being met.

It is worth underlining that in speaking here of the ordinary life, we are referring to *normative* standards – the standards held up on moral and political grounds as the proper goals – rather than the *actual* conditions prevailing in any particular time or place. By this definition, many people fail to reach the standard of the ordinary life and indeed in some communities hardly any one does. The ordinary life, as a normative conception, is not the same as the lives ordinarily lived – which may be may be much below what is desired.

The actual content of normative standards of ordinary life is, however, a deeply vexed question. The concept of social work as the realisation of ordinary life requires specific and concrete interpretations, which will frequently be contested. It was argued in the previous chapter that political liberalism, based on a thin theory of the good and a strong division between the public and private spheres, is insufficient to work out the purposes of the fulfilled life. The good life must also be defined by reference to the communal, the large area of social life that overlaps and interpenetrates the spheres of the private and the public. What is to count as the standard of ordinary life depends upon the communal, and as we have seen, the communal can no longer (if it ever could) be taken for granted.

Every specific conception of the ordinary life must therefore be open to revision as scientific knowledge, social standards and values change. Consequently, every type of social work is questionable in the long term. The history of social work provides ample illustration of this principle. A well-known example concerns the mothering of children. In the postwar years the influential research of Bowlby suggested that young children would be permanently damaged if deprived of the constant care of their mothers. Child care social work responded by aiming to prevent this separation wherever possible, and by trying to provide a close mother substitute in other cases. Later research by Rutter showed that Bowlby's conclusions were partly mistaken: it was constant mothering that was important, rather than the constant attention of the biological mother (Rutter, 1972). Social work responded by shifting the focus to the quality and constancy of care rather than the presence of the mother.

Once we go beyond the bare principles of liberalism in order to give specific interpretation, shape and substance to the aims of the good life, every substantive specification of the ordinary life can only be for today, and within a specific community. This makes setting out the requirements of the ordinary life hazardous. Nonetheless it is possible to give the idea a little more depth by setting out some prevailing ideas on the subject. A useful way of doing so is to consider the idea of normalisation, originally developed as a way of reformulating the aims of work with people with learning disabilities.

Normalisation theory, and the body of thinking about welfare and social values that has grown with and from it, suggests that the needs of individuals with disabilities might be classified under five headings (Booth, 1997; Braye and Preston-Shoot, 1995; Ramon, 1991). Indeed, what this represents is not so much a statement of the needs of people with disabilities as a statement of what *all* humans need, including incidentally people with disabilities. It contains, in prototype, a framework of minimum requirements for the good life. As with most lists of this kind, the requirements are not independent but interdependent.

- *Safety and psychological security:* Everyone needs physical care, security and safety. These must necessarily be provided within the context of healthy continuing intimate relationships, in families or substitutes for them.
- *Means of life:* Everyone needs access to the means of satisfying basic needs for food, shelter, income, health care, and so on. They should have appropriate independence in the choice of means.

- *Opportunity for creativity:* Everyone needs opportunities for education, rewarding work, personal growth, and the development and fulfilment of their creative potential.
- *Social participation and status:* Everyone needs recognition of their respected place in the community and the opportunity of fellowship. Everyone should be accorded moral status as a person and should have the opportunity to exercise and develop autonomy. They should not be excluded by unfairly discriminatory attitudes and practices.
- *Power and choice:* Everyone is entitled to exercise appropriate choice as regards their own circumstances, and participate in the wider political decisions of their community.

The ordinary life, by definition, attains the normative standards that are communally created. Departures from the standards of the ordinary life must attract concern or censure. The idea of social work as promoting the ordinary life proposes a general framework, within which the particular rationale and purposes of specific professional actions and programmes can be developed. Much of the business of social work is to repair the means of pursuing an ordinary life. The concerns of social work must indeed be broad, but obviously social workers cannot directly provide the means to meeting all life's needs should not pretend to do so. The special role of social work is to look right across the range of what is needed to fulfil an ordinary life, to correct deficiencies by procuring resources from elsewhere, and on occasion to create special new resources where the expectations of ordinary life cannot otherwise be met. The specialism of social work is the general conditions of the ordinary life.

Some issues and possible objections

Conservatism

Does defining social work in terms of the pursuit and support of prevailing social standards commit it to social conservatism? If the prevailing and accepted is to be given a privileged status, then any other ways of living will automatically be disfavoured by social work. This would be unjustifiable, since the inherent superiority of current values and ways of life should certainly not be assumed. The objection might be illustrated by reference to changing ideas about sexuality. Until quite recently homosexuality was widely thought of as either a sin or a mental illness; indeed, such views are still very common. In social work circles, however, these older views are now regarded as totally unacceptable and contrary to basic ideas of human rights. The codes of ethics of the British Association of Social Workers (1996) and the National Association of Social Workers (1996) prohibit discrimination on grounds of sexual orientation. If social work, the argument runs, allowed itself to be governed by conservative popular sentiment on this issue, it would remain bound to an obsolete, unscientific and morally unacceptable attitude.

To answer this objection we must return to the basis of community in liberal society. In the liberal polity the role of the state is limited to the protection of core rights and freedoms – those defined by a thin theory of the good. It was argued earlier that elaboration of the substantive goals and values that give individual lives their specific character and meaning lies in the sphere of the communal. Modern political communities based on the nation-state are large and inclusive, and contain within them many diverse communities of place and of interest; within them, most people belong to several more or less differentiated communities. The modern liberal state is inescapably pluralist; consensus over major questions of social values, morality and politics is often simply impossible.

Social work and other social interventions are inevitably geared to the standards and values of some community or other. The objects of the ordinary life are a matter for politics, in which the standards of one community have no prior or intrinsic authority over the standards of another. A social work committed to prevalent traditional standards would tend to conservatism, but it has no automatic superiority over a social work that would be considered radical in its chosen area of operation. It is just as possible for social work to be reformist as conservative. In the example just given, the morality of homosexuality must be treated as an open political question, to be resolved by a process of public debate. A radical position would question prevailing public sentiment. The error would be to assume that the issue is settled within the relevant communities when, in fact, it is not. Or, to take another example, if social workers in child care were to operate on the increasingly popular, but still minority view that parents should under no circumstances ever physically chastise their children, then their work would be reformist and not conservative in its intent.

Mundanity

The idea of social work as promoting the ordinary life might be felt to be lacking something in glamour. Defending the ordinary might seem the antithesis of exciting, whether for the practitioner or the client. Many outsiders, perhaps, imagine social work as worthy, but dull. This is a misconception. The usual general reason for social work intervention is that the identified or potential recipients of it are living in circumstances significantly below what is requisite for the ordinary life, from the pinched and narrow to the frankly appalling; or that they have entered ways of life so far unacceptable to ordinary society that they have to be restrained and if possible rehabilitated. The ordinary life is not a low standard of expectation: on the contrary, it is a high one, which all too many members of the community fail to, or are prevented from, attaining. Social workers, who must use large measures of worldly realism to help them retain a tolerable perspective on their daily tasks, often see their clients' attainment of some degree of relative normality in the context of ordinary life not as a trivial step but as a triumph. Workers and their agencies have to make daily judgements about which of the many potential calls on their time represent those cases so far below a standard of adequate, ordinary life that they demand a response, while other meritorious claims are left unheeded for lack of resources.

No one doubts that social work practice often does entail much repetitive effort in pursuit of rather mundane affairs: the everyday deficiencies of the public services; petty misdemeanours; commonplace kinds of personal difficulties and inconveniences; ordinary human failing and unwisdom; common disappointments. None of this detracts from the transcending importance of the life to the person who lives it. A person's affairs are uniquely and categorically important to that person. Within the welter of the mundane lies the absolute value of the individual's life. The uniqueness of every personal life transcends the often mundane circumstances in which it is played out. Thus, while each individual requires access to the means of ordinary life, the specific good that for them reposes in those means is indefinitely variable. For example, everyone requires (as part of the means of ordinary life) opportunities for mental enrichment through education and the arts; but for each individual, the ideal opportunities and the use they make of them will be different.

Relative injustice

The ordinary life is definable only in the context of community. In liberal democracies there exists a great number and diversity of communities, and their standards of the ordinary life differ. In more difficult cases this amounts to outright contradiction. For example, some ethnic and religious minorities have expectations about the respective rights and duties of men and women that are difficult to reconcile with the now standard presumption that women and men should have equal or even identical rights and duties. One approach to the issue of different standards is simply to say that different communities should be allowed and encouraged to foster their own standards; it is up to members of those communities to hold, and change, their standards as they see fit. There are several problems with this rather strong pluralism, however. In reality, individuals do not belong only to a single community. Communities overlap and interlock; individuals then perceive that different standards appear to be operating in different spheres. It becomes difficult to accept that a different standard, applied in a different place, is fair. For example, would it be right to expect, in one local area, that adults should be liable to contribute financially to the care of their dependent parents, while in a neighbouring area this was not required? Or could the requirement upon parents to maintain their children after separation or divorce be reasonably subject to different rules according to local ideas about family obligation? A sense of relative injustice in the treatment of individuals under essentially similar circumstances is very undermining of the sense of community as well as of practical public administration.

The British welfare state, predominantly centralist in character, has tended to allow only rather small variations between communities. Comparison with other advanced countries shows that there is certainly ample scope to permit much more variation within a general national framework. At bottom however this is an issue of how political institutions should function in a democracy. There have to be systems for arbitrating disagreements across the many intersecting communities that individuals find themselves involved in. At the same time it is necessary to question the basic presumption embedded in liberal political thought that the same standards of justice must apply across all communities and in all the respects. As Walzer (1983) has argued, there ought to be not sameness but difference. These and related issues are discussed in the next section.

Welfare citizenship

The aim of this chapter and the previous one has been to define the place of social work within the wider enterprise of welfare in liberal democracy. The freedoms and rights defended by liberal individualism comprise an essential core, but insufficiently substantiate the essentially social character of fulfilled lives. It is the contingencies of lives that give them their defining individuality; political theory cannot afford to neglect the means by which individualities are fostered and contingencies turned to good, and not bad, effect.

These issues can be reconceptualised in the idea of welfare citizenship. It will be argued that citizenship not only provides a vehicle for the rights and freedoms stipulated by liberal theory, but also offers a framework within which to accommodate the plurality and diversity of welfare practice necessary to the achievement of fulfilled ordinary lives.

Citizenship and community

Citizenship denotes membership of a political community, with concomitant rights and benefits, duties and burdens (Clark, 1996). It means some sort of compact of reciprocal obligation between the individual and the state, and between the citizen and other citizens – the community. It is obvious that this is a complicated bargain. In private relations between individuals, rights and duties are often complementary – Smith's duty to Jones is the obverse of Jones' rights over Smith. But citizenship is not based on straightforward reciprocal exchange. Take for example the state's undertaking (duty) to give its citizens protection against aggression. To make this possible, certain citizens may have an obligation enforced by law to serve in the armed forces. Despite this, protection for the individual is not in practice conditional on her agreeing to serve in the army. There are many grounds for legitimate exemption, such as age, physical incapacity, special value to the community of other work, or on the grounds that such duty would be unreasonably onerous in a given case, and even conscientious objection. Thus an individual's specific incapacity to contribute to some aspect of the state's work of discharging its duties to its citizens is not necessarily grounds for denying her the benefits of citizenship.

What are the obligations that a citizen must accept in order to qualify for the benefits of citizenship? A first expectation will be willingness to obey the law by, for example, paying taxes that go to fund the protections and amenities of citizenship. The archaic status of outlawry – effectively, non-citizenship – demonstrates the link between enjoying the protections of the rule of law and obeying the law. But limiting the obligations of citizenship to obeying the law would result in no more than a minimal, narrowly legalistic fulfilment of the role. There is also the difficulty that a citizen who disobeys a law on a matter of principle may perhaps be making a rather important contribution to the welfare of the community, as for example some political protesters.

Another approach is to postulate that the citizen's claim to aid and protection in the event of need or dependency rests on his implied willingness, had his luck been different, to contribute to meeting needs in the community. This is a model of indirect reciprocity in which the test of good citizenship seems to be the acceptance of some kind of voluntary undertaking to contribute to the common good according to one's abilities and personal choices. This is obviously a much weaker obligation than an explicit, legally sanctioned requirement to commit a specific personal resource. It would mean that the duties of the citizen would be to a very large extent the product of a series of contingencies such as age, gender, qualifications, class and so on; and this conclusion is difficult to reconcile with the traditional notion that citizens, by definition, should have equal standing in the community.

At this point the idea of citizen's rights is evidently in deep trouble. It appears to leave the fulfilment of rights at least partly dependent on the implied and untested altruism of others, and contingent on some deeply problematic boundary definitions. It defines only a flimsy and unpersuasive charter for the protection of rights, even if the satisfaction of citizens' rights is to be mediated by the institutions of the state rather than by direct transactions between citizens; ultimately the state is unlikely to be able to guarantee rights that are not supported by community opinion. This ambiguity of rights is matched by a corresponding ambiguity of the duties of citizenship. If the duties necessary to the fulfilment of social rights and the common good are merely voluntary, it is very difficult to see how enforcing action against citizens who seemed unwilling to contribute would be consistent with elementary justice. There is therefore a serious danger of highly anti-egalitarian outcomes.

The cause of this impasse is that there exist both active and passive conceptions of citizenship which, while seemingly contesting the same title, have entered the ring with rather different assumptions about human nature and projects for society. Oldfield (1990) identifies two rival conceptions of citizenship, the one associated with *liberal individualism* and the other with *civic republicanism*. Liberal individualism – the passive citizenship of rights – takes as its foundation the natural or human rights that inhere in persons. It treats individuals as self-determining, fully responsible moral agents. Action in the public realm is merely a matter for individual choice. This version of citizenship has dominated western thought since the seventeenth century. Oldfield suggests that it views citizenship as a *status*.

The opposing conception – the active citizenship of duty – arises from the classical tradition of civic republicanism. Here citizenship entails a 'shared responsibility for the identity and continuity of a particular political community' and public service is required, not optional; civic republicanism does not tolerate the abdication from politics which liberal individualism condones. Citizenship is seen as a *practice*. Moreover civic republicanism recognises that humans will not choose the path of civic duty unless they are constantly educated and re-educated into it; thus citizenship is an 'unnatural practice'.

Recent criticism of the postwar British welfare state has highlighted the culture of dependency it was said to create. As Ignatieff has persuasively put it:

> The ideal of citizenship current in post-war Britain gave special emphasis to the passive mode: equal entitlement to family allowance, free health care, the dole and the old age pension. (Ignatieff, 1989)

The climate for welfare has changed. Once the province of right-wing libertarians who saw little virtue in any state welfare system, discontent with the current state of welfare is now found at most points of the political spectrum. The whole idea of citizenship as a focus of political rights has been revived in both academic and popular debate (see Box 8.1).

BOX 8.1

The citizenship debate

After interest in Marshall's analysis (see Box 7.1) ebbed, the theory of citizenship was neglected until the later 1980s when it re-emerged rather suddenly as a focus of political debate – perhaps in reaction to the libertarian individualism which had been winning much of the political argument of the time. Charter 88, a pressure group, argued that civil rights in Britain needed a proper constitutional foundation. At around the same time the Speaker's Commission on Citizenship investigated the need to educate children for citizenship. Politicians seized on the idea as a vehicle for a wide range of mooted reforms. From 1987 the Conservative Home Secretary, Douglas Hurd, advocated the idea of 'active citizenship', stressing social responsibility. Paddy Ashdown, leader of the Liberal Democrats, perhaps sensing a bid to steal his colours, responded in 1989 with a call for a 'citizens' Britain' (Ashdown, 1989). Not long afterwards John Major, the Conservative Prime Minister, launched the Citizen's Charter (Great Britain, The Prime Minister, 1991) as a statement of rights, followed by a train of subsidiary charters relating to most of the public services. Various proposals were aired for forms of citizens' service for young people, usually voluntary but in some versions having at least an implicit element of coercion (for example Commission on Social Justice, 1994, pp. 361ff.).

Academics commented on the sudden revival of citizenship (Heater, 1991; Taylor, 1989, 1992) and began to redevelop its theory from the perspective of several different disciplines including legal and constitutional theory (for example Blackburn, 1993; Oliver and Heater, 1994), sociology (for example Turner, 1990, 1993), politics (for example Ignatieff, 1989; King and Waldron, 1988; Oldfield, 1990b; Oliver, 1991) and social policy (for example Andrews, 1991; Barbalet, 1988; Hill, 1994; Parry, 1990; Plant and Barry, 1990). The idea of citizenship has returned to the mainstream.

What does 'welfare citizenship' represent? There is no convincing case against the social rights of citizenship, as articulated by Marshall and broadly accepted by most ordinary members of society, writers and politicians. Only a tiny minority would seem to favour the abolition of education, health and other forms of state-sponsored welfare. What is now at issue is the form and content of state welfare: what should, and should not, count as a proper charge upon public responsibility; what should be the division between welfare provision directly provided or managed by the state, and provision that individuals are induced or compelled, by instruments of policy, into making for themselves; what should be the levels of deprivation permitted before welfare policy intervenes.

The point of framing the debate about welfare within the renewed discourse of citizenship is this. Welfare is no longer to be understood just as a passive entitlement of citizenship, but also as an active duty of citizenship. The duties of citizenship include, of course, paying one's taxes to finance welfare, but this minimal obligation does not discharge one's broad duties. Such duties will include contributions of time, concern and interest, and perhaps also of voluntary financial contributions. Welfare citizenship must be a citizenship of *obligation* as well as a citizenship of *entitlement*.

Social work, understood as the promotion of opportunities for the ordinary life, clearly requires the active conception of welfare citizenship. Ordinary lives are necessarily created and pursued within the defining context of the communities to which individuals belong. Within these communities, welfare officials can only have an occasional and relatively small part to play; a community or state dominated by welfare officials, even making the far-fetched assumption that it could be feasible, would represent an intolerable imposition on freedom. The role of social workers will naturally include direct service to those in immediate need, but it must also essentially include stimulating and shaping the active welfare citizenship of members of the relevant communities.

Institutions and welfare citizenship

On the whole, British social work has assumed that the state sector would play the leading role in shaping and providing social work services, just as it did in the other areas of the postwar welfare state. The philosophies of the Kilbrandon (1964) and Seebohm (1968) reports of the 1960s, which led to the foundation of the social work services in substantially their modern form, envisaged large organisations with far-reaching powers and duties under the direct authority and control of central and local government. While a place was left for community initiative, it was not expected or intended that *essential* services would be left to the vagaries of the somewhat anarchic voluntary sector; it was the local authorities that were made clearly responsible for implementing the key legislation in child care and protection, the care of the aged, and other sectors of social work activity. The main exception was the probation service in England, which was placed under even closer state control in central, not local, government.

The assumption of state dominance in social work services, just as in welfare more generally, led to a passive mentality of entitlement becoming the norm. Citizens were encouraged by professionals to think of what services they might expect from social work; they were rarely given to understand that social work might also lay obligations on them. On the whole, social work professionals willingly condoned this interpretation of their role; it gave them status and influence, and the ever-increasing range of statutory responsibilities bolstered the annual case for increasing the budget.

This assumption of state dominance is overdue for reappraisal; indeed it is already in recession. The first question is one of basic political principle: to what extent *ought* social work to be a directly run state service; in what respects would it be preferable to leave more of it to the initiative of private and voluntary organisations? That there is nothing inevitable about the British pattern of governmental dominance of social work service provision is readily illustrated by comparison with other western countries. A particularly striking example is Germany. Social policy in Germany is predicated on the principle of *subsidiarity*, which in essence requires that the higher, central levels of the state should always leave governance to the lower, local levels unless compelling reasons to the contrary exist. In the light of this principle, and from other historical reasons, social work services are run by a complex network of voluntary organisations and government bodies in which the voluntary sector has the greatest weight, while funding mostly derives from taxation. In striking contrast to the monolithic local government services found in Britain, social work is delivered by some 62,000 voluntary organisations grouped into six federations (Lorenz, 1994).

Although the state sector has dominated British social work, a number of contrasting models illustrate what has been left out of the dominant account. Broadly speaking, the alternatives propose either different methods of structuring and funding social work services, or different models and methods of face-to-face practice. The two aspects are often linked, since a particular mode of organisation may be held to support a particular method of practice. A good example is the concept of community social work advanced in the Barclay (1982) report, and especially the strong version in the minority report of Hadley (Brown *et al.*, 1982) and his associates. Community social work recognises that most social care is provided not by the formal systems of statutory and voluntary agencies, or in the commercial market, but within the ordinary help that family members give each other. Therefore, it is argued, formal social services must work in understanding and partnership with the informal sector. This requires different models of service organisation, especially a much stronger community presence, and more constructive attitudes by professionals towards the ordinary helping processes in the community.

Social expectations of welfare are too now large to be accommodated within the narrow liberal rights provided for in the institutions of liberal democracies. The restricted public sphere sanctioned by liberalism will increasingly fall short of meeting the standards of living demanded by the public. As standards rise, expectations laid upon the public sector do not moderate, but rise even faster. The underlying reason for the crisis of the welfare state is not rising expenditure, but a growing gap between the expectations of citizens and what public expenditure is able to procure. The social rights of citizenship can not be put back in the box, even if (improbably) that were thought desirable. To avoid this increasing gap between what citizens legitimately desire and what public institutions are able to deliver, the entailments of citizenship need to be rethought.

The implication for social work is that primary reliance on state-sponsored services for ensuring the conditions of the ordinary life will become increasingly obsolete. In reality of course, state services have only ever had a minority role; but in the perceptions of professionals and much of the general public, the publicly sponsored social work services have been expected to carry the crucial role for those individuals drawn into their net. This expectation needs to be replaced by the understanding that while social welfare is to a limited extent a public responsibility, it belongs primarily to the spheres of the private and the communal. There is no basis for an overriding political principle that social work should be primarily concerned with the delivery of welfare services by state-sponsored professionals to a rather small minority of identified needy individuals. But, contrariwise, citizens' participation in social work should not be limited to being a recipient; social welfare is a communal and citizenly responsibility.

9

Four Stocks of Ethical Practice

In earlier chapters the aim was to dissect and display the aspirations and practices conventionally wrapped up as social work values and exhibited as codes of ethics. It was shown that social work ethics are readily identified with the major traditions of western social thought. It was further argued that the conventional ethics of social work does not adequately answer key problems arising from moral and cultural pluralism, conflicts of multiple accountability, and the ambiguity of social work expertise. Social work raises not only moral issues but also questions of political obligation, legitimacy, and the rights and duties of the citizen.

The course of the argument was analytic: to map and explain central assumptions, trace their origins and consider their validity. Chapters 7 and 8 considered the arguments for public welfare and proposed that within welfare, the purpose of social work is to promote opportunities for the fulfilment of ordinary life within particular communities.

This chapter will proceed with a synthesis. It will propose and amplify a set of definitive principles for ethically sound social work. The principles will be spoken of as *stocks* of ethical practice. The metaphor alludes to the basic meaning of a 'stock' as a tree-trunk or stem, and thence figuratively as a source, progenitor or line of descent. A stock is organic, constantly changing and renewing itself as it interacts with its environment. A stock is also a supporting structure, and a fund or store for drawing on and supporting work in progress. The stocks of ethical practice are to be understood not only as ultimate goals that practice should aspire to realise, but also as antecedent sources in that practice should equally proceed from them as strive for them, and continuing guidelines by which we should orientate ourselves on a day-to-day basis. The stocks mark points of origin, intended destinations, and the way in between.

The argument of this chapter is that ethical practice in social work should both abide by and aim to develop the four stocks of *respect, justice, citizenship* and *discipline.* Of these, respect and citizenship have already been explored at some length in earlier chapters; the discussion here will move quickly to a conclusion. The broad and complex subject of justice will require a fuller treatment. The idea of professional discipline has been foreshadowed in the earlier critiques of professional knowledge, but is the least developed idea in social work and will require a full discussion.

Respect

Respect for persons has long been acknowledged as a key precept in the social work ethics literature (Banks, 1995; Butrym, 1976; CCETSW, 1976; Clark with Asquith, 1985; Downie and Telfer, 1980; Horne, 1987; Hugman and Smith, 1995; Plant, 1970), and was identified in Chapter 4 as one of the rules of social work ethics. It is a name for the intuitive common sense and universal teaching of morality that our dealings with our fellows should appreciate and give practical recognition to their interests, rights and feelings. Respect appeals immediately to ordinary beliefs about fair treatment. It may well convey a subtle, subliminal allusion to the religious attitude of deference to godly power. In some versions, respect also captures the idea of compassionate caring for human needs and vulnerabilities. Some writers argue that the principle of respect should be understood as the cornerstone of all morality.

The problem with any foundational principle of morality is that it may beg the question of moral action more than it helps to solve it. If respect is to serve as a defining principle of ethics it needs both amplification and justification: otherwise the argument becomes circular along the lines of 'moral conduct requires following the precept of respect for persons, because respect for persons is the foundation of morality'. The principle of respect, then, is intuitively attractive, and it may serve as a convenient abbreviation; but it will not justify action if it is posited as *self-evidently* true. The abbreviation needs to be expanded, and grounds for the principle need to be explored and not merely assumed.

Kantian ethics (summarised in Chapter 5) requires respect for people because they have the rational capacity to make decisions about moral right and wrong; to fail to acknowledge the rationality of the other person is to contradict one's own rationality. The Kantian perspective teaches that respect is obligatory because of the special, morally sensitive character of human rationality and the unique capacity of human beings to make *morally* significant decisions. On these grounds the principle of respect means that we should credit the authenticity of everyone's wishes and actions. If a person chooses a peculiar or aberrant course of action, we should assume, unless she has been externally deceived, that the choice was made with sound understanding of the moral consequences; if a person chooses to transgress against the respect due to others, we should assume that he understands and accepts the proper punishment. These ideas are often expressed in the notion of *autonomy,* or self-rule. Everyone should be free to live their own lives by their own decisions, at least insofar as these do not impinge on the like freedoms of others.

The Kantian argument expresses the highest moral aspirations of the intellect, but it is arguably centred on what is really a special, ideal case: the fully competent individual endowed with high abstract moral intelligence and the relative luxury of the opportunity to exercise it. It is obvious that many human beings do not have such an optimally developed capacity for making moral choices. Some are too young or immature; some have mental impairments resulting from injury or disease; some may be considered temporarily or permanently bereft of the capacity for rational thought. Many other individuals are forced to live under terrible conditions of deprivation, brutality or oppression; the practical scope of moral choice available to them is often much less than their status as intelligent beings presumably merits. The principle of respect will not serve as a foundation if it can do no useful work in relation to the very large numbers of individuals whose rationality is open to question or whose opportunity for making moral choices is constrained by brutalising circumstances. Included among both groups, of course, are many users of the helping professions.

The Kantian idea of respect works as the foundation for moral theory by specifying what it is that should be protected and enhanced above all else, namely the freedom of the rational will. A contrasting moral theory can be built, but on an analogous form, by substituting some other end. In this way a different version of the principle of respect can be derived from utilitarian premisses.

Whereas Kantianism frames morality within the highest capacity of
the human intellect, classical utilitarianism may be said to frame
morality within the lowest defining attribute of all sentient creatures,
the capacity for pleasure and pain. Utilitarianism proposes that
morality is to be judged by assessing the balance of pleasure over
pain. Respect can thus be stood on its head: what is to be respected is
not rationality but merely the capacity to feel. Respectful action is
that which produces the best outcome in terms of pleasure and pain.
This comes close in its outcomes to an ethic of reverence for life
itself, found in several systems of traditional and religious thought,
although the grounds may differ.

Both versions of respect sketched here are based on extreme
postulates: the highest capacity for moral action on the one hand, and
the lowest capacity for sensation on the other. In the real world, moral
choices have to be made by and among subjects who do not conform
to either ideal type, but have a combination of attributes and fall
somewhere in the middle. It is therefore unsafe to base a principle of
respect exclusively on either rationality or sentience; rationality and
sentience are both indispensable considerations. To address the
complexity of moral statuses that human beings are able to enact, and
the range of circumstances in which they find themselves, the
principle of respect will have to be a combination principle:
committed to recognising both to the freedom of the rational will and
the existential status of sentient but partly non-rational creatures.

The combination principle of respect is open to the same
objections as all pluralistic theories, that they involve comparing
incommensurables. The radical objection holds that respect based on
rationality and respect based on sentience invoke logically different
orders that simply cannot be weighed together in the same scale; any
attempt to do so is bound to be meaningless. The pragmatic
objection holds that even if in principle it might be conceded that a
common scale could be found, there is really no practically agreed
measure that will find common agreement. The response to these
charges is the common defence of pluralism suggested in Chapter 5:
that pluralism, for all its theoretical difficulties, is not demonstrably
worse than monistic theories, because monistic theories require
single-minded commitment to a single principle and the grounds for
establishing a single principle are controversial and insecure. Since
under unavoidable uncertainty we cannot have faith in any monism,
pluralism remains the better option.

In discussions of ethics, and especially professional ethics, respect is often closely linked to autonomy. Beauchamp and Childress (1989) posit *respect for autonomy* as one of their four foundation principles of medical ethics. Wilmot (1997) discusses autonomy as a key concept in community care. Generally within the social work literature, the concept of self-determination serves as a surrogate for autonomy. Self-determination is seen as either a corollary of, or a close second to, the principle of respect (see, in addition to references on respect given earlier, Ejaz, 1991; McDermott, 1975; Reamer, 1990; Rothman, 1989; Spicker, 1990). The common theme is the value of clients making their own choices about care and treatment, frequently invoking broadly Kantian grounds for respecting clients' rationality. The hybrid principle of respect suggested here is, however, broader than autonomy. It requires on the one hand that individuals should be enabled to make their own decisions as much as possible, but on the other that this should not be an overriding principle; the utilitarian perspective may require respect to be exercised by constraining choice, in order to get the best outcome on balance.

Justice

Justice is the acknowledged bedrock of right dealing between the many groups and interests that comprise society. In his primer on the subject Campbell (1988, p. 7) observes that 'justice is held to be the central and commanding concept of current mainstream normative political philosophy'. Justice plays a similar theoretical role to the principle of respect. As respect is said to be the key to right interpersonal relations, justice is held up as the key to right action for the public sphere and its institutions.

The necessity of justice is axiomatic, but the concept of justice is complex and multifaceted, and the import or practical consequence of justice is open to various interpretations. We shall begin by identifying five principal intuitions that animate the ideal of justice. These intuitions or primitive notions of justice can be thought of as representing the natural response to occasions of injustice; they embody the ordinary reaction to a range of ways in which it is possible to be wronged, cheated or duped.

Five primitives of justice

Justice as due process

Justice requires that decisions affecting people's interests should be taken according to rules and procedures that carry acknowledged authority and standing. When parties are in dispute, they need recourse to agreed methods of resolving the issue, and to office-bearers who have the appropriate responsibility. In order to avoid any suggestion of unfairness – the antithesis of justice – it is essential that those who have the responsibility for adjudicating disputes should have no stake in the interests of the disputants; and it is highly desirable, if not always achievable in practice, that the framework of rules should be in place before a specific issue has to be decided. Disinterested adjudication and independent rules are means of avoiding bias or favouritism, and ensuring that like cases are treated similarly.

These general principles are embodied in the legal requirement of due process, which demands that the proper rules of procedure should be followed (and be seen to be followed) if decisions are to count as legally sound. For example, the statements of persons arrested on suspicion of committing an offence can be invalidated as evidence if the individual has not received the proper formal caution. Because due process is seen to be essential to just outcomes it also informs decision-making outside the usual reach of the law. In sports for example, referees and umpires must follow the proper rules even if, on occasion, the rules seem to stretch ordinary notions of fairness and common sense; if the prescribed process is not correctly followed, the substantive decision is invalidated even if it might appear to be reasonable by some other criterion.

Justice based on desert

The second notion of justice is based on desert. An individual's attributes, actions, or failures to act have moral significance. We say that, out of justice, a brave and selfless soldier (morally) deserves a medal, that a hard worker deserves recognition and extra pay, that a leading scientist deserves a prize, that a significant and innovative artist deserves the opportunity to exhibit or publish his work. We accept that a lazy or dishonest employee deserves to be dismissed, that a deceitful person deserves not to be trusted, that a cheat deserves to be shamed and penalised, that a criminal deserves to be punished. Heroism and villainy are eternal themes of myth, art and morality.

Justice requires rewarding or punishing people according to desert. This means that individuals of particular merit should have preferential access to certain resources and positions. For example, access to jobs is normally on the basis of qualifications and skill. The distribution of honours and other non-material rewards is on the basis of excellence in the relevant attainment. The idea that wrongdoers should get what they deserve is practically universal.

Justice as human rights

The third notion of justice springs from the idea that individuals have certain fundamental rights or entitlements; abridging these rights constitutes an affront to justice. This is most easily appreciated in relation to paramount human rights including the rights to life, personal liberty and freedom of speech. It is difficult to disagree that their denial, for example by arbitrary imprisonment, constitutes an injustice. This conception of justice is strengthened by the close link that can be forged with the idea of respect for the person; injustice is the inevitable outcome of disrespectful treatment. A leading contemporary exponent of justice as rights is Ronald Dworkin. The key feature of Dworkin's theory is *equality of concern and respect*, a 'right [all men and women] possess not by virtue of birth or characteristic or merit or excellence but simply as human beings with the capacity to make plans and give justice' (Dworkin, 1977, p. 179; see also presentations of Dworkin's theory in Campbell, 1988; Kymlicka, 1990; Plant, 1991).

The idea of human rights has been very important historically and remains so politically, but presents several difficulties. It is difficult to ground rights solely on the concept of respect because it is less than clear how the apparently reasonable, but competing rights claims of individuals can be reconciled without some additional independent principle of decision making. Moreover, the content of human rights turns out to be forever disputable and inconclusive. There simply is not sufficient agreement about basic rights, and the more the list is extended, the less realistic it seems. This can be illustrated by attitudes to the possession of firearms. Most advanced countries permit individuals to own and use guns privately only in very restricted circumstances. In the USA however, a substantial number of citizens believe that there is a fundamental right to own and carry guns freely. In the end it is unsatisfactory to base justice itself on definitions of rights that remain controversial.

Justice as fair shares

The fourth notion incorporated within the idea of justice is about the equity or fairness of any person's treatment in comparison with others. It addresses the undoubted fact that goods and resources are usually in limited supply in relation to the number of potential consumers and beneficiaries. Since not everyone can have as much of everything as they might want, justice demands a way of dividing things up that ideally leaves everyone satisfied as to its political fairness even if, under extreme circumstances, basic needs might still not be well satisfied. Under conditions of water shortage, common-sense justice requires that water for purposes essential to daily life, such as cooking and drinking, should take priority over non-essential purposes such as lavish baths or ornamental gardens. Under conditions of extreme scarcity where survival is threatened, justice requires some equitable way of distributing the little water that is left.

The idea of fairness is undeniable, but there is much dispute about what, precisely, should constitute fairness. The simplest possible answer might be that everyone should receive equal shares of whatever commodities, such as water, are in limited supply. However, the presumption that fairness requires exact equality is does not answer to ordinary experience, which shows that needs are unevenly distributed. There can be little expectation that an initial, even distribution would remain workable in the long term. Moreover, justice based on strict equality would surely conflict with the other faces of justice. The problem then is to work out what uneven distributions will be fairest: and this is the question at the heart of theories of justice and more specifically, it is the focus of *social* justice.

Social justice thus hinges on the concept of needs: we say that justice demands that needs should be equitably satisfied, and we deem some kinds of unmet need an insult to justice. For example, most people think it would be highly unjust to deny victims of a road accident emergency medical care unless they could produce evidence of ability to pay for it. But while the notion of basic human needs seems quite intuitive, it is virtually impossible to define needs in a way that everyone agrees with (Doyal and Gough, 1991). At issue are the nature of human beings and the right mode of human existence. In traditional societies there was often consensus on these questions. In modern times science continually revolutionises our thinking about the human animal at the same time as prosperity offers incredible choices to a fortunate minority. In the face of such world-changing developments some writers conclude that it is futile to search for any definitive theory of human nature and human need. Others, however, remain convinced that whatever the difficulties, a theory of justice supported by a theory of need is indispensable to decent social institutions.

The leading theoretical stratagem for building a theory of social justice is the device of a social contract. Social contract theory is based on a thought experiment: it considers what rules and institutions for the regulation of social life free and rational persons would contrive in a situation where they could devise the rules before committing themselves to joining. The most famous and influential modern version of social contract theory is due to Rawls (1973). As we saw in Chapter 7, Rawls develops a 'thin', or minimalist, theory of primary goods essential to truly human life under any circumstances. In Rawls' scheme, the parties to the social contract confer behind a 'veil of ignorance' so that no one knows in advance whether he will be well or badly endowed by nature and circumstance. Rawls proceeds to argue that the parties to the social contract would rationally agree to two principles of justice:

1. equality in the provision of basic goods
2. inequality in other respects is just if the effect is to increase the welfare of everyone and especially the least well off in society.

Justice as liberation

A fifth idea of justice grows out of the belief that there is something radically wrong with conventional ways of apprehending human nature and capacity. Injustice results from faulty ideology, which incorrectly treats as natural fact what is really a constraint imposed by human error. Perhaps the clearest contemporary example is feminism. In its many forms feminism argues that women regularly receive unfair treatment compared with men – although the facts of this disadvantageous treatment may not always be agreed, the reasons for it may be disputed, and its existence may be denied and dissembled by men who wish to retain their power and advantages. Disadvantageous treatment for women is rooted in erroneous beliefs about the respective capacities of women and men and in attitudes that demean women, their needs, ways of thinking, values and priorities. Unfair treatment and discriminatory attitudes are congealed in widespread social practices and institutions whose reason for existence is the preservation of male domination. The object of feminism is liberation for women, and for men also affected by the negative consequences of sexism.

Other liberationist ideologies share a similar project of emancipating humanity from obsolete views of human nature and capacity; their logical structure is similar to the logic of feminism. Anti-racism substitutes race for gender in the terms of the argument outlined earlier. Advocates of the rights of homosexuals argue against prejudices over sexuality and sexual orientation, and the unjust treatment that some individuals consequently experience. Advocates of the interests of people with mental or physical disabilities argue that what is needed is equal status and entitlements in the face of social attitudes that tend to disparage their interests and deny their rights.

Developing justice

Modern physicists dream of a grand unified 'Theory of Everything' that would unite in one comprehensive theoretical system all the known fundamental laws of physics. Justice occupies a similar place in moral and political theory and is probably further from realisation than its counterpart in physics. A full theory of justice would incorporate at least the five primitive notions. It would offer solutions to the content and justification of rights, the problem of defining equity, the estimation of merit and the determination of desert. The radical aspect of justice challenges conventional ways of theorising social issues as well as the legitimacy of the existing social order. It is therefore no surprise that, as Beauchamp and Childress (1989, p. 256) say in their book on medical ethics: 'It has proved an intractable problem to supply a single, unified theory of justice that brings together our diverse views.'

The pursuit of a grand theory of justice, like the conquest of space, may be a magnificent and daunting prospect but practical ethics cannot wait for it to be concluded. Discussing the questions of abortion and euthanasia, Dworkin (1993, p. 29) contrasts two methods of philosophising about practical issues. In the first – 'from the outside in', or from the general to the particular – general ethical theories are first developed and from these a selection is made to deal with particular issues. In the second – 'from the inside out', or from the particular practical question to the wider theoretical issue – theories are 'bespoke' or 'homemade' for the occasion. Dworkin chooses the latter method for the discussion of abortion and euthanasia. The approach here will follow Dworkin's example and seek to develop a 'homemade' theory of justice serviceable as a stock of practice ethics of social work. It will be built around five themes that recall and explore further the five primitives of justice already mentioned. In the process we shall draw on established theories.

The defence of procedure

It was shown in Chapter 6 that social work is comprehensively interlocked with the institutions and practices of law. The law requires that individuals should be treated according to rigorously applied rules of procedure, such as those pertaining to the conduct of criminal investigations and trials. Similarly, there are legal rules for private contracts such as those relating to the purchase of goods or services; and there are rules governing the conduct of public administration, for example the spending decisions of local authorities. Contravening the decision-making rules often leads to the substantive decision being invalidated, even if on other grounds it might have been thought fair and reasonable.

The primitive notion of due process defends the existence and operation of rules of procedure. We expect that decisions will be made by the rules; this is normally a requirement of justice. We also require, however, that the rules themselves shall be just, since clearly the diligent execution of the correct formal procedure is not in itself a guarantee that the outcome will be just in the wider senses. Legal and quasi-legal procedures of the kind that dominate service bureaucracies are valuable insofar as they assure the regular and consistent application of authoritative principles and precepts. They help to procure similar treatment of similar cases, and tend to promote fairness between different categories of users who nevertheless will be in competition against each other for the allocation of scarce resources.

Rules of procedure and decision-making, then, are indispensable, but they also present a threat to justice. First, the application of rules tends to mask the individuality of users and the particularity of cases. Service users often complain that they feel they are being treated as impersonal units in a mechanistic process; the user is fitted to the service, not the other way about. Procedures are dangerous when they desensitise those who operate them to relevant individual differences. Second, procedures are inflexible. They embody a series of rules and assumptions that may not always match well with the characteristics of some of the cases that are treated under them. That is why the administration of justice requires the exercise of discretion; judges are empowered to vary the application of rules according to the circumstances of the case. So, for example, the actual punishment for killing can vary from immediate release to incarceration for the whole of life. The discretionary powers of social workers are, however, much more obscure. Third, procedures are very prone to take the place of analysis and reflection on the circumstances of individual cases. Following the procedure is apt to become the goal in itself, displacing and obscuring the broader principle that originally informed its creation. Officials who may have performed their role inadequately can then claim in their defence that since they correctly followed the proper procedure they should be exonerated of any blame, because they were merely the agents employed to carry out procedures of which they were not the authors.

Failures of service delivery or client protection routinely prompt a call for better and clearer procedures, or sometimes simply the better following of procedures already laid down. The unmistakable response is the ever-growing manuals of administration generated in all service bureaucracies of any size. Inevitably, the larger and more complex the systems of rules and procedures become, the harder it is for even the most conscientious employee to follow them diligently. The rules become too numerous to remember, and the more there are of them, the more likely it is that some will conflict with others. The wider sense of justice should warn us that the usefulness and just necessity of procedures will sometimes lead to substantive outcomes contrary to broader principles of justice. Justice entails, but is not satisfied by, due process; the rule of procedure should not be relied upon to do all the work of justice. In the following paragraphs we shall see what else justice requires.

Deserving clients

According to the second primitive, justice requires giving people what they deserve. For welfare professionals this means making judgements about what clients deserve to get or what treatment their case merits. This is partly about fair shares where rationing is necessary, an issue to be discussed further later. Aside from that, implementing welfare inevitably entails what is, in the end, a moral evaluation of the client. Like all members of society, professionals possess moral intelligence and are sensitive to the moral character of different needs, statuses and behaviours. They cannot extinguish their ordinary moral insight or avoid rating some categories and some individuals as more morally deserving of help than others.

There is a parallel for welfare professionals with the position of medical professionals. Doctors have to decide, for example, which patients with heart or kidney disease are to be offered a transplant. This is partly a technical matter about the suitability of the therapy for any given case. It is partly a question of resource allocation, since transplants are expensive and organs in short supply. But there are also issues of moral character. Is a patient of advanced age to be given lower priority for a kidney than a younger patient because his age makes him morally less deserving? Should a patient whose heart disease came from smoking be denied a transplant on the grounds that the condition was recklessly self-inflicted?

Social work grew partly out of the Poor Law, from which in its early days it inherited a strong concern to distinguish between the 'deserving' and 'undeserving' poor. The deserving poor were judged to be victims of misfortune, and merited assistance; the undeserving were judged to be morally irresponsible, and merited punishment and coercion to mend their ways. Nowadays this distinction would be regarded as inaccurate and prejudicial, but it is easy to observe the faults of our predecessors through the lens of history. Contemporary practice provides unlimited examples of judgements of moral character that might be equally open to challenge. For example, in assessing elderly people for domiciliary services it is often found that men are more likely to receive assistance with meals than women with similar degrees of incapacity, because cooking has traditionally been regarded as unbefitting to men. Or again, members of ethnic minorities have complained that they receive less help with their aged relatives from social services than the white community because of a judgement that prevailing traditions of family support render official help less relevant.

Having to make moral evaluations of clients is obviously fraught with the danger of injustice. The literature of counselling and traditional casework recognises this very clearly. Discussing the 'non-judgmental attitude' as one of the key principles of the casework relationship, Biestek attempts to maintain a distinction between finding guilt or innocence in the *client* and being indifferent to objective *standards* of right and wrong. The caseworker should refrain from making judgements of the person, which will be 'irrelevant, unmerciful and hazardous' (Biestek, 1961, p. 91). This is, however, a highly idealised position. It assumes that the counsellor is able to detach himself from any evaluation of the client's conduct, whether his own or that represented in the institutions and practices of society. That may be approximately possible where counselling is voluntarily undertaken on a private contractual basis, and where the client's accounts of his actions reveal no gross infringement of law and morality. Social work, however, is legitimated by state authority. Social workers cannot give priority to their private judgement of client actions over key principles of law and accepted morality. For example, if a client reveals abuse of a child, no one disputes that the information must be acted on to prevent the situation continuing. The person is judged: he deserves to be stopped. None of this negates a relevant aspect of the principle of respect, which is that even when the client must be judged wrong, he should still not be treated in a demeaning or belittling way.

Desert is also a consideration for people who may be affected by a client's actions, or social work intervention in relation to them. The child abuse may need to be stopped, but unfortunately trying to do so may have side effects for the child and her family that she does not deserve. The perfectly intelligible complaint of families in the Cleveland affair was that they had done nothing to deserve the apparently arbitrary removal of their children from home on inadequately established suspicion of abuse; the treatment they received was unjust.

In the field of criminal justice, desert has special resonance. One of the principal reasons for punishing criminals is retribution; we believe they should pay back society for the harm they have done. Thus for example, the drunk driver who kills another road user is imprisoned primarily to discharge a moral debt; relatives of victims in cases where only a light sentence is given often express disgust at the leniency of the sentence compared with the culpability of the offender. The logic of retribution is that the criminal deserves the penalty. As an adjunct of the criminal justice system, social work is implicated in the justice of such judgements. It is often suggested that social workers are somewhat reluctant accomplices to judicial retribution, and value their involvement rather because of its potential to soften the penalty or contribute to other valued goals, such as rehabilitation.

In the pursuit of justice, desert is a two-edged sword. Justice must plainly include desert: it is inherent in commonsense morality and its institutionalisation in law. The authority of social workers is generally legitimated by law, and much of their work consists in the implementation of specific laws: so social work begs the question of desert. Of course, deciding specifically who deserves what means treading treacherous ground, and even a mite of historical retrospection is sufficient to warn that notions of desert are fluid and fickle. This may well be why, as Campbell suggests, modern theories of justice have not been strongly desert based: 'It is argued that there are insuperable theoretical and practical difficulties in measuring desert' (Campbell, 1988, p. 161). (Campbell goes on however to expound a major contemporary example of a desert-based theory of justice.)

In the end the only escape from this conundrum may be to treat desert as a corollary of justice rather than the foundation of it. In other words, we may do better to invoke other principles in order to found the theory of justice, and expect that, in the process of applying them, desert will appear as one of the products of the theory.

Taking liberties

The third primitive of justice is the idea of fundamental, inalienable human rights that apply to all persons. In many contemporary contexts there is much dispute about the rights of persons as such. Nonetheless, it is universally agreed that, in general, people have a right to liberty. Any form of incarceration or restriction of movement therefore requires most stringent justification. This is directly relevant to social work and other welfare and caring professions, because one of their key roles is precisely to curtail the freedom of identified individuals. Social workers act to confine to mental hospital people who because of mental illness, appear to be a danger to themselves or others; they act to take guardianship powers over elderly people no longer capable of managing their affairs, including decisions about where to live; in the provision of care, they directly and indirectly prevent people with mental or physical disabilities from moving about freely as they might wish; they cause children to live in places and with people not of their choosing; they keep children in residential care, sometimes against their will and sometimes physically prevented from leaving the premises; they make recommendations about the sentencing and treatment of offenders, the effect of which may be to lead to imprisonment. Situations of risk to individuals' liberty are rightly recognised as one of the most crucial areas of decision-making in social work.

What steps should social workers take to ensure that in these and similar situations, they are not perpetrating injustice? There are several standards to meet, but since the requirements are complex they are liable to conflict. Deprivation of liberty should take place only after due process under law. This is to ensure that the reasons invoked to justify depriving someone of their liberty are based on democratic principles; and to ensure that the social workers, judges and others who implement decisions to curtail freedom do so in an accurate and disinterested manner. Unfortunately, matters are often not so clear. Many decisions to curtail freedom in the name of welfare are taken not through a clearly independent judicial process, but in a half-world where legally rigorous decision-making overlaps with customary practice, administrative convention and professional discretion. The legal defences against arbitrary deprivation of liberty may thus be compromised by system imperfections; the rules may be vague, poorly understood or badly implemented. Professionals should periodically question the integrity of these systems and seek necessary improvements.

As well as attending to proper legal process, social workers should periodically examine whether the provisions of the law, convention and practice are indeed substantively just. Assumptions about what constitutes good reason for legally curtailing freedom in the name of welfare change rapidly. For example, in the early and mid-twentieth century many women were permanently confined to mental hospitals or welfare institutions for having had an illegitimate baby. This now obsolete and objectionable policy was doubtless usually implemented in good faith by the welfare workers of the time. Justice is one key argument for deinstitutionalising individuals who may have been unfairly, but legally, confined.

Justice in welfare

All social services are based on a theory of human and social need. Humans need certain provisions of nutrition, shelter, health care, education, social support and so on; for some people to be deprived of the basics is deeply harmful to them and constitutes an affront to justice, especially in a world where others enjoy a superabundance of goods. Since the essentials of a decent life are not reliably delivered by a free market or any other accidental circumstance, deliberately crafted institutions and policies are necessary to ensure the meeting of human needs and the fulfilment of elementary social justice. These principles are timeless and just as well demonstrated in Towle's classic early textbook of social work (Towle, 1973), first published over half a century ago, as they are in the latest welfare policy papers.

Social work is implicated in at least three ways by the theory of needs and the pursuit of social justice. In the first place, it sets out to meet human needs that would generally be included among the basic, primary goods: care and nurturance at all points in life but especially in infancy and childhood, in dependency, ill health and infirmity. The primary character of social need is unmistakable where a child is emotionally abused or a dependent adult has no one to turn to for help with the ordinary essential tasks of daily life. Somewhat extending the idea of social care and concern are those types of social work that develop the capacity of communities to protect and enhance the lives of their members.

In the second place, social work is implicated by the theory of needs because its wide perspective on human living attends to the full spectrum of clients' needs and not merely the narrow segment that might befit a specialist in health, education or the relief of poverty. In social work practice a client's financial poverty or housing need is as much a matter for action as those matters of family relationships that could be considered the core of social work concern. In this way social workers are involved in the ministration of social justice – or injustice – across the whole range of social affairs.

Third, social work is especially implicated in social justice because a high preponderance of its clients manifestly suffer poverty, deprivation, disadvantage and exclusion. (This point is illustrated in Chapter 10.) The facts of poverty and other social maladies do not of themselves prove social injustice, if by that we mean humanly created, and humanly avoidable, frustration of basic needs; but generations of social theorists and practical reformers have argued that the problems which clients experience are indeed the product of defective administration or malign politics. Many theorists of public welfare have concluded that it is either a deliberate means of regulating the poor and in the process, denying them justice; or alternatively that it has this effect in practice even if its practitioners avow other, more benign aims.

Justice as a stock of ethical practice requires, then, that social workers take up a position about the basic unmet human needs in the society within which they work. To meet the standard of justice professionals must work from theory and explanation of the needs they deal with in practice. Of course, some unmet needs will be ascribed to natural facts about the world not attributable to human *political* failing, as for example many forms of ill health and disability. Many other problems, however, are primarily political failures to meet human needs as well as may be within natural constraints.

Oppression and liberation

The final idea of justice stresses that improvements to the human condition require not only the better satisfaction of rights and changes in the distribution of power and resources but also transformation of the very terms whereby we understand injustice. So, for example, under the influence of feminism, changing ideas about the respective roles of women and men have accustomed us to detecting injustice where previously none was visible. It is not that the frequent subservience and disadvantage of women in, say, the world of paid employment is new: it is rather that what was once accepted as more or less the natural order of things is now seen as a moral wrong to be challenged.

As an occupational group, social workers have often been quite receptive to new ideas and ideologies about the multiple forms of oppression. The radical social work movement was sympathetic to the socialist analysis of working-class powerlessness in capitalist society, and was influenced by revolutionary socialist ideas of new ways of living in which patriarchy and exploitation would be ended. Thanks to feminism, social workers along with most other groups in society began to question the traditional roles of men and women in, for example, gender relations and the parenting of children. Several authors have explored the import of feminism for social work (for a recent review, see Wise, 1995; also see Dale and Foster, 1986). Social work has particularly featured racism as a set of attitudes and ideologies that need to be eradicated from private and public life (for example Dominelli, 1988). Extending these paradigm cases of oppression, social work now routinely claims also to repudiate unfair treatment for reasons of culture and ethnicity, disability, sexuality, and other like bases of unjustified discrimination (Taylor, 1993).

The pursuit of justice as social liberation within state-authorised and sponsored welfare requires robust analysis and strong commitment. Feminism, anti-racism and other liberationist ideologies offer an exciting prospect to professionals trying to work with deeply intractable problems of justice and human living. Because they threaten accepted views and familiar practices, advocates of justice as liberation can count on often finding their message unwelcome. They need strong evidence and argument to persuade others.

The value of liberationist programmes is enhanced, however, by reading with a sense of irony. The abiding impression from any broad acquaintance of social work, unchallenged by research evidence to the contrary, is that it works more to sustain, rather than to overturn, those locales and practices that are said to be the seat of patriarchy, sexism, racism and other evils. In the regulation of family lives that have come so far off the norm that they attract the attention of welfare officials; in the management of mental illness and physical and mental disability; and in the control of offenders, social work procures social control within very largely conventional and traditional boundaries. Social workers should not confuse the reality of the actual effect of their work with aspirations captured in mere politically correct slogans.

Citizenship

In the last chapter citizenship was explained as the political status that defines the relationship between the rights of the individual and the obligations that flow from membership in the community. Citizenship as one of the four stocks of ethical practice requires social workers to pursue clients' rights as the means of realising their conception of an ordinary life. Indeed this is familiar ground, since 'welfare rights' work is staple fare in social work agencies. The idea that social work should sustain individuals in their contributions and obligations to the community is, however, less familiar and potentially much more controversial. Both aspects are discussed here.

Rights to welfare

The progressive development of state-sponsored welfare has given citizens an ever-widening range of social or welfare rights. Some services, such as education and health, are broadly aimed at the whole populace, while others are narrowly targeted at specific groups. Social work is often involved in securing the delivery of the broadly based services to individuals who for some reason have not received what they are entitled to. Welfare administration is complicated and error prone, and some individuals are defeated when the systems fail to function properly. It is undoubtedly part of the role of social work to correct and repair welfare mechanisms on behalf of clients who have been poorly served. Social workers should accept a duty to see that their clients receive the welfare entitlements intended by legislation and policy.

While some welfare services are broadly aimed, others are targeted at narrower segments of the population. Social work itself is a prime example, while under the umbrella of social work comes a diverse range of even more narrowly targeted services. The administration of targeted services invariably means the exercise of professional discretion. Officials decide who should receive services, at what intensity, and correspondingly they also decide whom to exclude. Decisions about the suitability of clients for services require professional judgement about the match of the need to the resource; and they usually take place in a context of shortage that means not everyone who could potentially benefit from a resource can be allocated it.

Guaranteeing the welfare rights of citizenship becomes progressively more difficult as services become more narrowly targeted, more specialised, more variable and more discretionary. This is partly because, practically, it is very difficult to administer complex and varied services comprehensively and consistently. Underneath the practical obstacles there are conceptual questions, for it is frequently less than clear what policy *intends* for entitlement to service, even assuming reliable administration. And underneath the question of intentions, there are normative questions about the criteria that *ought* to guide professional discretion. A well-known example of these problems is home care services for elderly or disabled people. A wide range of conditions may qualify (or disqualify) individuals for service, such as the degree of physical or mental impairment, the type of domestic equipment installed, the availability of family support and the gender of the user. Eligibility for service is often decided by practical rules of thumb loosely based on rationing, and not by any rigorous and objective measure of need; service delivery is often varied for arbitrary reasons related to the availability of staff or funds. The service is subject to industrial rules designed to protect the safety of workers but often at variance with what consumers actually want. Underneath all these difficulties is a range of unsettled questions about what domestic comfort and amenity people should be minimally entitled to in modern conditions.

For social workers, therefore, supporting the citizenship entitlements of welfare rights means more than merely ensuring that policy is correctly administered, important though that is. It means also engaging in a public dialogue about the intent and boundaries of discretion in publicly supported welfare, a dialogue which will turn on the expectations of ordinary life in communities. The need for this is not well recognised in the politics of welfare, and means for conducting it are not widely available. A parallel issue affects the obligations of welfare citizenship, which is now developed.

Contributing to welfare

In the second half of the twentieth century the concept of welfare as individuals' rights to state-sponsored benefits and services dominated social service professionals and the general public. There is, nonetheless, a contrasting and complementary perspective that instead of focusing mostly on entitlements also recognises and emphasises individuals' duty to contribute to the welfare of their communities. Community work, mentioned in Chapter 5, looks for explanations of social problems at the collective rather than the individual level and envisages the community as a source of help for its own problems. As a leading community activist has succinctly put it: 'The people here aren't the problem. They're the solution' (Bob Holman, quoted in Commission on Social Justice, 1994, p. 306). Chapter 8 reviewed a number of arguments for public welfare based on the good of the community rather than the rights of the citizen. Under the idea of welfare citizenship, the accepted social rights of citizenship entail duties to contribute to meeting the needs of the community.

Notwithstanding the traditions of communal duty in the maintenance of welfare, and despite overwhelming evidence that socially and politically desired levels of welfare are, quite simply, unattainable without the contributions of people acting together in the communal sphere, social workers are often reluctant to act as agents for developing the welfare of the community in general. They choose to work with individuals in evident particular need and they are trained and expected to focus their attention accordingly. They identify, first and foremost, with the interests of the client who, almost by definition, is someone who at that moment needs to claim their right to welfare. Social workers assume they have no authority to make demands upon non-clients except insofar as closely regards the manifest interest of clients. They are very sensitive to the derisory, stinging rebuke that they are 'do-gooders' who know, better than we know ourselves, how our affairs should be arranged. Especially in the public sector, they avoid areas of need not strongly legitimated by legislation.

The reluctance of social workers to set standards for individual and communal life is understandable in the light of established precepts such as respect for autonomy and acceptance of different values and ways of life. Social workers are properly cautious about drawing lines of right and wrong in a general social context of deep divisions of sincere opinion. Nevertheless, agnosticism is not a tenable position. While helping people to attain the conditions for the pursuit of an ordinary life, it is simply not possible to be neutral about what that should mean. Neither, therefore, is it desirable to aspire to neutrality, because the effect will be to pursue implicitly or covertly what ought to be declared explicitly. An example will illustrate the point.

Community care social work involves making arrangements for adults with various forms of disability or dependency who are considered unable to live a decent life without special support. The prime source of support for most people is family and close kin; when, therefore, an adult needs special help it is usually family members who are faced with the most far-reaching implications. Within families there is often disagreement about how such situations should be resolved; and in communities and society at large there are different views, ambiguously held and unclearly expressed, about the proper outcomes (Finch, 1989). In helping to create care arrangements, social workers have to patrol the lines of major social controversy: about the obligations of family members towards one another, the responsibility of the wider community to help neighbours or strangers in times of adversity, and the role of official welfare in meeting personal needs.

Fulfilling welfare requires social workers, who are charged with ensuring it, to look both ways as they patrol the lines: towards meeting the rightful claims of those with welfare needs, and at the same time towards supporting the duties of community members who have to contribute to the process. A longstanding but, until the 1990s, minority tradition in welfare theory and practice has wanted to emphasise the rights of 'clients' as fellow citizens within a common political society (for example British Association of Social Workers, 1980; Buck, 1993; Coote, 1992; Croft and Beresford, 1992; Jordan, 1976, 1989, 1990; King and Waldron, 1988). It has resisted the marginalisation of welfare users and stressed their equal rights to choice and participation.

The argument of welfare citizenship is that social workers (and other welfare professionals) have no special prerogative to impose their personal or collective ideas about individual and communal responsibility for welfare. Neither, similarly, should the social control that social workers are charged to assert over certain classes of individuals be left as an issue for them alone to determine. What social workers do have is a duty of democratic accountability in the settling of these questions. They should understand that the fulfilling of welfare is a deep and difficult issue for citizenship, to which they have a special professional duty to contribute. And not least, as professionals they do not cease to be citizens themselves, who should respect the rights of fellow citizens and meet their own obligations as citizens.

Discipline

Ethical practice in social work is usually taken to mean joining the refrain of traditional, humane values found in all discussions of professional ethics. This belief is not wrong, but as analysis it is incomplete and as prescription it is inadequate. In Chapter 4 it was shown that the conventional rules of practice ethics clearly require knowledge and competence. However, according to the exploration there and in Chapter 5, professional expertise is highly problematic in social work. Although no one doubts that social workers should have relevant knowledge and expertise, the content and character of their expertise is shadowy and disputable. The starting point here is that for practice to attain the goals of the profession and meet the expectations of the wider society, it must be informed by true knowledge and understanding as well as imbued with the right values. It will be argued that the concept of discipline best captures the character of professional expertise.

The root idea of discipline is learning from an authoritative teacher. By association and extension, the teacher is said to apply the discipline, and the learner is said to be disciplined when she takes the teaching to heart and mind. As a body of learning and teaching develops a more or less regular, predictable form when practised in different times and places, it takes on the identity of a discipline. Some are the familiar academic disciplines, such as mathematics or history; some disciplines are religious; some are artistic or aesthetic (music, painting), some physical (sports, dance), some technical and practical (engineering). Some disciplines transcend the conventional boundaries illustrated here, as, for example, religiously inspired meditation. While some disciplines aim to raise the spirit, others have a rational, practical and applied character. Disciplines become institutions, in the double sense: as bodies of belief and social practice regularly found in specific contexts; and as formal organisations in concrete situations, such as universities, conservatories, churches, courts of law and professional institutes.

Discipline is the container of structured, generalisable knowledge that extends beyond the immediate, first-hand experience of the individual. Without discipline there would be no culture, art or science; every child must learn her letters. But discipline is not only the liberating force that enables the individual to participate in society and culture; discipline may be stringent and repressive. Thus the individual who fails to observe the discipline is liable to be disciplined, which in this context means correction and possibly punishment. A standard ideal is that the person should be self-disciplined, which can be understood as the condition of having internalised the precepts of the discipline originally laid upon her by her teachers. The individual's eventual mastery of a discipline is the echo of the discipline originally imposed by the master.

The form and structure of disciplines is their strength, but their tendency to rigidity is an obstruction and a danger. Every healthy discipline is constantly under challenge and in flux. Disciplines that never change become closed and ossified, and ultimately sterile and irrelevant to everything except themselves. Challenges to a discipline may be external, as when one religion collides with another. More commonly perhaps, challenges to a discipline originate primarily from within, as its practitioners attempt to recreate and refashion it to solve new problems and meet the ever-changing needs of the times. Challenge means a departure from the orthodoxy of the discipline and requires creativity. Good practitioners of a discipline have not only mastery but also the creativity to challenge the established precepts of the discipline. In a discipline, mastery and creativity participate in a dialectical relationship as one approach first builds on, then denies, and finally transcends another (cf. Bernstein, 1972).

Work in the professions demands mastery of knowledge in the applied sciences and humanities that inform them. The traditional conception of discipline emphasises the academic aspects of a body of learning, a core of theory and a methodology of research. For example, intending doctors must study and pass examinations in subjects such as anatomy and physiology; intending engineers learn materials science and the theory of electromagnetism; intending ministers of religion learn the dead languages of the scriptures. During their education students learn the specific content of knowledge in their subject, and absorb the basic assumptions and methods of the discipline. They demonstrate their knowledge by the traditional academic exercises of problem-solving, essays, projects, examinations and so on.

In recent years it has increasingly been argued and recognised that the traditionally academic approach to a subject is not, by itself, a sound preparation for professional practice. This can be understood by comparing the respective goals of the academic and the profes-

sional service practitioner. The prime aim of the academic researcher
and teacher is to advance knowledge and theory in her subject. The
prime aim of the professional practitioner, however, is to serve the
needs of clients and society as a whole. Although these aims need not
necessarily be in conflict, the academic and the practitioner are ruled
by different priorities. The academic pursuit of a discipline means
concentrating effort on meaningful problems within the discourse of
the discipline. The practitioner, however, must orientate himself to
the expressed needs of clients and the expectations of paymasters.
Needs and expectations are no respecters of the current state of
knowledge and consequently, service practitioners are often obliged
to work on concrete problems that have no clear solution available
within current knowledge. Doctors, for example, have to treat
patients with incurable conditions; lawyers have to advise on
hopeless cases; social workers have to cope with the effects of irremediable poverty. Practitioners' way of thinking, governed by the
multifarious needs of service practice, has to be different from the
single-minded pursuit of current questions within the framework of
the academic discipline.

In step with questioning the traditional academic route to professional preparation, increasing concern about the capacity of
employees, professionals and their organisations to deliver what is
expected of them has appeared in many areas of policy and politics
over the last two decades. In Britain the unemployment crisis of the
1980s forced an overdue reappraisal of vocational training and led
eventually to the creation of new training methods and qualification
routes, especially for students and workers with lower educational
attainments. Throughout the public services there are vast new
systems intended to ensure accountability, quality and value for
money. The focus on employee and service effectiveness has
transmuted, for implementation at the individual level, into the
doctrine of competence. Officials devise codes of competencies,
which workers are expected to demonstrate by their actual behaviour
in practice on their way to vocational accreditation. British social
work has followed this route with its own competence codes, the
current template for professional qualification being the prime
example (CCETSW, 1996). Much debate has accompanied these
developments (for example O'Hagan, 1996; Vass, 1996; Winter,
1996; Yelloly and Henkel, 1995).

The limitations of the traditionally academic approach to discipline are widely acknowledged, but the doctrine that professional knowledge and understanding can be reduced to any sensible definition of competence is deeply mistaken (Clark, 1995). Attempting to equate what social workers need to know, understand and accomplish to a slew of bureaucratic formulae is a wrong turning down a dead end. Many writers have sought for a concept that would better capture the nature of professional discipline. In social work Schön's (1983) metaphor of the 'reflective practitioner' has enjoyed wide popularity – so much, indeed, that the point of the original insight has almost been forgotten. Others champion the concept of 'evidence-based practice', surely most puzzling for the implication that any other sort could be justified. Winter and Maisch (1996, pp. 44ff.) present a helpful formulation of the broader theory of professional work and its implications for learning, somewhat oddly embedded in the report of a project devoted to professional competence.

Professional discipline shows, then, that professionals should have care to master knowledge, theory and research in relevant academic subjects. More than this, academic knowledge must be complemented by the meta-knowledge of how to use it in the art of practice. Kronman makes the important point that 'to be professional is to have a certain identity or character, to be a person of a particular sort'; and he argues that what characterises the professional is the possession of practical wisdom, as distinguished from mere specialist expertise (Kronman, 1986). Discipline is one of the four stocks of ethical practice because the pursuit, mastery and renewal of knowledge, and its disciplined application, are indispensable to morally defensible practice.

What should be the content of professional discipline in social work? The broad, all-encompassing aims of social work are both a strength and a weakness. Adopting the definition of social work as promotion of the means of realising the ordinary life, the daunting range of its discipline becomes obvious. The ordinary life, for any particular individual, could potentially entail any imaginable project. If, for example, we say that the ordinary life should include the opportunity for physically adventurous pursuits, then social workers who work with physically disabled people need the knowledge, skill and understanding to translate this into reality for their client. The range of knowledge relevant for social work is indeed well illustrated in the 86 (very conservatively enumerated) knowledge base items stipulated by CCETSW in its *Rules and Requirements for the DipSW* (CCETSW, 1996). Covering a range as diverse as 'economic, social, demographic, cultural, religious, linguistic, environmental and political factors, and their implications for social work practice in the United Kingdom' to 'social and emotional impact of physical, sensory and learning disabilities, ill health and mental illness on children, adults, families and carers', it can only inspire the depressing thought that no ordinary mortal could hope to master more than a tiny fraction of it even in a lifetime's study.

In the real world of broad and complex needs, and limited resources, social workers must first be generalists. They will often have to rely on specialists to supply specific services and resources. What they need is a broad framework that will enable them to understand the general nature of a problem, and in what direction it should be pursued. Box 9.1 offers, for the sake of illustration and argument, a skeletal outline for the professional discipline of social work. The reader may reflect on it, with the aim of improving, rejecting or transcending it.

Conclusion

Ethical practice in social work is to be fostered by bending its goals and methods onto the four 'stocks' or cardinal principles of respect, justice, citizenship and discipline. The organic metaphor signifies that the content of these concepts is not crystallised and determinate, but on the contrary capable of different interpretations according to the values and world views of different agents. Their effect is not fixed over time, since the content of respect, justice, citizenship and discipline are constantly dissolved and reformed in an endless dialogue. We should concentrate our attention on finding specific interpretations of the four stocks or principles suitable to the age and the circumstance, and we should form welfare practice accordingly.

The political process of constant dialogue is best safeguarded by the human and political rights of liberalism. Such rights, however, do not furnish an adequate conception of the goals of welfare. Social work, it has been argued, is devoted to promotion of the ordinary life and that is something to be sought and contended in the arena of the

BOX 9.1

Elements of social work discipline

1. The value(s) of human living

A reflective understanding of the goals and values of human life and living. The tradition of social work is western, liberal, humane; other cultural, religious and philosophical positions may well need to be more fully considered.

2. Interest in people and relationships

A deep interest and good insight into human nature, behaviour and relationships; a capacity for empathy and ability to form various types of (non-possessive) professional relationship. These qualities provide a foundation for understanding of social and psychological problems, life problems.

3. Interest in community and society

A deep interest and good insight into the descriptive and normative theory of social life in the public realm, community and society. These qualities provide a foundation for understanding of sociology and social problems, also politics. Extends to grasp of legal reasoning and uses of law; welfare policy and politics, functioning of public agencies.

4. Scientific curiosity

A striving to describe, analyse, explain and perhaps predict the phenomena of our experience; the thirst for (research) knowledge and its application, skills of research and enquiry.

5. Service ethic

A motivation towards the service and reform ethic; adherence to precepts of diligence, duty, accountability, consideration for others, action not for self-interest, improvement of social conditions.

6. Command of specialised social work knowledge

Ability and readiness to learn about models and methods of social work intervention and the evidence for their effectiveness; also statutory and procedural requirements.

7. Ready to learn instrumental skills

Ability and readiness to learn job-relevant instrumental skills of practical effectiveness, such as communication skills, information handling skills, recreations and sports, crafts, driving.

Source: Clark, 1996.

communal. The actual content of respect, justice, citizenship and discipline cannot be fully specified with the resources of liberal thin theory of the good: they have to be elaborated in the context of real lives in real communities. The means and ends of social welfare, as part of the good life, are never settled, but always in the process of being abolished and recreated.

10

Issues and Applications

This final chapter looks at a selection of practical issues in social work ethics. It first considers the wider question of whether professionals are subject to different standards of morality from ordinary citizens. It goes on to explore four important generic problems of practice ethics. These problems are prefaced with exercises that can equally be tried before or after reading the main text. The discussion will apply the concepts and approaches developed earlier in this book, especially the idea of four stocks of ethical practice featured in Chapter 9.

Personal and professional ethics: the separatist thesis

A basic question for all professional ethics is whether being a professional entails ethical standards and obligations different from those of ordinary members of the community. There are broadly three views about this. The first is that the professional role obligates the professional in a number of special ways, which may sometimes run counter to ordinary morality. Gewirth (1986) calls this the *separatist thesis* that professionals, by virtue of their expertise, have rights and duties not only different from but occasionally contrary to ordinary morality. The separatist thesis may defend such practices as the physician's lying to the patient or circumventing an absence of informed consent, or the lawyer's not revealing that the client is lying on oath. Referring to lawyers, Tur (1996, p. 59) declares that:

> On the standard conception lawyers are not morally accountable for the results of their efforts and cannot be made accountable without destroying their essential function. Lawyering thus appears to involve an institutional exemption from the normal dictates of moral conscience.

According to this position, professionals maintain that although their actions may seemingly infringe standard moral rights, the desirable end of their role-based practice justifies the effective means.

The second position, notably advocated by Goldman (1980), is opposite to the first: it holds that the moral obligations of professionals are no different from those of other members of society. However, while we might prefer that professionals should be allowed no privileges or licences denied to the rest of us, it is surely true that in professional work there are special situations and responsibilities not clearly covered within ordinary morality. The BASW Code of Ethics (1996, Foreword, 2) claims that 'membership of any profession entails obligations beyond those of the ordinary citizen'. Hardin (1990) argues that ordinary morality provides an inadequate guide to decision-making in social work because the aims of welfare policy are essentially political matters; what social workers (and doctors) ought to do has become a matter of policy and law, not of individual morality. We might instance here the special responsibility of social workers to advise upon or carry out measures that legally limit the freedom of, for example, certain children, offenders and people with mental health problems. These pose issues that ordinary moralities hardly touch upon.

The third position is intermediate; in Koehn's terms, it sees 'professional ethics as an institutionalized expression of prevailing public morality' (Koehn, 1994, p. 150). This means that although professionals will have a range of special obligations and privileges, these are not contrary to but lie within the principles of ordinary morality. Gewirth presents an intricate argument based on respect for the equal rights of all persons to the necessary conditions of human action (a version of the principle of respect). He concludes that the separatist thesis is correct in that rules of professional practice may justifiably require actions and policies that are different from those required by the direct applications of the general principle of morality; but the separatist thesis is mistaken in that professional rules and modes of operation must conform to the general principle of morality. Thus 'the autonomy of professional ethics... is strictly limited' (Gewirth, 1986, p. 300). Flores and Johnson (1983) ask whether professionals, such as engineers, who hold narrow roles in large organisations can be held responsible for collective failures, such as the catastrophic failure of an aircraft. They argue that individuals acting in professional roles are not exempt from bearing responsibility. This argument has considerable resonance in social work, where failures are frequently organisational failures of collective responsibility: for example, the failure of public authorities over many years to control cruelty and sexual abuse in residential care homes. In a controversial article, Hollis and Howe (1987) argue that social workers cannot escape moral responsibility for failures of practice even if they could not be reasonably held negligent or guilty of error in the particular case.

The remainder of this chapter will assume that some version of the intermediate position is the only credible possibility. This is based on pluralistically accepting as indispensable principles that:

- professional practices that are demonstrably incompatible with fundamental principles of ordinary morality are intolerable
- there are several morally significant features of professional practice – especially its institutional entailments – upon which ordinary morality is largely silent and unhelpful.

Koehn (1994) points out that accepting professional ethics as legitimate insomuch as their underlying principles reflect the morality of the community leaves open the possibility that professionals in an immoral community will simply have sanction to practise immorally. As argued at several points in this book, the principles of public and private morality are complex and plural, and they must be resolved in a public political process.

Autonomy, paternalism and citizenship

The cognate principles of respecting persons, protecting their self-determination and enhancing their autonomy are universally accepted in professional ethics. In practice however, professionals often have to deal with vulnerable individuals whose capacity for self-determination seems doubtful, or whose circumstances raise questions about whether they should be allowed to exercise it. Such occasions suggest a need for paternalistic intervention. Paternalism can be roughly defined as interference with a person's liberty for his own good (Beauchamp and Childress, 1989; Dworkin, 1979). To act paternalistically means to constrain someone's autonomy on the grounds of his own interests and without his fully informed consent.

BOX 10.1

Exercises on autonomy and paternalism

(a) Miss A, aged in her sixties, lives alone and has been intermittently supported at home by the social work agency for many years. She has learning disabilities, a severe alcohol problem and numerous chronic health problems. Her ability to manage her affairs is very limited. Eventually, her health deteriorates so much that she needs hospitalisation, and her house has become filthy and virtually uninhabitable. It is decided, against Miss A's wishes, to take legal guardianship powers. As her social worker, you are concerned to protect her rights to make her own decisions.

(b) Valley Hospital is a Victorian institution that now provides care for people with long-term mental health problems. Many of the patients have been institutionalised for years. They have become accustomed to the limited privacy, amenity and recreational opportunity of the traditional hospital wards. Social work support is limited to occasional contacts and negotiations with patients' relatives, most of whom rarely visit. It is suggested that the patients should be given more opportunity to express their views about their care and treatment. The nursing staff are well intentioned but struggle to keep the system going with minimal resources. They are reluctant to disturb the patients' equilibrium, feeling that in reality there is not much new that can be offered.

There are, of course, other grounds for interfering with a person's liberty, such as protecting the interests of others; but then we are not speaking of paternalism.

The common assumption is that paternalism towards adults is intrinsically objectionable, illustrated by the frequent use – by writers of both the left and the right – of 'paternalistic' as a pejorative term (for example Braye and Preston-Shoot, 1995; Croft and Beresford, 1990; Marsland, 1992; Minford, 1991). However, some forms of paternalism in professional welfare practice are practically unavoidable (Clark, 1998; Lindley, 1988; Mason and McCall Smith, 1994; Sainsbury, 1989). It is convenient to speak of justified paternalism where a convincing case can be made out for interference on the grounds of the supposed beneficiary's interest; and unjustified paternalism where the case for such interference, against the presumption for liberty, is on balance unsatisfactory. The following paragraphs examine the grounds for justified paternalism and consider its application to social work.

Classic grounds for paternalism

A convenient starting point for the analysis of paternalism is with Locke (Laslett, 1965). Locke very plausibly suggests that the parental exercise of power over a child is necessary and justified in the early stages of development; later this becomes progressively obsolete as the individual attains adulthood. A similar kind of care is necessary towards 'lunaticks and ideots', 'innocents' and 'madmen' as they do not have full mental capacities. Full and effective status under the civil law is acquired as we attain full capacities. Locke specifically refutes the view that the significant but temporary power of the parent over the child is an appropriate model for the power of the prince over the subject. The implication is that individuals, born free and rational, and not excluded by immaturity or incapacity from the proper exercise of their will under the law, ought not to be constrained by the civil authorities for reasons of their (alleged) own good.

Mill's famous argument that it is only harm (or threat of harm) to others, and not to oneself, which justifies interference with the liberty of persons of 'full age, and the ordinary amount of understanding' is initially more radical than Locke's (Warnock, 1962). Mill would expose those who intend something self-detrimental to reason, persuasion or public censure, but not to legal coercion. However, Mill does later admit the necessity of preventing some actions whereby the actor would limit his freedom, on the grounds that freedom to undermine one's own freedom is absurd. Mill appears to have been struggling to reconcile his intuition on liberty with his utilitarian theory, and seems to have been left with some major unresolved questions. Nonetheless Mill's defence of freedom in the sphere of self-regarding actions has become the benchmark, and posed problems which if anything are even more relevant in our time than in Mill's.

Types of paternalism

A person may take a paternalistic action in a purely private capacity, as in the classic example of the passer-by who restrains the intending suicide on the bridge. There is no legal or formal requirement here (although there may be laws about what is permissible in such circumstances). This may be termed *private* paternalism. As a contrast to that, much paternalistic intervention is sponsored by the state through legislation and public policy. For example, restrictions on dangerous sports may be at least partly paternalist in intention. Paternalism also features in some kinds of professional practice, notably medicine, which are substantially sponsored and mediated by public institutions. This is *public* paternalism. Public paternalism is similar to what Feinberg (1973) and others term legal paternalism, but is somewhat broader in its scope.

A second distinction is between those interferences or restraints applied to the intended beneficiary, and those applied instead to some intermediary agency. The parent's control of the child is an example of *direct* paternalism. On the other hand, *indirect* paternalism restricts the liberty of other parties in the expectation of good, or avoided harm, for the (vulnerable) beneficiaries. Indirect paternalism, as Dworkin (1979) suggests, characteristically takes the form of restraints upon the suppliers of dangerous commodities rather than the end users. Examples include laws about gambling or the supply of intoxicants, and laws about protecting the population from charlatans.

Justified paternalism

When is paternalism justified? It is already obvious that Locke's assumption that full citizenship, and therefore freedom from government interference, should go with adult years and possession of normal faculties does not match the expectations of public policy in modern society. Such a strongly anti-paternalist position does not give sufficient protection to the vulnerable, such as the users of social services.

It will be argued here that paternalism is justified when the following two conditions are *both* met:

1. the intended beneficiaries are at significant risk of serious harm
2. there exists a material and irremediable discrepancy between the intended beneficiaries' defective knowledge and understanding of the situation and the intending benefactors' superior knowledge and understanding.

Risk of harm

Deciding what constitutes significant, and what merely trivial, risk of harm is a perennial issue in the literature (Feinberg, 1973). There are two main components of the calculation: the level of risk (that is to say, the probability that a damaging event will occur) and the seriousness of the potential harm. The assessment of risk is complicated by time; one may be more or less at risk, now or at future times, as a consequence of decisions made now. The assessment of harm is also complicated. A harm may comprise an obvious worsening of one's current situation, such as grave injury. More problematically, harm may be construed as damage to one's long-term best interests, or failure to gain access to a widely regarded benefit. We say, for example, that failure to get a good education will have harmful consequences. These calculations have to be made against a rapidly changing background of public knowledge and opinion about the gravity of risks and harms. Thus for example public action to curb smoking has hugely intensified as results of research demonstrating its harmful effects have entered common knowledge.

The estimation of risks and harms entails a somewhat different procedure in the respective cases of private and public paternalism. The private individual who undertakes a paternalist action does so upon her own opinion of benefit and harm, which may or may not be generally supported by the community. In taking her action she proceeds on her own belief that the intended beneficiary is unable properly to assess the situation. Public paternalism, however, is implemented through a system of laws and public administration, which in a democratic polity are (or should be) open to public debate, scrutiny and accountability. Public paternalism ought to be authorised by the considered view of the political community as a whole, and cannot be sanctioned by the unrepresentative views of individuals in advantageous positions of influence.

Knowledge and understanding

The second issue to consider is the supposed beneficiary's knowledge and understanding of his situation. This is crucial because paternalism, by definition, means a restriction of the subject's freedom without his *informed* consent (uninformed, naive or 'idiotic' consent is worthless in this context). Whether informed consent exists must be appraised against the subject's ability to understand what he might be consenting to.

A beneficiary may fail to possess the relevant knowledge and understanding in at least three main types of situation.

1. *Lack of information:* The beneficiary is in a state of avoidable ignorance, by accident; he does not possess the relevant facts. For example, one might be unaware that, despite appearances, the ice on the lake is too thin for safety.
2. *Misinformation:* The beneficiary has deliberately been kept in a state of partial ignorance or misunderstanding, so that an element of manipulation or deception enters the scene. For example, a patient might be told less than the whole truth about his medical condition or the treatment proposed in order that he should be more amenable to the doctor's intended intervention.
3. *Cannot be advised:* The beneficiary is in a state of ignorance because he cannot be given the relevant understanding. This can happen in a variety of situations, such as:

   – he is a child whose cognitive and emotional capacities are not yet fully developed
   – he is insensible
   – he lacks the education to understand, at least in the short term, the nature of the hazard faced, as for example the stone age tribesman will probably not appreciate the danger of radioactivity
   – the necessary knowledge and understanding is considered to be potentially harmful in itself, as for example an unfavourable medical diagnosis may precipitate despair
   – his mental capacity is temporarily or permanently impaired or insufficient through conditions such as emotional stress, psychosis, brain injury or dementia.

   Under circumstances such as these, the intended beneficiary's ignorance is irremediable.

Under what conditions of defective knowledge and understanding might paternalism be justified? The first two are relatively straightforward to dispose of. Mere lack of information would not generally constitute strong enough grounds; the obvious answer to this type of situation is to give the subject the information and let him decide for himself. An exception could be allowed for very urgent cases where it is not possible to give the subject the information before he exposes himself to the risk, such as stepping inadvertently into the path of a moving bus. In public policy the presumption must similarly be against mere public ignorance as legitimate grounds for paternalism; it is normally possible to educate the public about the dangers they may be exposed to. Again, there could be scope for some exceptions under conditions of grave public emergency or disaster.

Ignorance as a consequence of misinformation equally cannot *of itself* be grounds for paternalism. The real use of misinformation is to smooth interventions that might be resisted if those affected had the full picture. Agents may claim that they are presenting a partial picture (or being economical with the truth) in order to better the conditions of beneficiaries in ways that they could not fully appreciate. This is a dangerous form of false paternalism which ought to be resisted. Nevertheless it may be possible to defend the use of misinformation as an adjunct where paternalism is *independently* justified on other grounds, in order to minimise needless harm. This is the classic defence of medical paternalism (Goldman, 1980). In public policy Weale (1978) suggests that the withholding of information may count as justified public paternalism if not to do so might result in the exercise of more forceful compulsion instead. Thus misinformation, a tool of soft control, could perhaps be permitted if the alternative involves the use of greater force or the infliction of more harm.

The third type of defective knowledge and understanding, labelled earlier as 'cannot be advised', presents the trickiest decisions, requiring discrimination between adequate and inadequate levels of mental competence. Competence is specific to the problem and the context, and is most commonly a matter of degree rather than a matter of absolute distinction (Beauchamp and Childress, 1989). Furthermore, the definition of adequate mental competence within any given community is highly perishable; views about it are liable to radical transformation in the space of just a few years, let alone across different societies and historical epochs. Yet the definition of mental competence is no mere philosophical, psychological or legal exercise, but a key practical concept that informs all human action in both the private and public spheres. Since the issue cannot be postponed pending a definitive answer, how can acceptable boundaries be placed on paternalism?

Reasonable public paternalism must again involve the wide consent of the political community arrived at through a process of public debate. For example, the concept of mental illness used to justify compulsory detention in hospital on the grounds that the patient is a danger to himself must be supported by the community. The principle of community consent will not however necessarily preclude practices that subsequently come to be seen as reprehensible, as history amply illustrates. In this democratic model it will be up to individuals who object to current practice to persuade others that it must be changed; it should not be the prerogative of those who claim superior knowledge or values to impose their views by covert or forceful means.

The conclusion is that paternalism is justified when the intended beneficiary is at significant risk of serious harm; *and* when he has irremediably defective knowledge and understanding of the situation. As a corollary of the latter circumstance, he will be unable to give informed consent to the intervention. But since the criteria for establishing all these conditions are highly contestable, we should be cautious. There is every reason to support the conclusion of both utilitarian and deontological philosophers that paternalism is to be avoided unless the arguments for it are compelling (Husak, 1981).

Because of the requirement for democratic accountability, the occasions for indirect public paternalism must be highly exceptional, principally concerned with the preservation of general safety in a genuine emergency (natural disasters, external aggression). Otherwise paternalistic restrictions ought to be justified through an open political process so that they are, in effect, self-imposed by the people according to democratic principles. For example, if there are to be laws controlling or banning, on paternalistic grounds, dangerous pursuits like motor racing, they should be adopted only after full and informed public debate.

Direct public paternalism, on the other hand, has wider legitimacy. This is where laws, administrative regulation or publicly sponsored intervention restrain the liberty of individuals who must be specifically identified, for example those apparently intending self-mutilation or suicide. The legitimacy of public direct paternalism then rests on showing that the specific, identified individuals are at particular, extraordinary risk. This is the most acute problem for social work and other welfare services. How should such decisions be sanctioned?

Difficult cases: justified paternalism and the practice of citizenship

Paternalism is justified when the intended beneficiary is at significant risk of serious harm, and is in a state of irremediably defective knowledge and understanding of the danger such that he cannot be advised. However, the determination of these conditions – 'serious harm' and 'cannot be advised' – is frequently contentious and problematic. For this reason the exercise of paternalism must be coupled to the practice of citizenship. This applies to those on both sides of a paternalistic transaction, beneficiaries and benefactors, clients and social workers.

Potential beneficiaries (or victims) of paternalism ought to have their rights as citizens safeguarded, more particularly so since they are by definition especially vulnerable to the power of others. But it is only half the story to consider their putative rights to freedom and non-interference, which figure in the case against paternalistic intervention. It is equally necessary to think of their potential rights of welfare recipience, a legitimate call on the resources of the community because of some kind of special need. Thus to protect the rights of potential candidates for paternalism, the duty of (other) citizens may be either to promote paternalism or to resist it, according to the merits of the case.

On the other side of the relationship, benefactors who would exercise private paternalism, and individuals who carry responsibility for public paternalism, ought to conceive their power as a duty governed by citizenship. Their actions should be guided not merely by their private estimate of the potential benefits and harms of paternalism, but by the community's conception of citizens' rights and obligations. Paternalism is an exercise of the responsibilities of citizenship, and bound by its duties.

For public paternalism, since the beneficiary cannot give informed consent, government and its agents ought to seek authority elsewhere so that vulnerable individuals are protected from arbitrary powers. Public paternalism is justified only where the community as a whole has sanctioned the determination of a harm as serious; it should not rest solely upon individual opinion. It follows that the evaluation of harms that might be thought to warrant paternalism counts as a duty of citizens. The views of professionals and experts on the potential gravity of harms should be subjected to the scrutiny of disinterested citizens to ensure that paternalist practices are responsive to community opinion. This does not preclude delegation of responsibility, but insists on maintaining effective accountability. The control of paternalism therefore requires a citizenship of duty, or what might also be described as a citizenship of participation.

Providing for the needs of dependent adults, which is a key responsibility of social work, often entails justified paternalism, private or public. In the process, the citizens' rights of adults with dependencies, such as their entitlement to special services, are all too liable to conflict with the citizenship rights of those who in the event must care for them, such as their freedom to pursue their own legitimate projects without hindrance. The liberal individualist version of citizenship outlined in Chapter 8 guarantees vulnerable individuals neither the special help, nor the special protection from paternalism, that their condition merits. The essentially negative rights or freedoms of liberal individualism will not reliably mobilise the special resources needed by vulnerable adults; nor will they ensure that the exercise of paternalism is properly scrutinised by the community on behalf of those who may need it. Something much closer to the active citizenship of civil republicanism is needed to realise the participation of the community in managing welfare. Thus the exercise of justified paternalism in social welfare is fundamentally a political problem of citizenship; and social workers must cultivate citizenship as the regulator of justified, and the counterweight to unjustified, paternalism.

Confidentiality, privacy and disclosure

It is probably the best known precept of professional ethics that the professional should not divulge the content of the client's communications unless the client clearly authorises otherwise. It is conventionally associated with one's relationship with his priest, doctor or lawyer. Beauchamp and Childress (1989, p. 330) note that 'some rule of confidentiality appears in virtually every code of medical ethics'. Stipulations of confidentiality appear equally regularly in social work codes of ethics. Professionals are figures with whom, it is held, the client must feel free to communicate his personal experience, thoughts and feelings without fear that they will be transmitted elsewhere.

BOX 10.2

Exercises on confidentiality

(a) Consider a case from your professional experience (especially a case involving conflicts of interests between different clients, or a serious threat to someone's safety and welfare). List everyone in your agency, in other agencies and elsewhere who had knowledge of the case or access to information about it, whether with formal permission or otherwise. Specify whether they knew the identity of those involved or merely knew about the circumstances of the case anonymously. Examine whether this represents ethically sound practice.

(b) You are a social worker specialising in child and family social work in a small local 'patch'. Over years of work there you have come to know many local families and you have a friendly relationship with the community. You learn from confidential social work sources that a convicted child sex offender is about to be released from prison and is to be offered housing in the area where you work. Do you let it be known in the community?

The arguments for confidentiality are, in summary form, as follows (Beauchamp and Childress, 1989; Biestek, 1961; Bok, 1984; Koehn, 1994; Reamer, 1990; Rhodes, 1986; Tur, 1996; Wilmot, 1997).

- Lack of confidentiality violates the client's rights to protect his reputation and keep his secrets, which defend his privacy and autonomy.
- If the client cannot believe that what he says will not be passed on without his permission, truthful communication necessary to providing proper help will be inhibited. For example, a lawyer in a criminal case may need to know in private from his client what really happened in order to devise the best courtroom defence.
- Failing to keep confidentiality may unfairly prejudice the client's interests because it could pass on to other parties information they might use against the client.
- Where (as is usual) professional service is offered and accepted on the implicit or explicit promise of confidentiality, breaking confidence is straightforwardly a breach of a promise or contract.
- The general welfare will be damaged if individuals are discouraged from seeking professional help through fear of

unwarranted exposure. For example, someone with an infectious disease such as AIDS might not confide it to their doctor if they thought this could result in disadvantageous treatment.

These general arguments for professional confidentiality are usually assumed to be broadly applicable to social work. An official government code on social work confidentiality reads in part:

> *All* personal information should be regarded as confidential... Information supplied by a donor for one purpose should not be used for another purpose... Information supplied by a donor should not be disclosed without the donor's consent in other than exceptional circumstances. Social work departments should give an undertaking to donors to this effect, and explain where exceptional circumstances may apply. (Scottish Office, 1989, p. 3; emphasis original)

However, as Biestek plainly puts it, 'the principle of confidentiality appears to be deceptively simple at first glance, but is actually very complex and difficult to apply to concrete casework situations' (Biestek, 1961, p. 121). A comparison with medicine confirms the complexity. Mason and McCall Smith (1994) show that there may be many good reasons to relax the doctor's rule of confidentiality. Especially important are reasons based on danger to people other than the patient, or benefit to society as a whole, if the presumption of confidence is not broken.

The core proposition of confidentiality is that, unless good reasons to the contrary are shown, nothing that the client communicates to the worker should be passed on to anyone else. This might be termed the strong version of confidentiality, or *absolute confidentiality*. It is found side by side, and usually undifferentiated from, a weaker version, which stipulates that nothing that the client communicates should be transmitted to anyone else in such a way that the identity of the client is revealed; this will be termed *non-identification*. The weak version permits communicating case histories with names and other identifying details removed; it is the weak version which is usually envisaged and practised. Both the strong and the weak versions of confidentiality are subject, however, to a large range of exceptions based on a several different reasons.

A considerable amount of personal and confidential information about clients circulates in agencies and is transmitted to staff not directly involved in the case as an incidental consequence of the way service bureaucracies operate. Shardlow (1995) illustrates how the effects of this may be experienced by clients. Case notes, usually typed and filed by administrative staff, will be inspected by managers and consulted by supervisors and colleagues who may have to deal with the case in the main worker's absence. In practice, files are usually available on demand to virtually any professional member of the agency, even if they have no clear cause for viewing a file. Supervisors of front-line workers and students often need a detailed knowledge of service users' circumstances to ensure the proper conduct of the work, but the users are seldom aware of who has knowledge of their case. Workers may intend to practise weak confidentiality or non-identification, concealing the identity of clients while being free to discuss cases on appropriate occasions; but in small places and in unusual cases circumstantial information may make it all too easy to guess the identity of the subject. Social workers often pass on information about their clients without rigorously verifying that the client has truly consented or that the recipient of the information has a legitimate interest. Reception areas and other office spaces are often woefully lacking in privacy. Workers in open-plan offices inevitably overhear their colleagues conducting clients' personal business on the phone. Workers converse informally about their clients' affairs with no strictly professional purpose in mind; others overhear these conversations, including members of the public and casual visitors to the agency. The difference between proper exchange of information and mere gossip is apt to be neglected.

There is obviously huge scope for inadvertent or careless leakage of information which ought to be protected by the principle of confidentiality. Biestek characterises the information about clients held within the agency as a *group secret*, binding equally every member of it (Biestek, 1961, p. 125). But this blurs a distinction that ought to be preserved, between the personal knowledge of the client that the worker directly involved should reasonably keep secret because it is irrelevant to the business of the case, and the information that the worker should properly communicate to colleagues in order that the client's interests be best served. During contact with the client the worker will probably learn incidentally about aspects of the client's past history, or work, domestic and financial circumstances, or attitudes, or relationships, or political views, that are not material to the work of the agency with the client. A strict interpretation of confidentiality might require that the worker should only communicate to agency colleagues, and record in agency documents, information strictly necessary to the work in hand. The other personal information incidentally gained should, perhaps, never even become the group secret of the agency, but remain a personal secret of the worker's.

Equally worrying are the supposed occasions for disclosing client information deliberately. The above-mentioned official code, which is probably broadly representative of accepted current practice, lists eight categories of staff and others within the 'normal' limits of disclosure. They comprise not only many staff within the agency but also other agencies working in cooperation, students and their teachers, researchers, informal carers and members of an official committee of enquiry. The same code also authorises 'exceptional' disclosure, suggesting that 'in certain circumstances the law or the public interest may override a person's right to have information kept confidential' (Scottish Office, 1989, p. 4). These exceptional circumstances are defined by statute and by judicial processes in particular cases, such as a court order; there is also an expectation to disclose information to the police in cases of serious crime.

Departures from a strict interpretation of confidentiality have important implications for the privacy, and therefore the liberty and opportunity, of the people affected. Social workers are authorised to obtain the criminal records of offenders who require assessment or treatment, of potential foster and adoptive parents, of intending workers in child care, of intending new staff of the agency and students who will work in it. Individuals with a criminal record may understandably wish it to be kept as little known about as possible, but the legitimate interests of service users and the wider community may justify transmitting the information which a social worker has gained. The wide circle of people to whom information about a criminal record may legitimately be passed curtails the ex-offender's privacy and opportunity to pursue his personal choices. The problem does not end there; once a secret about someone's past becomes quite widely known in official circles, practically, it becomes very difficult to prevent it leaking into general circulation.

The principle of confidentiality in social work thus seems to comprise a rather general and indeterminate presumption that client information should be confidential at least to the agency. Set against the presumption is the reality that truly keeping information in confidence is practically very difficult to achieve in social work agencies. Moreover, there is a large range of circumstances where disclosure of personal information is not merely acceptable, but positively required. There appear to be few effective institutional safeguards against lapses of confidentiality. The whole concept of confidentiality appears inadequately defined and decidedly thread-bare in practice. How else might the problem be addressed?

It would be better to discard the blanket presumption of confidentiality, since the arguments and situations for abandoning or overruling it seem to be at least as powerful as those for observing it. Schellenberg (1996) makes a similar suggestion in the context of child protection. The traditional principle of confidentiality is based on a mistake of means for ends. It holds up confidentiality as a basic requirement, but confidentiality is better understood as the outcome of other, more fundamental first principles. The arguments of this book suggest that instead of aiming for confidentiality as a good in itself, the handling of personal information about clients ought to be informed by the four stocks or basic principles of social work ethics: respect, justice, citizenship and discipline. The following paragraphs explore some implications of these concepts, all four of which are relevant to confidentiality.

The idea of respect and its alter ego, the promotion of autonomy, indicate that it will often be right for the social worker to keep private the information she gains about the client, whether that information is deliberately sought as essential to the work in hand or irrelevant (but still sensitive) information gained incidentally in the process of contact. Indeed respect is the traditional basis of confidentiality, as the arguments cited earlier show. The social worker's obligation to respect others and promote their autonomy is not limited to her relationship with her client, however. Respect must be shown to all moral subjects, and the worker must consider the respect she owes to others as well as to the client. There are clearly occasions when respecting others will require the worker to disclose information about the client without his consent. Well-known examples are where a parent communicates information that suggests a probable danger to a child, or where a client admits or threatens criminal action that would endanger others unless the social worker takes steps to prevent it.

Two concepts from the sphere of justice are especially relevant to confidentiality. The primitive notion of due process translates into professional practice as, among other things, the requirement to follow authorised rules and procedures. Justice will be best served if personal information about clients is indeed correctly handled in accordance with clear rules, and if those rules are known and understood by everyone with a material interest. Agencies should therefore make every effort to define rules of confidentiality, publish them effectively, and enforce their observance.

Justice as empowerment also has clear implications for confidentiality. Service users are very easily disempowered if information about them circulates in quarters where it does not belong, and especially so if they are unaware that it does. Service users may also be unfairly treated if, contrariwise, personal information about them fails to reach the proper quarters; the consequence may be that they fail to receive the right treatment or the best resource for their circumstances. Professional service must take particular care that information transmitted about clients is accurate, pertinent, sufficient and timely.

One of the key questions about confidentiality concerns what information about herself the citizen should be entitled to regard as protected from retransmission by public or voluntary agencies, which hold it legitimately, to other parties or the general public. The classic position is that agencies should not reveal even the identity of their clients, even to family members or others with close legitimate interests; it regards involvement with the agency as a strictly private matter for the client alone. Such a policy can be found among, for example, voluntary agencies that deal with homeless people and those that offer advice on contraception and sexuality to young people. However, this position invokes a very strong concept of privacy and concomitantly, a weak notion of citizenship in community. A more usual assumption would be that when, for example, an adult approaches a social agency because of difficulties through illness or disability, the agency would certainly expect to involve family members even if the individual who sought help felt reluctant to do so. This is often extended to members of the immediate community, such as friends and neighbours, who are likely to be involved as well. At the other end of the spectrum, a strong version of community responsibility and involvement underlies community social work and community work. Workers actively encourage citizens to take a part in supporting members of the community; they must share information about community members, treating as public personal details that arguably might be regarded as private. This may also be extended to encouraging surveillance of neighbours who are thought to be at risk in some way or another. The responsibility and role distinctions of professionals and members of the public are deliberately eroded.

The worker's and the agency's conceptions of the rights and duties of citizenship therefore affect the determination of the boundaries of confidentiality. There seems to be a wide range of prevalent views on this issue, illustrated in agency policies about their own public visibility. Some social work agencies present themselves as points of public concourse and reference, which anyone might frequent just as they would a library, health centre or supermarket. Other agencies minimise or altogether conceal a public profile, as if to be associated with them were a matter of shame to be shaded in the deepest discretion, or on the argument that secrecy is necessary to protect clients. The tension between these views is about the role of citizens in the community, both as users of services and as contributors to the public welfare. In this as in other questions, the tension must be addressed through public political processes.

The fourth concept, of professional discipline, underwrites the practices of professional confidentiality and disclosure of personal information. While it is abundantly clear that no simple rule or rules of confidentiality will answer the complexity of handling personal information, this strengthens rather than removes the need for disciplined practices. Workers should not be expected to tackle such complex issues without positive guidance and assistance from authoritative sources. Unless disciplines are positively articulated, there is no good safeguard against arbitrary decisions, inconsistent policies and sloppy performance. Of course, workers who have been offered, and who have mastered, a sound discipline of confidentiality may eventually conclude that it is, in some respects, ill founded; they may then seek to redefine good practice.

Two strategies for improving discipline on confidentiality suggest themselves. The first is that every agency should create and publish explicit policy statements and codes of practice for the guidance of workers and for the information of service users. They should make it explicit to clients who exactly will have access to – or be actively informed about – information they may disclose to the worker, what matters disclosure may relate to, under what conditions and with what safeguards. Although such codes are already fairly common, they are usually vague. They seldom state, for example, who exactly within the agency and outside it will have access to personal information, and they rarely make the distinction, drawn above, between absolute confidentiality and the weaker principle of non-identification. It is very likely that a close and public examination of these matters would provoke inconvenient controversy, which agency managers might prefer to avoid. But this is a debate that ought to be held in public; it should not be left to bureaucrats to devise rules in quiet obscurity.

The second discipline would focus on individual clients. General policy statements have some value in defining confidentiality, but are inevitably laden with complex conditions and provisos. Rhodes suggests that 'social workers should make explicit contracts about confidentiality with each client' (Rhodes, 1986, p. 78). There is much to commend the idea of translating a general policy into specific stipulations on an individualised basis, demanding though it will sometimes be. The individual 'contract' of confidentiality needs to be specific to particular issues being addressed in the case, and needs to be appropriate to the client's understanding, ability and emotional capacity to deal with them. It will also, as Rhodes argues, reflect the worker's personal ethical and political beliefs. Making explicit the rules of confidentiality that will apply in particular cases gives at least some scope to the client to consider whether they feel satisfied with the contract on offer.

Accountability, social control and connivance: the range of professional responsibility

Social work, which aims to promote the realisation of ordinary life, takes a broad view of human needs and interests. It is both necessary and inevitable that workers will discover things about the people they come into contact with that might be a cause for concern. Sometimes these matters will not be obviously or directly relevant to the business in hand, but the worker's knowledge of them, once gained, cannot really be denied or undone. A few familiar examples will illustrate the point. Social workers sometimes discover or receive reports of reasons for suspecting that a child is being maltreated by a parent, or is being exposed to danger through ignorance or neglect, or that a disabled adult is being maltreated within the family. Social

---

BOX 10.3

Exercises on responsibility

(a) You are off-duty, shopping in the district where you work as a social worker. You notice a mother with two children under five. The mother is loudly, severely and apparently disproportionately reprimanding the children for bad behaviour. She slaps the toddler irritably for grasping at an alluring display of sweets. You notice that the mother looks inexperienced, stressed and unwell. What do you do? Explain your reasons.

(b) You work in a residential unit for young people aged 13 upwards. Nearly all of them smoke. Policy is to allow those over 16 to buy and smoke cigarettes, but everyone knows that the younger residents also smoke out of sight of staff. As a parent in private life, you do not permit your children to smoke. You are concerned for the long-term health of all the young people in the unit. You also find the amount of smoking that goes on in the unit personally objectionable.

---

workers become aware that clients are fraudulently claiming welfare benefits or appear to be engaged in petty crime and dishonesty. Clients show unmistakable signs of using illegal drugs. Social workers learn of young people who are conducting sexual relationships below the age of consent, or of people with learning disabilities who are entering illegal sexual relationships. Probation officers find out or suspect that a client on probation has committed a further offence.

The issue that runs through all these examples is about what activities of other people social workers have a professional duty to intervene over, and what actions they should connive at, allow to pass as though unwitnessed. The question is plainly one of judgement and degree. At one extreme, no one doubts that social workers do certainly have a professional responsibility to take decisive action if they receive a report of alleged child abuse; they would otherwise be held at least partly accountable for any avoidable harms that ensued. At the other end of the scale, it would obviously be intolerable and counterproductive for social workers to report officiously on every minor unwisdom, misdemeanour or incivility they happened to come across. Social workers do have a significant role in social control; what is less clear is the range of matters over which they ought to exert it. This issue is probably more difficult for social work than other professions. The nurse or doctor can reasonably say that their concern is only with the patient's health, so other matters are not their business; the lawyer properly confines himself to legal advice; the specialist therapist or adviser claims a remit only for the specialist help the client seeks. For social work with its holistic perspective it is not clear that any matter in the client's life is definitively excluded, even when other specialists are involved.

Two distinctions will offer some purchase on the problem. The first is about the extent of citizens' duties. There are infringements of rights and dangers to others that ordinary morality expects every citizen to act upon if it is within his or her power to do so. Anyone who witnesses a life-threatening accident or a serious crime is rightfully expected at the very least to report the matter and summon help. If they can also give direct assistance, such as defending someone from attack or giving first aid, then that might also be expected and would often be admired. On the other hand, there are innumerable minor transgressions in respect of which ordinary morality lays no strong expectations on the casual witness. It may be admirable to remonstrate with people who allow their dog to foul the footpath, or ignore no-smoking signs, but failure to do so is not ordinarily regarded as a serious fault of the witness. Broadly speaking, citizenship requires us to respond to *serious* offences. This restates the requirement, but does not determine its content: what counts as a serious offence is something for political argument and consensus, and various enormously in different times and places. For example, people accustomed to common western fashion in dress would hardly regard as significant infringements of morality, modes of dress that some religious traditions regard as unacceptable immodesty. The definition of seriousness is a matter of custom within particular communities.

The second distinction is between the ordinary duties of the citizen and the special duties that fall upon professionals by virtue of their role and expertise. When there is a call for a doctor in the house, this only lays a special duty on doctors and not on other people. For social work this poses a particularly awkward question. Under what circumstances would one call for a social worker in the house? It requires us to identify what special professional attributes distinguish social workers from other citizens; or as it might equally be put, to explain the content of professional discipline in social work. From this would follow a specification of those situations where social workers have a special professional responsibility; those areas of social life where they should be specifically expected to exert social control; those actions and failures to act at which social workers should not connive.

The breadth of concerns that disciplined social work properly requires makes good discipline especially difficult to achieve. For example, child and family social workers need to know the difference between adequate and inadequate standards of nutrition, hygiene and safety in the home, but they are not normally experts in these fields. They need to be able to tell when a child is suspiciously injured or failing to thrive, but they are not physicians. In the frequent absence of good training or authoritative and timely specialist advice, they fall back on commonsense ideas and routine practices. In so doing, they raise doubts about whether social work really has any special expertise to offer. In this context it is interesting that some social work agencies have identified themselves as holding key responsibilities in public disasters such as the Piper Alpha oil rig fire and the crowd control failure at the Hillsborough football stadium. The expertise offered has especially featured emotional support and counselling to survivors and relatives, implying that agency leaders regard this as a distinctive feature of social work expertise. But disaster relief will never be more than a very small part of social work activity; the heart of social work expertise must lie elsewhere.

The conclusions so far are that social workers, like other professionals, do have a number of special duties and rights associated with their professional status, but these special duties and rights should accord with the key principles of ordinary morality. As professionals they are accountable to society, through its political institutions, for taking action over certain serious failures by other citizens, and for responding to certain types of social need and problem. The question of which failures and which needs are specifically the concern of social workers is vexed by the ambiguity of social work expertise. A better edge to the definition of what social workers should, and should not, take action over can be given by invoking the principle of justice.

The range of social work responsibility is not a question for social workers to determine alone. To do so would unjustly exclude the voice of ordinary citizens while simultaneously placing professionals in the untenable position of being judges in their own case. It is nonetheless something that agency procedures should routinely address. While not forgetting the inherent retrograde tendency of procedures to defeat their own objectives, regular practice should aim at a workable clarity over what to do about commonly occurring problems. Procedures should ensure, among other things, that people – clients, non-clients and potential clients – receive what they deserve. The formalisation of procedure and the definition of desert are commonly already very highly institutionalised for some problems, most notoriously alleged child abuse. In contrast, procedures are very poorly institutionalised for other issues that might be rated of equivalent importance. Examples of the latter include the prevalence of poverty and its consequences in communities with a high demand for social work services; the debilitating effects of crime; or the devastating consequences of bad neighbourly behaviour, to name but three.

The range of social work responsibility implies and requires a conception of freedom. Professionals are practitioners, sometimes unwittingly, of some policies of freedom and some of restriction of freedom. Typically, workers and their agencies have to balance citizens' rights to freedom from unnecessary and unwarranted interference by official bodies with clients' and citizens' rights to freedoms from avoidable harm and deprivation. Equally, social work implies and requires a theory of human welfare. The ideals of freedom and welfare have many interpretations and raise many perpetual controversies. Social workers – obligated, like other professionals, by the principles of ordinary morality – have no privileged view on freedom and welfare. What they do share is a civic responsibility to contribute to the ongoing debate, and the specific answers which every age and culture contrives for itself.

Individual needs, structural disadvantage and politics

Social work concerns itself with a wide range of human and social problems, but it does so in a characteristic way: its prime focus is on affected individuals and not on wider social processes. When, for example, a social worker is helping to devise new living arrangements for an adult with disabilities, the objective is to make the best for that individual's welfare. The social worker is not concerned to address

BOX 10.4

Exercises on needs and politics

(a) You are a social worker in a traditional one-industry community, in which there are very strong networks of family and neighbourhood support. Times have just got much harder with the closure of the factory, putting most families into poverty. The social work agency offers a conventional casework service. There is now a significant increase in general demand. How should the agency attempt to respond to the crisis of employment and confidence in the community?

(b) The local authority has announced its intention to close down its remaining old people's homes. It has decided that private and voluntary homes will be able to meet local demand more cheaply than the public sector. As a social worker you are aware that the local authority home in your area is highly valued by users and their families. Do you take any action in your professional capacity? If you challenge the decision, what are your reasons?

the root cause of the person's disability, which might for example be industrial injury, poor health services, unhealthy life styles, inadequate housing or discriminatory social attitudes, to mention only some of the possibilities. Nor is the social worker concerned with why that individual, and not others, should be receiving official support. As observed in Chapter 5, the characteristic perspective of social workers is case centred: they focus their interventions on a series of individuals who have acquired an identity as agency cases. It is much less usual for social workers to adopt a social problem-centred perspective, which is associated with social reformism. So, to continue the example, if a local industry has a bad record with the health of its employees, it would be very unusual for social workers to bend their agency's efforts to improving health and safety in that industry. The case-centred perspective runs through social work like the letters in rock candy, visible in the common vocabulary of the 'caseload' as the measure of work, in countless introductory textbooks, in policy papers, in research studies of practice, and in workers' anecdotal accounts.

There are various opinions of this trademark of social work. Probably the dominant one is simply that it is right for social workers to focus on individual cases: that is their task and their skill. Pinker (1982) made the case eloquently in his minority contribution to the Barclay (1982) report on community social work. A recent ministerial speech affirms the conventional view as follows: 'Social work services are not about redressing the major injustices in our world. Their remit is not to battle with the major forces that drive social exclusion – poverty, unemployment, ill health and disability' (Galbraith, 1998). The conventional view is that while social reforms to address the underlying causes of the problems that bring clients to the door are doubtless necessary, they are not social work's main business. To this it may be added that social workers and their agencies are already very overpressed with current commitments, many of them statutory, and cannot afford the resources for excursions into areas outside social work proper.

Against the conventional view there are two sorts of argument. The first is that the problems that social work engages with cannot be effectively addressed, even at the individual level, unless their origin in broader social processes is properly understood. A key example is poverty. In a detailed review, Becker (1997) shows that the vast majority of social work clients – perhaps nine out of ten – are directly affected by poverty and its fellow traveller, unemployment. In spite of this, and notwithstanding the limited powers of British social work agencies to dispense financial aid, social workers have generally shown little practical awareness of the significance of poverty in their clients' lives. The social services departments, Becker maintains, have had a key role in 'managing the poor', and more recently have tended to withdraw from addressing poverty issues altogether.

Paradoxically, social workers' stance on poverty is not because they lack understanding of its structural nature. Jones (1997) traces it to the individualistic attitude that runs deep in social work's roots. The point of this first critique is that focusing intervention on individual cases is very inefficient. Disregarding the significance of poverty for nearly all social work clients implies neglecting the obvious possibility that global reduction of poverty, through broader measures of social policy, might be a more effective way of meeting the needs of clients than individualised social work. This point can be generalised to many of the issues that commonly affect social work clients, including health, housing, difficulties in education, and so forth. One of the signs of inefficiency in social services that often coexists with misdiagnosis of the underlying problem is a great preoccupation with resource allocation and rationing. Workers and agencies find themselves on a constant treadmill of trying to deal with overwhelming demand on painfully thin resources.

The second kind of argument against the conventional individualised view of social work problems claims it is wrong on political principle. Critics say it creates an unwarranted status barrier between worker professionals, who are deemed virtually innocent of the causes and exempt from the effects of social problems, and clients, who as ordinary members of the community are treated as the locus and perhaps the cause of social problems. Such critics advocate modes of practice that will positively address oppressive policies in social work agencies and elsewhere; their targets are racism, sexism, disablism and other like prejudices. What is crucial is that the issues are seen to lie just as much within the policies of the state and the agencies it supports as they do in the outside world of clients and the problems they bring.

The critique of the conventional, individualised view is well supported by plausible readings of the four stocks of social work ethics. The principle of respect does indeed remind us that every case, including the case which is merely typical of a widespread common problem, merits individualised attention to its particularities. Although individuals may present instances of common problems, they should nonetheless not be treated as impersonal examples of categories. However, attention to the problem should not end with the individual affected. Thus social workers should not view poverty merely as an incidental circumstance of most of their cases, occasionally meriting individualised, if rather ineffectual, alleviation. Their policies should be also be informed by the principle of justice. Many social workers agree that policies in welfare are unjust both in conception and in operation. The stock of justice requires that the agencies and institutions of social work should positively address those policy intentions and effects that, on due deliberation, are unjust. Ignoring injustice in the spheres that social work particularly operates in cannot meet the requirements of ethical practice.

In trying to meet individuals' needs while also addressing wider social problems, the concept of citizenship is once more extremely pertinent. Jordan, notably, has long argued that 'clients are fellow citizens and are due the respect that all citizens owe each other'

(Jordan, 1990, p. 74). In a fairly similar vein, Holman has proposed that relationships between clients and social workers ought to be placed upon a new footing of 'mutuality', defined by 'the recognition of mutual obligations towards others, stemming from the acceptance of a common kinship, expressed in joint action, towards a more equitable sharing of resources and responsibilities' (Holman, 1993, p. 56).

Welfare does not discount the citizenship rights and duties of service users, or indeed those of professionals. Citizenship does draw attention to defective professional–client relationships and conventional modes of agency function. All too often clients are not treated as fellow citizens, but as mere consumers, or supplicants, or units of demand, or ignorant obstructions to the smooth functioning of the agency. In agencies under heavy pressure, the public can too easily become the enemy. Agency practices are often weak in the practicalities of facilitating citizen involvement, partly through ineptitude, but more especially because they are not guided by any clear perspective on citizenship.

Conclusion

This chapter has examined several significant issues in social work ethics. As well as being important in their own right, they serve as test examples of the approach that is argued in this book. The right way to practise is not something that can be read off from the 'values' of social work, which are altogether too vague, generalised and disputable to enable useful discriminations at the points where decision making becomes difficult. The culture of social work does contain a recognisable body of ethical precepts, however, partly expressed in formal codes of ethics but also carried unconsciously as part of the profession's taken-for-granted baggage. The earlier chapters inspected this baggage for its strengths and shortcomings.

The door to good professional practice is opened by the key of cogent and justified purpose. This book has argued that the aim of social work is to promote the realisation of ordinary life; but that in our time, the ordinary life is ineluctably controversial. For that reason, and others too, the ethics of social work are matters for political argument. In order to found practice ethics we should concentrate on the principles of respect, justice, citizenship and discipline. These concepts, too, are controversial. Their value is that they target the argument in the right places. As citizens we must work to find reasonable consensus and tolerable compromises on these core principles, in a debate ruled by the spirit and methods of democracy. As professionals who are related to their clients primarily as fellow citizens and only secondarily as service users, social workers should contribute positively to this debate and answer to its conclusions. That is the only guarantee of an authentic practice ethics.

Appendix

BRITISH ASSOCIATION OF SOCIAL WORKERS
The Code of Ethics for Social Work

1. Social work is a professional activity. Implicit in its practice are ethical principles which prescribe the professional responsibility of the social worker. The primary objective of the Code of Ethics is to make these implicit principles explicit for the protection of clients and other members of society.

2. Membership of any profession entails certain obligations beyond those of the ordinary citizen. A profession's code of ethics sets down in general terms these special obligations and specifies particular duties which follow from them.

3. Members of a profession have obligations to their clients, to their employers, to each other, to colleagues in other disciplines and to society.

4. To carry out these obligations, professionals have complementary rights which must be respected if work is to be effective.

5. Any professional association has the duty to secure, as far as possible, that its members discharge their professional obligations and that members are afforded in full necessary professional rights.

The Foreword (paras 2–5) is a statement about the purposes of the Code. The Statement of Principles attempts to make explicit the values implicit in the practice of social work, and the Principles of Practice attempt to set out a basic Code for the individual social worker.

The Foreword expresses the view that the acceptance of special ethical obligations is part of the definition of any professional worker. This is a basic assumption which underlies any code of professional ethics (para 2). Paragraph 3 challenges, as being over simplifications, suggestions that the professional's only obligation is to the client, or that the employed professional's only obligations are to the employer. Paragraph 4 refers to the rights of professionals. Chief among them is the right to exercise professional discretion.

Statement of Principles

6. Basic to the profession of social work is the recognition of the value and dignity of every human being, irrespective of origin, race, status, sex, sexual orientation, age, disability, belief or contribution to society. The profession accepts a responsibility to encourage and facilitate the self-realisation of each individual person with due regard to the interest of others.

   Basic ethical principles in social work are necessarily extremely wide, in view of the wide focus of social work. A narrower basis than recognition of the value and dignity of every human being' would not be adequate. The social workers basic values must relate to individuals, whether working with individuals, groups or communities, since it is the welfare of the individuals in a group or community which is the social worker's basic concern even if indirectly. The phrase 'irrespective of origin, race, sex, sexual orientation, age, disability, belief or contribution to society' is intended to be interpreted widely. 'Origin' includes national, social, cultural and class origins, distant or recent.
   'Status' refers to an individual's current situation and includes social marital, health, citizenship status and status in an institution or organisation. 'Age' does not mean old age only. 'Belief' is not confined to religious beliefs and includes beliefs which might be regarded as delusions.
   The second sentence avoids the term 'self-determination', which sounds a little too open-ended, and attempts to recognise the limitations which real-life situations impose. Social workers are often concerned with trying to harmonise conflicting interests and, failing harmony, to arrive at the least damaging solution for all concerned. It is, therefore, sometimes not possible to ensure that there will be no detriment to the interest of others, or to the client's interest. Hence the phrase 'with due regard for the interest of others'.

7. Concerned with the enhancement of human well-being, social
    work attempts to relieve and prevent hardship and suffering.
    Social workers thus have a responsibility to help individuals,
    families, groups and communities through the provision and
    operation of appropriate services, and by contributing to social
    planning and action. Social work has developed methods of
    practice, which rely on a growing body of systematic knowledge,
    research and experience.

    *In the first sentence, limits to what social work can achieve have to
    be recognised. Being concerned with the enhancement of human
    well-being implies a responsibility to promote social functioning as
    well as relieve suffering. The Codes of Ethics of the American and
    Canadian Associations state that the social worker renders
    appropriate service in a public emergency. All citizens are expected to
    do this but social workers may be required by their professional
    values to undertake specific tasks in emergencies.*

8. The professional obligation must be acknowledged, not only to
    increase personal knowledge and skill, but also to contribute to
    the total body of professional knowledge. This involves the
    constant evaluation of methods and policies in the light of
    changing needs. The worker recognises that the competence of
    any particular discipline is limited, and that the interests of the
    client require co-operation between those who share professional
    responsibility for the clients welfare.

    *In statements about obligations, commitments or responsibilities, it
    is important not to impose obligations which cannot be fulfilled. It is
    not reasonable and proper to demand, for example, that a social
    worker should feel concern for a particular client, since feelings
    cannot be summoned at will. At the same time, it would be reason-
    able to expect social workers to declare a position if clients aroused in
    them feelings which obstruct their capacity to help.*

9. The social workers responsibility for relief and prevention of
    hardship and suffering is not always fully discharged by direct
    service to individual families and groups. The worker has the
    right and duty to bring to the attention of those in power, and
    of the general public, ways in which the activities of government,
    society or agencies create or contribute to hardship and suffering

or militate against their relief. Social workers are often at the interface between powerful organisations and relatively powerless applicants for service. While social workers are accountable to those under whose authority they work, and responsible for the efficient performance of their professional task and for their management of the organisations resources, their primary responsibility is to those for whom they work, clients, groups, communities. In view of the lack of power of some of these clients, social workers have a special responsibility to ensure as fully as possible that each persons rights are respected and needs satisfied.

The first two sentences in this paragraph relate back to the statement in Paragraph 7 about social planning and action. The paragraph then comments on the social workers own particular position in relation to planning, policy-making and the giving of service. The word interface is intended to denote a place where contacts take place, contacts which may be active or passive and which may lead to harmony or to conflict. The paragraph goes on to try to balance the social worker's responsibility to the employer against the responsibility to the client. The clients frequent lack of power must be taken into account in weighing these responsibilities.

The Principles of Practice

The Principles of Practice are based on and derived from the Statement of Principles, but are more personal and in more concrete terms. They move from general principles to principles to guide practice, while recognising that social workers must exercise personal judgement. The preamble identifies the Statement of Principles as giving the primary, underlying or basic objectives of social workers. All the undertakings which follow are qualified by the words 'to the best of their ability'. It is therefore, recognised that, to take the first principle as an example, the opportunity to contribute to the formulation of policies may in a particular case be extremely limited. Social workers' willingness to give their best is also required.

10. In accepting the statement of principles embodying the primary obligations of the social worker, members of the Association undertake that, as individuals and as part of their professional responsibilities that to the best of their ability,

   i. They will contribute to the formulation and implementation of policies for human welfare, and they will not permit their knowledge, skills or experience to be used to further dehumanising or discriminatory policies and will positively promote the use of their knowledge, skills and experience for the benefit of all sections of the community and individuals.

   This Principle is fundamental and carries the recognition that dehumanising and discriminatory policies may be the result of ignoring the needs of some sectors of the community as much as positive action to harm them. Observance of it may lead the social worker to resign from a post in certain circumstances.

   ii. They will respect their clients as individuals and will seek to ensure that their dignity, individuality, rights and responsibility shall be safeguarded.

   This Principle has general implications, but particular attention should be paid lest a person suffers loss of dignity or rights by the very act of becoming a client.

   iii. They will not discriminate against clients, on the grounds of their origin, race, status, sex, sexual orientation, age, disability, beliefs, or contribution to society, they will not tolerate actions of colleagues or others which may be racist, sexist or otherwise discriminatory, nor will they deny those differences which will shape the nature of clients needs and will ensure any personal help is offered within an acceptable personal and cultural context. They will draw to the attention of the Association any activity which is professionally unacceptable.

   This Principle requires social workers to be aware of the actions of others and to recognise that each of us has a responsibility to challenge the unacceptable practices of colleagues and others. It also places emphasis on the need to promote different provisions for different groups and gives support to social workers attempting to change their own and others practices. See also the comment on Paragraph 6.

iv. They will help their clients both individually and collectively to increase the range of choices open to them and their powers to make decisions, securing the participation, wherever possible, of clients in defining and obtaining services appropriate to their needs.

This Principle holds good in all circumstances but a social worker also has a duty to enable the client to identify realistic choices. This applies equally when working with community groups who have a right to help in making effective political choices relating to community resources and in channelling their activities in directions which will ensure a return on their effort. The responsibility of the social worker is to provide such individuals and groups with full information on which they can base their decisions and to encourage self-advocacy by any identifiable client or community.

v. They will not reject their clients or lose concern for their suffering, even if obliged to protect themselves or others against them or obliged to acknowledge an inability to help them.

This Principle raises the problem of what can legitimately be said about the worker–client relationship. It is not possible to lay down requirements about the social worker's feelings, but 'rejection' includes action as well as feeling. Rejecting the client is, of course, different from closing the case. The reference to the need to protect themselves is to acknowledge the need to set boundaries if clients are physically violent.

vi. They will give precedence to their professional responsibility over their own personal interests.

This Principle recognises the opportunities for conflict between personal and professional responsibilities. It does not imply that at all times the social worker must put responsibility to a client above all other responsibilities as a citizen. It places on the social worker an obligation not to pursue personal interests at the client's expense. It also includes the responsibility of a social worker not to engage in sexual relationships with clients or the family members of clients.

vii. They accept that continuing professional education and training are basic to the practice of social work, and they hold themselves responsible for the standard of service they give.

This Principle recognises that qualifying training does not complete a social worker's education. The importance of continuing education is also increased by the need to keep abreast of changing social factors, legislation and in the light of expanding knowledge. The assumption of personal responsibility for one's work is crucial to professionalism. A completely bureaucratised service cannot be a professional one.

viii. They recognise the need to collaborate with others in the interest of their clients.

This Principle places an obligation on social workers not only to be alert to the need to collaborate, but to take appropriate action.

ix. They will make clear in making any public statements or undertaking any public activities, whether they are acting in a personal capacity or on behalf of an organisation.

x. They will acknowledge a responsibility to help clients to obtain all those services and rights to which they are entitled; and will seek to ensure that these services are provided within a framework which will be both ethnically and culturally appropriate for all members of the community; and that an appropriate diversity will be promoted both in their own agency and other organisations in which they have influence.

xi. They will recognise that information clearly entrusted for one purpose should not be used for another purpose without sanction. They will respect the privacy of clients and others with whom they come into contact and confidential information gained in their relationships with them. They will divulge such information only with the consent of the client (or informant) except where there is clear evidence of serious danger to the client, worker, other persons or the community or in other circumstances, judged exceptional, on the basis of professional consideration and consultation.

This Principle was published some years ago in the Association's Discussion Paper No.1 on Confidentiality in Social Work. The sanction referred to in the first sentence of the Principle is the sanction of the person giving the information to the social worker. The multi-purpose agency, in particular, has to consider what administrative arrangements should be made to guard against the misuse of information. The paper on confidentiality, after outlining situations in which the clients right to confidentiality might be overridden, states: 'In all the foregoing circumstances the breach of confidence must remain limited to the needs of the situation at that time and in no circumstances can the worker assume a carte blanche to reveal matters which are not relevant to that particular situation'.

xii. They will work for the creation and maintenance in employing agencies of conditions which will support and facilitate social workers acceptance of the obligations of the Code.

There is a clear implication in this Principle that employers should recognise the whole Code. The Principle also acknowledges the difficulties of the employed professional, especially the social worker who works in an agency whose role is not specifically therapeutic.

This Code was revised and re-adopted by AGM in 1996. The original Code was adopted by the BASW Annual General Meeting in Edinburgh in 1975. It was amended following the 1985 Annual General Meeting in Swansea to remove all gender specific language and by BASW Council in June 1986 following the Sheffield Annual General Meeting at which BASW took a positive stance against racism.

ALL MEMBERS OF THE ASSOCIATION ARE REQUIRED TO UPHOLD THE CODE AND MAKE COMMITMENT TO IT AT THEIR ANNUAL RENEWAL OF MEMBERSHIP

BASW maintains a Disciplinary Board, as required by the constitution, which considers allegations of professional misconduct against members of the Association. Misconduct is defined to include actions or omissions which are likely to be:

- harmful to clients or members of the public, or
- prejudicial to the development or standing of social work practice, or
- contrary to the Code of Ethics.

Members have a duty to draw such concerns about individual members to the Associations attention. Referrals to the Disciplinary Board should be made to the Director, who can advise members on procedure and interpretation.

References

Abrams, P., Abrams, S., Humphrey, R. and Snaith, R. (1989) *Neighbourhood Care and Social Policy*, London, HMSO.

Acton, H.B. (1970) *Kant's Moral Philosophy*, London, Macmillan.

Andrews, G. (ed.) (1991) *Citizenship*, London, Lawrence & Wishart.

Ashdown, P. (1989) *Citizens' Britain: A Radical Agenda for the 1990s*, London, Fourth Estate.

Atiyah, P.S. (1995) *Law and Modern Society*, 2nd edn, Oxford, Oxford University Press.

Ball, C. (1996) *Law for Social Workers*, 3rd edn, Aldershot, Arena.

Ball, C. (1997) 'The law', in Davies, M. (ed.) *The Blackwell Companion to Social Work*, Oxford, Blackwell, Chapter II.2.

Ball, C., Harris, R., Roberts, G. and Vernon, S. (1988) *The Law Report: Teaching and Assessment of Law in Social Work Education*, London, Central Council for Education and Training in Social Work.

Bamford, T. (1990) *The Future of Social Work*, Basingstoke, Macmillan.

Banks, S. (1995) *Ethics and Values in Social Work*, Basingstoke, Macmillan.

Barbalet, J.M. (1988) *Citizenship*, Milton Keynes, Open University Press.

Barclay, P.M. (chair) (1982) *Social Workers: Their Role and Tasks*, London, Bedford Square Press.

Baron, M.W., Pettit, P. and Slote, M. (1997) *Three Methods of Ethics: A Debate*, Malden, MA, Blackwell.

Barry, N. (1990) *Welfare*, Milton Keynes, Open University Press.

Bartlett, H.M. (1970) *The Common Base of Social Work Practice*, New York, National Association of Social Workers.

Beauchamp, T.L. and Childress, J.F. (1989) *Principles of Biomedical Ethics*, 3rd edn, New York, Oxford University Press.

Becker, S. (1997) *Responding to Poverty: The Politics of Cash and Care*, London, Longman.

Bellamy, R. and Ross, A. (eds) (1996) *A Textual Introduction to Social and Political Theory*, Manchester, Manchester University Press.

Bernstein, R. (1972) *Praxis and Action*, London, Duckworth.

Biestek, F.P. (1961) *The Casework Relationship*, London, Allen & Unwin.

Blackburn, R. (ed.) (1993) *Rights of Citizenship*, London, Mansell.

Blom-Cooper, L. (1987) *A Child in Mind: Protection of Children in a Responsible Society*, London, London Borough of Greenwich.

Bok, S. (1984) *Secrets*, Oxford, Oxford University Press.

Booth, T. (1997) 'Learning difficulties' in Davies, M. (ed.) *The Blackwell Companion to Social Work*, 1st edn, Oxford, Blackwell, Chapter IV.6.

Braye, S. and Preston-Shoot, M. (1995) *Empowering Practice in Social Care*, Buckingham, Open University Press.

British Association of Social Workers (1980) *Clients Are Fellow Citizens*, Birmingham, British Association of Social Workers.

British Association of Social Workers (1996) *The Code of Ethics for Social Work*, Birmingham, British Association of Social Workers.

Brown, P., Hadley, R. and White, K.J. (1982) 'A case for neighbourhood-based social work and social services', in Barclay, P.M. (chair) *Social Workers: Their Role and Tasks*, London, Bedford Square Press, Appendix A.

Buck, T. (1993) 'The disabled citizen', in Blackburn, R. (ed.) *Rights of Citizenship*, London, Mansell, Chapter 9.

Bulmer, M. (1987) *The Social Basis of Community Care*, London, Allen & Unwin.

Butcher, T. (1995) *Delivering Welfare: The Governance of the Social Services in the 1990s*, Buckingham, Open University Press.

Butrym, Z.T. (1976) *The Nature of Social Work*, London, Macmillan.

Campbell, T. (1988) *Justice*, Basingstoke, Macmillan.

Canadian Association of Social Workers (1994) *Social Work Code of Ethics*, Ottawa, Canadian Association of Social Workers.

CCETSW (1976) *Values in Social Work*, London, CCETSW.

CCETSW (1996) *Assuring Quality in the Diploma in Social Work – 1: Rules and Requirements for the DipSW*, 2nd edn, rev. 1996 edn, London, CCETSW.

Clark, C. (1995) 'Competence and discipline in professional formation', *British Journal of Social Work* **25**: 563–80.

Clark, C. (1996) *Paternalism and Citizenship in Community Care*, Edinburgh, University of Edinburgh.

Clark, C. (1998) 'Self-determination and paternalism in community care: practice and prospects', *British Journal of Social Work* **28**: 387–402.

Clark, C.L. with Asquith, S. (1985) *Social Work and Social Philosophy: A Guide for Practice*, London, Routledge & Kegan Paul.

Clark, C. and Lapsley, I. (eds) (1995) *Planning and Costing Community Care*, London, Jessica Kingsley.

Commission on the Future of the Voluntary Sector (1996) *Meeting the Challenge of Change: Voluntary Action into the 21st Century*, London, National Council for Voluntary Organisations.

Commission on Social Justice (1994) *Social Justice: Strategies for National Renewal*, London, Vintage.

Conrad, A.P. (1988) 'Ethical considerations in the psychosocial process', *Social Casework* **69**: 603–10.

Coote, A. (ed.) (1992) *The Welfare of Citizens: Developing New Social Rights*, London, Rivers Oram.

Coulshed, V. (1988) *Social Work Practice: An Introduction*, Basingstoke, Macmillan.

Croft, S. and Beresford, P. (1990) *From Paternalism to Participation: Involving People in Social Services*, London, Open Services Project.

Croft, S. and Beresford, P. (1992) 'The politics of participation', *Critical Social Policy* **12**(2): 20–44.

Dale, J. and Foster, P. (1986) *Feminists and State Welfare*, London, Routledge & Kegan Paul.

Davies, C. (1983) 'Professionals in bureaucracies: the conflict thesis revisited', in Dingwall, R. and Lewis, P. (eds) *The Sociology of the Professions*, London, Macmillan, Chapter 8.

Davies, M. (ed.) (1997) *The Blackwell Companion to Social Work*, Oxford, Blackwell.

Deakin, N. (1987) *The Politics of Welfare*, London, Methuen.

DHSS (1978) *Social Service Teams: The Practitioner's View*, London, DHSS.

Dobrin, A. (1989) 'Ethical judgements of male and female social workers', *Social Work* **34**: 451–5.

DoH (1989) *Caring for People: Community Care in the Next Decade and Beyond*, London, HMSO.

Dominelli, L. (1988) *Anti-racist Social Work*, Basingstoke, Macmillan.

Downie, R.S. and Telfer, E. (1980) *Caring and Curing: A Philosophy of Medicine and Social Work*, London, Methuen.

Doyal, L. and Gough, I. (1991) *A Theory of Human Need*, Basingstoke, Macmillan.

Dworkin, G. (1979) 'Paternalism', in Laslett, P. and Fishkin, J. (eds) *Philosophy, Politics and Society: Fifth Series*, Oxford, Blackwell, Chapter 5.

Dworkin, R. (1977) *Taking Rights Seriously*, London, Duckworth.

Dworkin, R. (1993) *Life's Dominion: An Argument about Abortion and Euthanasia*, London, HarperCollins.

Ejaz, F.K. (1991) 'Self-determination: lessons to be learned from social work practice in India', *British Journal of Social Work* **21**: 127–42.

Esping-Andersen, G. (1990) *The Three Worlds of Welfare Capitalism*, Cambridge, Polity.

Fairbairn, G. and Fairbairn, S. (eds) (1988) *Ethical Issues in Caring*, Aldershot, Avebury.

Feinberg, J. (1973) *Social Philosophy*, Englewood Cliffs, NJ, Prentice Hall.

Finch, J. (1989) *Family Obligations and Social Change*, Cambridge, Polity.

Flores, A. and Johnson, D.B. (1983) 'Collective responsibility and professional roles', *Ethics* **93**: 537–45.

Frankena, W. (1963) *Ethics*, Englewood Cliffs, NJ, Prentice Hall.

Galbraith, S. (1998) *Modernising Social Work*, Edinburgh, The Scottish Office.

Gambrill, E. and Pruger, E. (eds) (1997) *Controversial Issues in Social Work Ethics, Values and Obligations*, Needham Heights, MA, Allyn & Bacon.

George, V. and Wilding, P. (1994) *Welfare and Ideology*, Hemel Hempstead, Harvester Wheatsheaf.

Gewirth, A. (1978) *Reason and Morality*, Chicago, University of Chicago Press.

Gewirth, A. (1986) 'Professional ethics: the separatist thesis', *Ethics* **96**: 282–300.

Goetschius, G.W. (1969) *Working with Community Groups*, London, Routledge & Kegan Paul.

Goldman, A.H. (1980) *The Moral Foundations of Professional Ethics*, Totowa, NJ, Rowman & Littlefield.

Goodin, R.E. (1993) 'Utility and the good', in Singer, P. (ed.) *A Companion to Ethics*, Oxford, Blackwell, Chapter 20.

Gray, J. (1993) *Post-Liberalism: Studies in Political Thought*, London, Routledge.

Gray, J. (1995) 'Agonistic liberalism', *Social Philosophy and Policy* **12**(1): 111–35.

Great Britain, the Prime Minister (1991) *The Citizen's Charter: Raising the Standard* London, HMSO.

Griffiths, R. (1988) *Community Care: Agenda for Action*, London, HMSO.

Halmos, P. (1978a) *The Faith of the Counsellors*, 2nd edn, London, Constable.

Halmos, P. (1978b) *The Personal and the Political*, London, Hutchinson.

Hardin, R. (1990) 'The artificial duties of contemporary professionals', *Social Service Review* **64**: 528–42.

Heater, D. (1991) 'Citizenship: a remarkable case of sudden interest', *Parliamentary Affairs* **44**(2): 140–56.

Hill, D.M. (1994) *Citizens and Cities: Urban Policy in the 1990s*, Hemel Hempstead, Harvester Wheatsheaf.

Holland, T.P. and Kilpatrick, A.C. (1991) 'Ethical issues in social work: toward a grounded theory of professional ethics', *Social Work* **36**(2): 138–44.

Hollis, H. and Howe, D. (1987) 'Moral risks in social work', *Journal of Applied Philosophy* **4**(2): 123–33.

Holman, B. (1993) *A New Deal for Social Welfare*, Oxford, Lion.

Horne, M. (1987) *Values in Social Work*, Aldershot, Wildwood House.

Horton, J. (1992) *Political Obligation*, Basingstoke, Macmillan.

Hugman, R. (1991) *Power in Caring Professions*, Basingstoke, Macmillan.

Hugman, R. and Smith, D. (eds) (1995) *Ethical Issues in Social Work*, London, Routledge.

Hunt, G. (ed.) (1998) *Whistleblowing in the Social Services: Public Accountability and Professional Practice*, London, Arnold.

Husak, D.N. (1981) 'Paternalism and autonomy', *Philosophy and Public Affairs* **10**(1): 27–46.

Ignatieff, M. (1989) 'Citizenship and moral narcissism', *Political Quarterly* **60**(1): 63–74.

Jones, C. (1997) 'Poverty', in Davies, M. (ed.) *The Blackwell Companion to Social Work*, Oxford, Blackwell, Chapter IV.1.

Jordan, B. (1976) *Freedom and the Welfare State*, London, Routledge & Kegan Paul.

Jordan, B. (1989) *The Common Good: Citizenship, Morality and Self-Interest*, Oxford, Blackwell.

Jordan, B. (1990) *Social Work in an Unjust Society*, Hemel Hempsted, Harvester Wheatsheaf.

Lord Kilbrandon (chair) (1964) *Report of the Committee on Children and Young Persons (Scotland)* , Edinburgh, HMSO.

King, D.S. and Waldron, J. (1988) 'Citizenship, social citizenship and the defence of welfare provision', *British Journal of Political Science* **18**: 415–43.

Koehn, D. (1994) *The Ground of Professional Ethics*, London, Routledge.

Kronman, A. (1986) 'Practical wisdom and professional character', *Social Philosophy and Policy* **4**(1): 203–34.

Kugelman, W. (1992) 'Social work ethics in the practice arena: a qualitative study', *Social Work in Health Care* **17**(4): 59–77.

Kymlicka, W. (1990) *Contemporary Political Philosophy: An Introduction*, Oxford, Oxford University Press.

Laslett, P. (ed.) (1965) *Two Treatises of Government*, New York, Mentor.

Levy, C.S. (1993) *Social Work Ethics on the Line*, Binghamton, NY, Haworth Press.

Lewis, J. and Glennerster, H. (1996) *Implementing the New Community Care*, Buckingham, Open University Press.

Lindley, R. (1988) 'Paternalism and caring', in Fairbairn, G. and Fairbairn, S. (eds) *Ethical Issues in Caring*, Aldershot, Avebury, Chapter 6.

Loewenberg, F. and Dolgoff, R. (1982) *Ethical Decisions for Social Work Practice*, Itasca, IL, Peacock.

Loney, M., Bocock, R., Clarke, J., Cochrane, A., Graham, P. and Wilson, M. (eds) (1991) *The State or the Market: Politics and Welfare in Contemporary Britain*, 2nd edn, London, Sage.

Lorenz, W. (1994) 'Personal social services', in Clasen, J. and Freeman, R. (eds) *Social Policy in Germany*, Hemel Hempstead, Harvester Wheatsheaf, Chapter 7.

Macdonald, G. and Macdonald, K. (1995) 'Ethical issues in social work research', in Hugman, R. and Smith, D. (eds) *Ethical Issues in Social Work*, London, Routledge, Chapter 3.

Macdonald, K.M. (1995) *The Sociology of the Professions*, London, Sage.

Marshall, T.H. (1950) 'Citizenship and social class', in Marshall, T.H. (ed.) *Citizenship and Social Class, and other essays*, Cambridge, Cambridge University Press, Chapter IV.

Marsland, D. (1992) 'The roots and consequences of paternalist collectivism: Beveridge and his influence', *Social Policy and Administration* **26**(2): 144–50.

Marsland, D. (1996) *Welfare or Welfare State? Contradictions and Dilemmas of Social Policy*, Basingstoke, Macmillan.

Mason, J.K. and McCall Smith, R.A. (1994) *Law and Medical Ethics*, 4th edn, London, Butterworths.

May, T. and Vass, A.A. (eds) (1996) *Working with Offenders: Issues, Contexts and Outcomes*, London, Sage.

Mayberry, J.F. (1996) 'The views of professionals and patients on compulsory removal from home to an institution (Section 47, National Assistance Act)', *Health and Social Care in the Community* **4**(4): 208–14.

McDermott, F.E. (1975) *Self-determination in Social Work*, London, Routledge & Kegan Paul.

Mills, C.W. (1970) *The Sociological Imagination*, Harmondsworth, Penguin.

Minford, P. (1991) 'The role of the social services: a view from the New Right', in Loney, M., Bocock, R., Clarke, J., Cochrane, A., Graham, P. and Wilson, M. (eds) *The State or the Market: Politics and Welfare in Contemporary Britain*, 2nd edn, London, Sage, Chapter 5 .

NASW (1996) *Code of Ethics*, Washington, DC, National Association of Social Workers.

Norman, R. (1983) *The Moral Philosophers: An Introduction to Ethics*, Oxford, Oxford University Press.

Novak, K. (ed.) (1998) *Is There a Third Way? Essays on the Changing Direction of Socialist Thought*, London, Institute of Economic Affairs.

O'Hagan, K. (1996) 'Social work competence: a historical perspective', in O'Hagan, K. (ed.) *Competence in Social Work Practice: A Practical Guide for Professionals*, London, Jessica Kingsley, Chapter 1.

Oldfield, A. (1990a) 'Citizenship: an unnatural practice?', *Political Quarterly* **61**(2): 177–87.

Oldfield, A. (1990b) *Citizenship and Community: Civic Republicanism and the Modern World*, London, Routledge.

Oliver, D. (1991) 'Active citizenship in the 1990s', *Parliamentary Affairs* **44**(2): 158–71.

Oliver, D. and Heater, D. (1994) *The Foundations of Citizenship*, Hemel Hempstead, Harvester Wheatsheaf.

O'Neill, O. (1993) 'Kantian ethics', in Singer, P. (ed.) *A Companion to Ethics*, Oxford, Blackwell, Chapter 14.

Parry, R. (ed.) (1990) *New Perspectives on Citizenship*, Edinburgh, University of Edinburgh.

Paton, H.J. (1991) *The Moral Law: Kant's Groundwork of the Metaphysic of Morals*, London, Routledge.

Payne, M. (1995) *Social Work and Community Care*, Basingstoke, Macmillan.

Pettit, P. (1993) 'Consequentialism', in Singer, P. (ed.) *A Companion to Ethics*, Oxford, Blackwell, Chapter 19.

Pierson, C. (1991) *Beyond the Welfare State? The New Political Economy of Welfare*, Oxford, Polity/Blackwell.

Pike, C.K. (1996) 'Development and initial validation of the Social Work Values Inventory', *Research on Social Work Practice* **6**(3): 337–52.

Pinker, R.A. (1982) 'An alternative view', in Barclay, P.M.C. (ed.) *Social Workers: Their Role and Tasks*, London, Bedford Square Press, Appendix B.

Pinker, R. (1991) 'On rediscovering the middle way in social welfare', in Wilson, T. and Wilson, R. (eds) *The State and Social Welfare: The Objectives of Policy*, Harlow, Longman, Chapter 15.

Plant, R. (1970) *Social and Moral Theory in Casework*, London, Routledge & Kegan Paul.

Plant, R. (1991) *Modern Political Thought*, Oxford, Blackwell.

Plant, R. and Barry, N. (1990) *Citizenship and Rights in Thatcher's Britain: Two Views*, London, Institute of Economic Affairs.

Proctor, E.K., Morrow-Howell, N. and Lott, C. (1993) 'Classification and correlates of ethical dilemmas in hospital social work', *Social Work* **38**(2): 166–77.

Rachels, J. (1993) *The Elements of Moral Philosophy*, 2nd edn, New York, McGraw-Hill.

Ramon, S. (1991) *Beyond Community Care: Normalisation and Integration Work*, Basingstoke, Macmillan.

Raphael, D.D. (1981) *Moral Philosophy*, Oxford, Oxford University Press.

Rawls, J. (1973) *A Theory of Justice*, Oxford, Oxford University Press.

Reamer, F.G. (1990) *Ethical Dilemmas in Social Service*, 2nd edn, New York, Columbia University Press.

Reamer, F.G. (1995) *Social Work Values and Ethics*, New York, Columbia University Press.

Rees, S. (1991) *Achieving Power: Practice and Policy in Social Welfare*, Sydney, Allen & Unwin.

Rees, S. and Wallace, A. (1982) *Verdicts on Social Work*, London, Edward Arnold.

Rhodes, M.L. (1986) *Ethical Dilemmas in Social Work Practice*, Boston, Routledge & Kegan Paul.

Rokeach, M. (1973) *The Nature of Human Values*, New York, Free Press.

Rothman, J. (1989) 'Client self-determination: untangling the knot', *Social Service Review* December: 598–612.

Rutter, M. (1972) *Maternal Deprivation Reassessed*, Harmondsworth, Penguin.

Sainsbury, E. (1989) 'Participation and paternalism', in Shardlow, S. (ed.) *The Values of Change in Social Work*, London, Tavistock/Routledge, Chapter 7.

Sainsbury, E., Nixon, S. and Phillips, D. (1982) *Social Work in Focus: Clients' and Social Workers' Perceptions in Long-term Social Work*, London, Routledge & Kegan Paul.

Schellenberg, D.H. (1996) 'Confidentiality and media attention: a discussion concerning denial and public education', *Social Policy and Administration* **30**(3): 263–75.

Schneewind, J.B. (1993) 'Modern moral philosophy', in Singer, P. (ed.) *A Companion to Ethics*, Oxford, Blackwell, Chapter 12.

Schön, D.A. (1983) *The Reflective Practitioner: How Professionals Think in Action*, London, Temple Smith.

Scottish Office, Social Work Services Group (1989) *Code on Confidentiality of Social Work Records*, Edinburgh, Scottish Office.

Seebohm, F. (chair) (1968) *Report of the Committee on Local Authority and Allied Social Services*, London, HMSO.

Shardlow, S. (1995) 'Confidentiality, accountability and the boundaries of client–worker relationships', in Hugman, R. and Smith, D. (eds) *Ethical Issues in Social Work*, London, Routledge, Chapter 4.

Shardlow, S. (ed.) (1989) *The Values of Change in Social Work*, London, Tavistock/Routledge.

Singer, P. (ed.) (1994) *Ethics*, Oxford, Oxford University Press.

Spicker, P. (1990) 'Social work and self-determination', *British Journal of Social Work* **20**: 221–36.

Statham, D. (1978) *Radicals in Social Work*, London, Routledge & Kegan Paul.

Stirk, P.M.R. and Weigall, D. (1995) *An Introduction to Political Ideas*, London, Pinter.

Taylor, D. (1989) 'Citizenship and social power', *Critical Social Policy* **26**(2): 19–31.

Taylor, D. (1992) 'A Big Idea for the nineties? The rise of citizens' charters', *Critical Social Policy* **33**: 87–94.

Taylor, G. (1993) 'Challenges from the margins', in Clarke, J. (ed.) *A Crisis in Care? Challenges to Social Work*, London, Sage/Open University, Chapter 5.

Thane, P. (1996) *Foundations of the Welfare State*, 2nd edn, London, Longman.

Thomas, D.N. (1983) *The Making of Community Work*, London, Allen & Unwin.

Thomson, I.E., Melia, K.M. and Boyd, K.M. (1993) *Nursing Ethics*, 3rd edn, Edinburgh, Churchill Livingstone.

Timms, N. (1983) *Social Work Values: An Enquiry*, London, Routledge & Kegan Paul.

Timms, N. and Watson, D. (eds) (1976) *Talking about Welfare*, London, Routledge & Kegan Paul.

Timms, N. and Watson, D. (eds) (1978) *Philosophy in Social Work*, London, Routledge & Kegan Paul.

Titmuss, R.M. (1970) *The Gift Relationship*, London, Allen & Unwin.

Towle, C. (1973) *Common Human Needs*, London, Allen & Unwin.

Tur, R.H.S. (1996) 'Accountability and lawyers', in Chadwick, R. (ed.) *Ethics and the Professions*, Aldershot, Avebury, Chapter 5.

Turner, B.S. (1990) 'Outline of a theory of citizenship', *Sociology* **24**(2): 189–217.

Turner, B.S. (ed.) (1993) *Citizenship and Social Theory*, London, Sage.

Utting, W. (1997) 'A view from central government', in Davies, M. (ed.) *The Blackwell Companion to Social Work*, Oxford, Blackwell, Chapter VI.4.

Vass, A.A. (ed.) (1996) *Social Work Competences: Core Knowledge, Skills and Values*, London, Sage.

Walden, T., Wolock, I. and Demone, H.W. (1990) 'Ethical decision making in human services: a comparative study', *Families in Society: The Journal of Contemporary Human Services* **71** (2): 67–75.

Walzer, M. (1983) *Spheres of Justice*, New York, Basic Books.

Warnock, M. (ed.) (1962) *Utilitarianism*, London, Collins.

Watson, D. (ed.) (1985) *A Code of Ethics for Social Work: The Second Step*, London, Routledge & Kegan Paul.

Weale, A. (1978) 'Paternalism and social policy', *Journal of Social Policy* **7** (2): 157–72.

Willmott, P. (1989) *Community Initiatives: Patterns and Prospects*, London, Policy Studies Institute.

Wilmot, S. (1997) *The Ethics of Community Care*, London, Cassell.

Winter, R. and Maisch, M. (1996) *Professional Competence and Higher Education: the ASSET programme*, London, Falmer Press.

Wise, S. (1995) 'Feminist ethics in practice', in Hugman, R. and Smith, D. (eds) *Ethical Issues in Social Work*, London, Routledge, Chapter 6.

Yelloly, M. and Henkel, M. (1995) *Learning and Teaching in Social Work: Towards Reflective Practice*, London, Jessica Kingsley.

Index